HONOR KILLINGS IN THE TWENTY-FIRST CENTURY

HONOR KILLINGS IN THE TWENTY-FIRST CENTURY

Nicole Pope

First published in hardcover in 2011 by PALGRAVE MACMILLAN® in the United States—a division of St. Martin's Press LLC, 175 Fifth Avenue, New York, NY 10010.

Where this book is distributed in the UK, Europe and the rest of the world, this is by Palgrave Macmillan, a division of Macmillan Publishers Limited, registered in England, company number 785998, of Houndmills, Basingstoke, Hampshire RG21 6XS.

Palgrave Macmillan is the global academic imprint of the above companies and has companies and representatives throughout the world.

Palgrave® and Macmillan® are registered trademarks in the United States, the United Kingdom, Europe and other countries.

ISBN: 978–1–137–37143–0

The Library of Congress has cataloged the hardcover edition as follows:

Pope, Nicole.
    Honor killings in the twenty-first century / Nicole Pope.
        p. cm.
    Includes bibliographical references.
    ISBN 978–0–230–33978–1 (alk. paper)
        1. Women—Violence against. 2. Honor killings. 3. Honor killings—Case studies. 4. Women's rights. 5. Honor—Social aspects. I. Title.

HV6250.4.W65P635 2011
306.87—dc23   2011024737

A catalogue record of the book is available from the British Library.

Design by Integra Software Services

First PALGRAVE MACMILLAN paperback edition: December 2013

10 9 8 7 6 5 4 3 2 1

To my daughters Vanessa and Amanda
And to my parents Pierre and Lisi Bernet

Contents

PREFACE

I beg the ancient privilege of Athens,
As she is mine, I may dispose of her:
Which shall be either to this gentleman
Or to her death, according to our law
Immediately provided in that case.
Egeus, father of Hermia
Act I, Scene I
A Midsummer Night's Dream,
by William Shakespeare

When I set out to write about "honor" killings, I had no idea that I would embark on an emotional journey that would last a decade and would prove challenging, professionally and personally.

I had a fairly simple—simplistic, it turned out—idea in mind. I had spent more than 20 years in the Middle East and in Turkey. In the course of my work as a journalist, I had stumbled upon cases of murders committed in the name of honor. Like most people who hear about these crimes, I was appalled and moved by the deaths of innocent young women. But I was also intrigued and wanted to find out more about the circumstances that led to their deaths. The individual stories described in news reports suggested that entire communities were involved.

I struggled with the idea that an attachment to an unwritten social code could be powerful enough to override human instinct and push parents to kill the children they had brought into the world. I wanted to examine the social mechanisms that could drive them to such extremes and find out what went on in the minds of perpetrators.

I started by looking at specific cases of what I thought of as "textbook honor killings." The pattern, it then seemed to me, was quite clear: a young woman is perceived to have tarnished the family honor, her relatives gather to decide her fate, and one family member is given the mandate to kill her.

But I soon realized that a blanket of "honor" was thrown over a much broader variety of crimes and abuses, and that cases of honor killings that seemed to follow a kind of tribal pattern were in fact only the tip of the iceberg.

Violence committed in the name of honor has to be examined in the wider context of a patriarchal structure that assigns specific roles to its members according to their gender. Crimes committed in the name of honor, often wrongly described in Western media as an Islamic practice, can only be properly addressed when studied in conjunction with practices such as forced marriages and bride exchanges, as well as with the cult of virginity and the expectation of total obedience on the part of women, which provide the social backdrop to these crimes wherever they occur.

Many of the cases outlined in this book do not involve informal family courts handing down death sentences. They may not neatly fit the stereotype of honor killings as described in Western media. Some of them do not even result in a murder. But all the tragedies outlined in this book are linked by a common thread, and each shines a light on a different aspect of what is sometimes described as the "honor culture."

Inverted commas are needed to frame the word "honor" because discrimination and violence against women are never honorable, even if the perpetrators believe they are redeeming their or their family's reputation. For practical reasons, I did not use them throughout the text but they are always implied when "honor" is attached to the notion that women should be obedient and conform to a behavior determined by male members of the community.

Culture, in this context, does not refer to the set of customs of one specific country or religion. Patriarchal values, and the practices that evolve from them, take on different forms from one country to the next. They can even vary between neighboring villages. Although many of these practices have roots that reach back in time, they are neither monolithic nor immutable. In fact, they are constantly evolving.

Different lifestyles also coexist within a country. In places where honor-based violence is still reported, I also met educated or well-off women, who enjoyed rights and freedoms similar to their counterparts in the West. The harmful practices outlined in this book were largely alien to them. And even among men and women from less privileged backgrounds, I met many who rejected the harmful aspects of their traditions and bravely fought from within their communities to effect change.

While my research led me to closely examine gender relations in countries where crimes are still committed in the name of honor, it also forced me to take a closer look at the situation of women in developed Western countries. I had not really anticipated that this project would take me down this path. Observed from the safe distance of newspaper clippings, honor-based violence seemed to stem from traditions so different from the ones I had grown up with that they appeared to have no bearing on gender issues in Western societies.

A closer examination of the global situation of women, however, reveals a continuum of violence against them. Honor killings are undoubtedly at the extreme end of the spectrum, but they cannot be entirely detached from forms of violence that Westerners are more familiar with and therefore often less sensitive to. I personally believe that an arch of patriarchal bullying links honor killings to crimes committed against women in Western societies, even if the narrative and the sociopolitical background are different.

I went looking for traditions and found instead a scourge that, in many cases, takes on very modern forms. Honor killings may have existed for centuries or even millennia, but they have also evolved to maintain their grip in a rapidly changing world.

I therefore felt that it was important to look at them from a broader perspective and examine how they take place in different environments. I collected essays and media reports from various countries, but narrowed the area of field research to Turkey, where I live and have easy access to information, partly through women's rights groups; to Pakistan, a country where honor killings remain frequent but are also well documented thanks to the tireless efforts of human rights activists; and to the United Kingdom, a country that has "discovered" honor killings and related issues such as forced marriages in recent years.

Comparing stories in these three locations allowed me to identify similarities, but also differences in the interpretation of honor. Above all, I realized that, contrary to widespread Western prejudices, often fuelled by sensationalist media reports, honor killings are not an inevitable part of some cultures. In the course of my investigation, I was privileged to meet remarkable activists, lawyers, and community organizers who are actively challenging the status quo to remove discriminatory practices against women from their culture, while preserving its positive aspects. These courageous people have already succeeded in amending the legislation in several countries and are gradually forcing a change of mentality.

It is largely thanks to their efforts that past victims have found a voice and thanks to their work that more women can be saved when they are under threat.

ACKNOWLEDGMENTS

I could not have written this book without the numerous people who have helped me along the way. I am grateful to the committed activists and NGO representatives in several countries who gave me their time and generously shared their expertise. Their dedication to human rights and the courage they display in the face of often strong opposition are truly inspiring. Nebahat Akkoç and her dynamic team at Kamer in Diyarbakir raised awareness of honor killings in Turkey; they also helped me on several occasions. Women under threat, relatives of victims, and people closely involved in tragic cases granted me access and accepted to recount painful personal stories. Special thanks to Masooma Qazilbash for her assistance and her hospitality during my visit to Pakistan.

The support of close friends was crucial in bringing this project to fruition. Anya Schiffrin, Robin Stephenson, and Maureen Freely bravely offered to read drafts at various stages of completion and contributed useful comments. Virginia Brown Keyder provided coffee breaks, Froukje Santing was always at the end of the telephone, and Irene Banias was a steady supporter. Toria Field believed in the project from the beginning. I am also grateful to my agent, Diana Finch, for her patience and her efforts on my behalf. And finally, thanks to my daughters, Vanessa and Amanda, for being there and encouraging me.

CHAPTER 1

ROJIN*

"I have an interesting case for you. It is an unusual one with a happy ending," a female lawyer of my acquaintance said when I visited her in her office in Diyarbakir, the capital of Turkey's Kurdish region, located in the southeast of the country. "The relatives have decided not to kill the girl. I know them well and I'm sure they'll agree to talk to you."

By the time I came across Rojin's story in 2002, I had been collecting information about crimes committed in the name of honor for a couple of years and had interviewed quite a few people who had been involved in or had witnessed the murder of girls killed by their relatives for allegedly violating the social code of honor. But this was my first opportunity to get closer to the internal debate that takes place within a family when a scandal erupts.

Rojin, sexually assaulted by a middle-aged man twice married and father of several children, had gotten pregnant as a result of the rape. The woman who put me in touch with the victim's relatives was one of several feminist lawyers who had taken on the case and represented the victim during the perpetrator's trial.

Frightened of her family's reaction, Rojin, a poorly educated village girl, had kept silent for months about the rape. The truth only emerged seven months later when she could no longer hide her swelling belly. She eventually gave birth to a baby boy who was given up for adoption.

Rojin would undoubtedly have been killed by her relatives had it not been for the swift intervention of her half-sister Zekiye. She was born of their father's first marriage and was old enough to be Rojin's mother. She had nine children of her own, several of them older than her youngest half-sibling.

The forceful Zekiye had reacted quickly, taking Rojin under her wing before the news of her pregnancy broke out in the family. She later managed to convince male relatives to spare the teenager's life.

The lawyer's offer to introduce me to the family gave me a unique opportunity to hear their side of the story. I hoped to get a better understanding of how significant honor was in the lives of the family members, and what dynamics determined why some women, such as Rojin, could be saved, while others were brutally murdered.

* * *

The next day, after phoning ahead to make sure that I would be welcome, I boarded a bus for Nusaybin, some 130 kilometers away from Diyarbakir. It was late April and the sun was already scorching this remote corner of Turkey.

The journey, on a wheezing vehicle without air-conditioning, was not particularly comfortable. I was allocated a seat next to a large peasant woman wearing a flowery skirt over her traditional baggy pants. A white kerchief, with hand-crocheted lacy edges, was tightly wound around her head. She was obviously returning from a shopping expedition to the regional capital and was laden with heavy parcels that spilled over her lap and onto mine. Pinned to my seat, I turned to the window and watched the scenery unfold. The vastness of the landscape in this rural part of Turkey never fails to enchant me.

I knew that this apparent peacefulness hid seething political tensions. This region at the southeast corner of Turkey, hemmed in by the borders of Iraq, Iran, and Syria, had long been the stage of a violent upheaval. Between 1984 and 1999, armed clashes between separatist guerrillas of the Kurdistan Workers' Party (PKK) and Turkish military forces had claimed some 40,000 lives and caused widespread misery. I had spent most of the nineties reporting (for the French daily *Le Monde* and other publications) on the conflict and on the widespread human rights violations that occurred.

According to conservative official figures, at least 350,000 people had been displaced by this internal war—forced out by the PKK, according to the official version; pushed out by the Turkish military, which burned villages to deny the rebels access to supplies, according to information gathered on the ground. The displaced probably numbered close to a million. Most of them ended up in the suburbs of regional urban centers, eking out a meager existence after losing the land and livestock that provided their subsistence.

The level of violence dropped drastically in 1999 after the Turkish authorities arrested PKK leader Abdullah Öcalan, who had fled from his previous refuge in Damascus to Kenya, and sentenced him to life imprisonment. But the authorities, having claimed victory, failed to take advantage of the truce to address the roots of the problem. A cease-fire declared by the rebels that year was only followed by limited cultural reforms, and after several years of relative peace, the militants resumed armed operations in 2004.

Further clashes ensued, fueled partly by the U.S. intervention in Iraq, which left the north of the country in the hands of Iraqi Kurds, who were sympathetic to their Turkish cousins' plight. In 2009, the Turkish government, led by the conservative Justice and Development Party (AKP), finally broke with decades of rigid policy and recognized that denying Kurds their cultural identity had been a mistake. A "democratic opening" to expand cultural rights and convince militants to put down their weapons followed, but the process faced such strong resistance from Turkish nationalists that the government was forced to retreat.

At the time I visited Zekiye and her family in April 2002, the unilateral cease-fire declared by the PKK was still in force and the region was largely peaceful. Most of the roadblocks and security checks that had made travel across the region very difficult, and often hazardous, in the previous decade had been removed and a sense of normality had returned, although no long-term political solution to Turkey's perennial Kurdish problem had yet been found, or even been seriously sought.

After leaving behind the imposing basalt fortifications, built between the eleventh and thirteenth centuries, that stretch for 5 kilometers and surround the city of Diyarbakir, the bus meandered alongside the Tigris River for a while, passing a few hamlets along the way. Fields on gently rolling hills bordered the road and lonely shepherds—dwarfed by the vast expanse of empty space—could occasionally be spotted in the distance, escorting flocks of sheep with fierce-looking dogs.

After an hour, the road started curling up to the city of Mardin, an old Arab town of breathtaking architectural beauty. Sand-colored stone houses with lace-like carvings and arched windows, separated by narrow alleyways, clung precariously to a rocky promontory. Below the city's terraces, the vast plain of Mesopotamia stretched as far as the eye could see, beyond the border with Syria, in a monochromatic patchwork of fields.

After zigzagging down the cliff and driving across a flat expanse of land, the bus finally arrived at the Nusaybin bus terminal. It was little more than a dusty stop on the side of the road. When I phoned my hosts to signal my arrival, I was told to wait. A young man, who appeared to be in his late twenties, soon came to fetch me. As we walked through the potholed streets of the town, I tried to make light conversation but he was clearly unwilling to chat. From his stony face, I gathered that he did not think it a good idea to allow foreigners to probe delicate family matters.

At the house, a large two-storey concrete villa with a pretty garden in front, Zekiye received me with the warmth and hospitality that characterizes most encounters in this part of the world. She was a tall and commanding figure, a rotund middle-aged woman with a broad, open face under her colorful headscarf. Her demeanor immediately identified her as a matriarch who wielded a lot of authority within the family.

After marrying a civil servant employed by the ministry of public works—therefore marrying well by local standards—Zekiye had left her village of origin and her siblings to settle in the town of Nusaybin where her family had gradually expanded to include nine children.

Zekiye's male relatives had stayed in the village and were still working the family land. Rojin, the rape victim, was one of five children born of Zekiye's elderly father's second marriage. After the death of his first spouse, who had given birth to three children, he had brought in a much younger partner.

I didn't get the impression that the two branches of the family were emotionally close, but they were all part of an extended clan. As customs dictate, the older siblings dutifully provided financial and moral support to the younger ones, who had been abandoned by their mother after the death of their father. No details were provided about the circumstances that had pushed their mother to leave, but the younger siblings appeared to be treated as poor relatives who were a bit of a burden.

When Zekiye was alerted by Rojin's sister that the young girl might be pregnant, she wasted no time and rushed to the village some 40 kilometers away from her home.

She was aware that news of Rojin's pregnancy would have the effect of a bombshell in the extended family and the men would soon be baying for blood. Unless she acted fast, not only would her young half-sister risk being killed by irate relatives but a blood feud could erupt between their and the rapist's family. Clan vendettas in this part of Turkey can last for generations and claim many lives.

She fetched Rojin and immediately drove her to the safety of her own home. Only then did she inform her elder brother Hüseyin of the situation. He was the oldest male and therefore officially the head of the familial group (the *aile reisi*). Zekiye knew she needed to convince him, before any of their other relatives, to spare Rojin's life.

At the house, I met Zekiye's teenage daughter Fatoş, a high school student, who stepped in and acted as a translator when her mother struggled to find the right Turkish words. Like many women of her generation in this poor and underdeveloped region of Turkey, Zekiye had not attended school. Kurdish was spoken at home, and Zekiye had few opportunities to practice her Turkish.

Lively and pretty with her hair tied up in a ponytail, wearing jeans and a T-shirt, Fatoş looked no different than a Western teenager. There seemed to be a wide gulf between the rural setting her mother had known in her own childhood and the small-town environment her daughter was growing up in. Yet traditional perceptions still had a strong grip on the younger generation.

"*Namus* (honor) is very important for the villagers," Fatoş explained when I asked her about Rojin's ordeal. "At first we couldn't believe such a thing could happen to our family. My mother nearly fainted when she heard."

I asked Fatoş about her personal views. I expected her to feel some sympathy for a girl barely a year or two older than she was, but I was taken aback by her vehement reaction.

"I hardly know her, but I cannot stand her," she said fiercely. "How could she do such a thing? How could she mess up our family in such a way! She is nothing but filth."

I pointed out that Rojin had been a victim of rape, but Fatoş just shrugged and carried on ranting against the girl she held responsible for the catastrophe that had befallen their family.

Zekiye, mature and more aware of the complexities of life, was upset and perturbed rather than angry. She was torn between her sense of fairness and justice, and the traditional notions of honor and chastity that had been drummed into her head as she grew up.

Her common sense told her that Rojin was a victim, but the young girl's pregnancy was a threat to the family reputation and Zekiye could not help but be affected by the scandal. Killing Rojin would be the easy option: it would put an end to the sense of social alienation the extended clan, which she said counted some 150 members, was experiencing.

Talking to her and to other members of her family gave me a sense of their internal turmoil and the burden that the code of honor places on communities and individuals. Listening to Zekiye and her relatives, I felt like an atheist confronted with the unshakeable faith of believers: their belief in the honor system was utterly alien to me, but it was evidently very real to them. The sheer power of it almost took my breath away.

Rojin's rape had torn a gaping hole into their lives. Once a respectable family, they all felt dirtied by the scandal and could not hide their shame.

"Since this happened, mom cannot eat, she cannot sleep," Fatoş told me.

However misguided their attachment to honor appeared, their suffering was real. Zekiye believed that her teenaged half-sister did not deserve to die, but she could not bring herself to exonerate her entirely.

"The girl is guilty, she should have told us. She is a stupid, ignorant girl," Zekiye proclaimed, shaking her head in disbelief. "Why didn't she run away instead of leaving this burden on our shoulders?"

But she accepted that there were mitigating circumstances: the girl was young and uneducated. Had Rojin announced her pregnancy earlier, "something could have been done," Zekiye suggested, hinting perhaps at a discreet abortion that might have allowed the family to cover up the sexual assault.

Later, Hüseyin joined us and took over the discussion. Unlike his sister who had moved up the social ladder when she married and become a town dweller, Hüseyin had remained in the village, and he still lived modestly on the family land.

He had the wiry body and leathery skin of a man who spends most of his life outdoors, and he was clearly proud of his prominent position within the clan.

Watching him interact with his sister Zekiye, it was immediately clear to me that she exercised a strong moderating influence over him. Hüseyin believed that he was in control, but she was smarter and more worldly wise than he was. She bowed to tradition and deferred to him respectfully, manipulating him into believing that he was making his own decisions. But, like many older women in patriarchal societies, she was a clever operator, using her power in a roundabout way rather than through direct confrontation.

She had achieved the remarkable feat of getting her nine children educated, some of them at postdoctoral level, in a region where many kids still don't even attend primary school. According to official figures published in June 2009, 220,000 children of school age, among them 130,000 girls, were not registered in school, even though primary education is compulsory in Turkey.[1]

One of Zekiye's sons was a doctor, while another was in medical school. A daughter was among the lawyers who fought to get Rojin's rapist convicted, while another trained as a nurse. Another member of the brood owned a publishing house, which fell foul of the authorities for publishing political texts, and one was attending graduate school in Germany.

Zekiye's open-mindedness helped tip the balance in favor of Rojin's survival, but I could see that it had been a hard-fought battle and that the resulting victory was fragile.

* * *

The jumble of conflicting emotions unleashed in the family by Rojin's rape was even more apparent during my conversation with Hüseyin, who oscillated between anger and patronizing leniency as he told me his version of events.

He was furious with Rojin, cursing her for bringing dishonor on the family one minute, then magnanimously accepting that she was "ignorant" and therefore "not entirely" responsible for what had happened to her. But an element of doubt was always at the back of his mind—the niggling thought that Rojin might have been consenting or at least must have tempted her attacker with her unbecoming behavior.

"Girls are guilty, but of course if they are forced it is different," he said, apparently unaware of the contradiction inherent in his statement. Then he added almost immediately: "Of course, no one was there to see how it happened."

The belief that women run wild as soon as men have their back turned is often given as justification for the need to maintain constant control.

The debate on retribution was still raging within the clan. Hotheaded young males, in particular, believed that the family's pride could be restored only if blood was spilled. Hüseyin, to some extent, shared their views.

Their customs were clear on the matter. "If a girl is touched by someone who is not legitimately entitled to touch her, or who hasn't asked for her father's permission, then we have to kill or we would show a lack of strength," he explained. "This is according to our religious laws. You have to ask a girl's father first. They should have come and asked for the girl in marriage. We could have said yes or no," he said, bitterly.

The grievous harm that had been caused to the young girl was not Hüseyin's main concern. He was primarily incensed that Seymo, the rapist, had violated tradition and not sought his permission, in loco parentis, before approaching the girl. The rapist had thus left their family group facing an impossible decision.

"If only this dog had abducted her, then the situation would have been better," Hüseyin grumbled. "We could have accepted a girl from their family in compensation, and this messy situation would not have arisen." The harm done to Rojin was a secondary matter; the main issue was the lack of a marriage proposal. Hüseyin and his male relatives felt slighted.

In their home village, Seymo's interest in Rojin had not gone unnoticed. The man was well known for having a roving eye and being attracted to young girls. Zekiye told me that he had kidnapped and married his second wife when she was still in her early teens. This episode was noted by the judges during the trial and apparently contributed to his heavy sentence.

Before they had even heard of the rape, Rojin's relatives had paid a visit to the *muhtar*, the elected village headman, who happened to be the rapist's brother. They had asked him to keep Seymo away from "their" girl. Rojin was due to marry someone else shortly, and she should be left alone, they warned. Little did they know that their warnings had come too late. By the time the family delegation visited the *muhtar*, Rojin was already pregnant.

Hüseyin was seething with anger when he mentioned Seymo's family. His mind was clearly swimming in a confusion of feelings. He was proud of his decision not to kill Rojin, which he said showed his degree of "enlightenment." "We think it's wrong to kill her. She was deceived. She was young, she was ignorant," he said. But the emotional roller coaster would push him into a different mood a few minutes later, when he talked of Rojin as "a dirty girl," who had contaminated the rest of the family with "filth."

"Now all the girls in our family have lost points. Nobody wants to marry her sister. This is why the tradition is to kill them," he explained. "It is to show that no other girl in the family will follow the same path."

* * *

I, too, was experiencing contradictory feelings. These people had been hospitable and received me with great kindness. I could see that operating within the narrow constraints of their traditional community they were genuinely trying to do the right thing. Their efforts had saved Rojin's life, but their attachment to honor could not guarantee the teenager a decent life.

She was the one I had really hoped to see. I wanted to hear her side of the story, and understand how she had found the mental strength to withstand the unbearable pressure placed on her in the previous 18 months. But I had to bide my time: my hosts had shown remarkable openness in agreeing to discuss a topic that was a source of pain and deep shame, something normally never discussed outside the family.

I had to tread carefully. But throughout my conversation with her relatives, my thoughts kept wandering toward Rojin. Eventually, I seized an opportune break in the discussion and asked, tentatively, if I could talk to her. To my surprise, they immediately agreed but warned me first, rather contemptuously, that she was "a stupid and uneducated girl and wouldn't be able to speak to me in Turkish."

Until that moment, I hadn't realized that Rojin was still living under their roof. It was a shock to discover that while we were discussing her fate, the teenager was kept isolated in a room on the ground floor. Her relatives fed her, leaving plates in front of her door, but they could not bring themselves to look at her, let alone communicate with her. She was not allowed to share family life.

"I saw her twice in court, but for the past year I have not spoken to her and will never talk to her again," Hüseyin informed me. "We brought her brother over from the village with his family to look after her. His wife brings meals into her room every day."

No lock was needed to keep Rojin a prisoner. She knew she would risk death if she ventured outside, and she had nowhere else to go. "If our relatives had access to her, they might lynch her," Hüseyin admitted. I found it hard to reconcile the kindness these people had shown me with the apparent lack of compassion that caused them to ostracize a teenage rape victim and keep her in solitary confinement.

While I talked to Hüseyin, Zekiye retreated to the kitchen to cook lunch. When she brought me a tray with a grilled chicken breast, fried potatoes, and a light salad of tomatoes and cucumber, my hosts both withdrew from the room to let me eat: it would have been improper for a female stranger to eat in front of a man. Eating my meal alone felt strange. I thought of the teenage girl who, for over a year, had eaten her food alone day after day and lived in almost complete isolation.

* * *

It was with great trepidation that I finally stepped down to the ground floor to meet Rojin. She had suffered the shock and humiliation of rape, feared for her life throughout her pregnancy, and then experienced the pain of childbirth only to have her baby snatched away from her. What state could she be in?

Keeping the baby was never an option. In fact, Rojin's lawyer, who had seen her at the hospital shortly after her son was born, said she held the newborn awkwardly, at a distance from her body, and would not look at him.

The baby was visible proof of her shame and she could not afford to bond with a child she would not be allowed to bring up. As soon as the results of the paternity test were confirmed, the little boy was handed over to the state-run orphanage in Mardin.

The sullen young man who had guided me through the streets of Nusaybin turned out to have been Rojin's brother Fadil. Despite his young age he looked pale and unhealthy: he was suffering from tuberculosis, I was told, and had been hospitalized on more than one occasion. In fact, it was during one of his absences, when his sisters were not under the direct supervision of a male relative, that the rape had taken place.

Unable to work, he had been ordered by the family elders to move to Nusaybin, with his wife and two young children, in order to look after Rojin. Nobody wanted any contact with her, least of all him, but family hierarchy required him to obey. He clearly resented the task. Strict patriarchal rules do not just apply to women. Young men too are expected to accept the diktat of their male elders.

Fadil and his wife took me into a concrete room devoid of furniture. The walls were whitewashed and carpets covered the hard cement floor. I wanted to sit on the colorful cushions that lined the walls, but they insisted on bringing a white plastic garden chair for me and planted it right in the middle of the room.

The door opened, and Rojin entered with her head bowed. I was almost as intimidated as she was. Fadil sat cross-legged in one corner of the small space, while his wife occupied another. Both were silently staring into empty space.

The situation was awkward and extremely uncomfortable: I was sitting on the chair as if on a throne, while the young girl crouched at my feet. Her entire body was trembling and she was oozing animal fear. She could not look at me and kept fiddling with the edge of her cotton headscarf, decorated with handmade crochet lace. She was a fairly tall, solidly built girl with a round face—pretty in a peasant sort of way. A few pimples betrayed her young age.

She looked so helpless and childlike that I felt the urge to hug and comfort her, but her relatives' hostile attitude kept me in check.

I touched her shoulder, trying to convey as much warmth and sympathy as I could, through this simple touch, and asked if she was willing to tell me her story. She opened her mouth to answer, then shuddered and bowed her head even deeper, in shame this time, more than fear. Her lips quivered and a tear came to her eyes. I felt I was torturing her with my questions.

From the opposite side of the room, I could feel waves of contempt and disgust emanating from Fadil and his wife. Their anger expanded to fill the empty space. They kept their eyes averted, as if looking at her would make them dirty.

Rojin felt their antagonism and remained silent. I asked her if she felt vindicated by the verdict that had sent her aggressor to jail for over 11 years. She mumbled "yes," barely moving her lips. Then she stopped talking. After a while, the silence became unbearable. I could take it no longer. I thanked her and asked her what I could do for her. I reminded her that she was a victim and had done nothing wrong. As I wished her luck and got up to leave, her brother and sister-in-law led the way out of the room.

As soon as they had passed the threshold, ahead of us, she turned to me, grabbed my hand, and talked in urgent tones. "Please help me, I would be so grateful if you could," she said, looking at me with eager eyes.

We conversed in whispers for a few minutes as the other two stood in icy silence a few meters away. She told me briefly about the rape. "He had been laying his hands on all the girls that went past him," she said. "He said if I told anyone about the rape, the two families would kill each other, and I would be killed too. I begged him to leave me alone, I told him I was too young, I was afraid."

She knew that her family had decided to spare her life, but she was not entirely convinced that she was safe. I tried to reassure her, but I wasn't very confident either about her future. Rojin said that she was properly fed, but had no control over her own fate.

"It is not in my hands. I don't know what will happen."

Contrary to what her relatives had told me, I got the impression that despite her lack of education she was sharp-witted, and her Turkish was quite good.

The judges' decision to hand out a heavy sentence to her rapist had given Rojin's account of the rape an official stamp of authenticity and had undoubtedly saved her life. Her attacker had initially denied having intercourse with her, but when it became clear that a DNA test could easily prove his paternity, he changed his tune and claimed Rojin had been consenting. The judges did not accept his last minute editing of events.

But the teenager's situation remained precarious nonetheless. Her relatives, although well meaning, would not keep her under their roof permanently. The longer she stayed, the more likely it was that frustration would eventually boil over.

Their own lives had been suspended, and they felt that they would breathe freely only after she had exited the family once and for all. They were desperate to find a way out that did not involve murder, but they didn't know what to do with a disgraced girl no one wanted to take off their hands.

"The decision is to send her away, marry her off, and never see her again for as long as she lives," Hüseyin told me. Easier said than done, it turned out. Relatives had been searching high and low for a potential husband, but no candidate had come forward.

"Her life is finished. No honorable man would marry a girl in her situation. Could you find a family that would look after her in Istanbul?" Hüseyin asked me.

I excused myself and stepped out into the garden to make a phone call to a friend who ran a women's rights organization in Istanbul. I was tempted to fly Rojin back to Istanbul with me, but I was also hesitant. Despite her dire straits, the young girl might find it difficult to adapt out of her own environment. Shelters were rare in Turkey at that time, and I was not certain I would get help from the authorities.

But I wanted to support Rojin in some way. Her life was not in immediate danger, but her long-term prospects were bleak. My friend in Istanbul said she would look into the options available and would call me back. Perhaps the social services could take Rojin under their protection.

Outside, the sun was shining, but Rojin had gone back to the dark room where she lived. She could probably hear the roosters crowing in the distance, but she could not see the ducks frolicking on the banks of the stream that ran past the house. Nor could she go out into the garden to admire the rose bushes Zekiye was justly proud of.

After my brief encounter with Rojin, I found it harder to make polite conversation and exchange pleasantries with my hosts. They were decent people, trying to find the best way out of an unfortunate situation, but it was difficult to understand how they could isolate the young victim of a horrendous assault without feeling some compassion.

As I left, I thanked Zekiye profusely for her hospitality and for the meal she had cooked for me. "You've worked very hard," I said politely.

Before she could even respond, Hüseyin stepped in. "It is her duty," he said. "That's what women do."

* * *

I flew back to Istanbul, shaken by Rojin's tragedy. I had read about many horrific cases that ended in murder, but this particular story, which allegedly had a "happy ending" because the girl did not die, was just as disturbing.

For the first time, I had really come face to face with so-called honor, not as an abstract notion, but as a reality in people's lives.

It would have been easier to be able to label all perpetrators of honor killings as homicidal sociopaths, but the day I had spent with Zekiye and her family had shown that even ordinary, apparently reasonable people could come very close to committing murder to protect their reputation.

Rojin's relatives could not explain concretely how the scandal had affected them, but the opprobrium of the community—real and imagined—weighed heavily on them. The stain on their reputation affected every fiber of their beings. They felt that the world they knew had collapsed around them.

In their eyes, Rojin had ceased to exist the minute her rape became public knowledge. They had not killed her physically, but she was dead to them and the community.. The blood ties, usually so strong in this part of the world, had all but disintegrated. All they wanted was to find a way to get rid of her for good.

While I chatted with Hüseyin, the conversation had strayed to politics. The 15-year guerrilla war that had killed tens of thousands of people in Turkey's Kurdish area was still fresh in people's memories. The region, already underdeveloped, had sunk further into poverty as villagers were forced to leave land and livestock behind as they fled.

One of Zekiye's sons was among the estimated 40,000 dead. He had "gone to the mountains" at a young age, joining the armed militants who fought the Turkish armed forces in the rugged terrain of the border area, and had died during an armed confrontation.

Like many Turkish Kurds, Hüseyin and his family wanted the right to speak their language freely, recognition of their separate ethnic and cultural identity, and more political autonomy. They rightfully complained about state neglect and the heavy-handed way the Turkish authorities had dealt with the rebellion. The brutal and often indiscriminate methods used to crush the uprising had been extensively documented by organizations like Amnesty International in countless reports of human rights abuses.

Casually running his fingers through his prayer beads, Hüseyin complained bitterly about state oppression. "Why," he asked, "do the authorities always oppress the weak and the poor?".

I could not help but see a parallel between the state's attitude to the aspiration of the Kurds and the patriarchal pressure his community was imposing on women like Rojin. Did the state not demand total obedience from its citizens, whatever their ethnic origin, in the same way the head of a family expects unquestioning allegiance from his female relatives?

Such thoughts had clearly never crossed Hüseyin's head. He could talk about democracy in political terms, but freedom of choice within the family was not on offer.

When I turned to Rojin's sad-looking brother Fadil to ask him how he saw his sister's situation, the head of the clan stepped in before the young man could even open his mouth.

"There is no need to ask for his opinion," he said. "What he thinks is irrelevant. I'm his senior, and he has to do what I say."

I wondered how Zekiye's educated children, who were young and living in big cities, in more cosmopolitan surroundings, felt about the whole drama. It had emerged in the course of our discussion that I knew one of her sons, who lived in Istanbul. By sheer coincidence, I had attended the opening of his trial at a state security court a week earlier.

Hikmet ran a publishing house and was being tried for translating foreign books on the Kurds, deemed unsuitable by Turkish officialdom. Human rights activists from Western countries had attended the hearing and urged the Turkish authorities to drop the case. He was eventually acquitted several months later.

What would an educated man who benefited from the support of international human rights groups when his right to free expression was violated make of the tragedy that was playing out in his own family?

Shortly after my return to Istanbul, I called to make an appointment. In the meantime, I had inquired about possible solutions to Rojin's plight. My feminist friend suggested the family should contact the social services in Mardin province. They sometimes took young women into care, moving them to shelters at the other end of the country where they could be educated and taught new skills, safely out of reach of their relatives. Another option was to help her apply for asylum in a Western country: cases of women granted refugee status for gender violence were still rare, but a few had been successful.

Hikmet and I had friends in common and he had heard of me, but he was apparently unaware that I had spent time with his mother and uncle at the family home.

When I mentioned Rojin, he looked a bit sheepish. Yes, he said, he had heard of her story. Although she was a relative, he had not met the girl personally. He was aware that she was in a bad situation, but what could he do? His parents had asked him to take her off their hands and shelter her in Istanbul, but he felt that he could not take responsibility for her well-being.

I outlined the two main options that I had been told were available to Rojin and asked him to relay the information to his family.

"I doubt they will accept to involve the social services," he said, "because they don't trust them."

The family feared, above all, that if Rojin settled in a state institution, her whereabouts would eventually be discovered and the rapist's family might try to have her kidnapped. Under the penal code in force in Turkey at the time, a rapist could avoid serving his sentence if he married his victim, who was of course rarely consulted. Even if she was, she probably saw it as the only way to escape death.

In this particular case, the family felt honor could only be redeemed if the perpetrator served his full sentence. A blood feud in the village had been averted, but men in Rojin's and her rapist's extended families still carried guns and saw the other clan as the enemy. Mediation attempts between the two families had failed: the girl's relatives were determined to get legal redress for the insult they had suffered.

A new penal code was introduced in Turkey in 2005. Under pressure from feminist groups, several articles detrimental to women were replaced or removed, including the provision that let rapists off the hook if they married the woman they had assaulted.

Hikmet was cautiously optimistic that his parents might be interested in sending Rojin abroad. He promised to consult them and let me know what transpired.

I did not have to wait long. A few hours later, the telephone rang. Hikmet had spoken to his mother: the crisis had been successfully resolved, he said. Rojin had been sent to Şırnak, a mountain province near the Iraqi border, and married off to a man too poor to afford a bride price. In fact, I later learned, he had been paid to take her on.

My heart sank. For Rojin's relatives, this was a sensible way out. They had now officially transferred "ownership" of the young woman, and she was no longer their problem. But a woman married in such circumstances was unlikely to ever shake off the stigma of her past. Not only would she suffer a life of poverty, but probably also be victimized by in-laws, who would never fully forgive her "sin."

For a while, I toyed with the idea of returning to Nusaybin to ask for Rojin's address. Eventually, I decided against it. Her relatives would not welcome my interference, a reminder of the scandal that they were trying hard to put behind them. And even if I discovered where Rojin was living, I risked jeopardizing her chances of integrating into the new environment if I turned up looking for her.

I could only hope that she had married into a decent family and had a husband who treated her with some respect. Perhaps her neighbors did not know the circumstances surrounding her arrival. I still often think of her, and wonder how she is doing.

She will never fully overcome the tragic events that have marked her teenage years, but I hope she can find some contentment and raise children who will bring her the warmth and affection that was so cruelly lacking when she needed it most.

I later learned from her lawyer that the Court of Appeal had overturned Rojin's rapist's conviction and reduced his sentence. He was freed after serving less than 20 months in jail—a very cheap price for the life that he had ruined.

CHAPTER 2

HONOR AND SHAME

Despite the best efforts of women's rights activists over the past decades, thousands of women around the world are killed every year for defying an unwritten patriarchal code of conduct. Many more are ostracized, like Rojin, or face unbearable pressure in their daily lives.

A conservative and much quoted United Nations Population Fund (UNFPA) estimate suggests that at least 5,000 women are murdered every year in defense of "honor," or perhaps more accurately, in support of social mores that require girls to be obedient and chaste.

Often perceived in the West as an Islamic custom, honor killings are in fact a pre-Islamic tradition that prevailed in many countries for centuries and whose roots are lost in time. Today's perpetrators no doubt believe that they are acting to protect an abstract notion of honor they hold as sacred, but honor killings may initially have had a more practical purpose.

As scholar Leila Ahmed, who has written extensively about patriarchy, explained in her landmark book, as soon as tribes settled and began to acquire land and other assets, "the patriarchal family, designed to guarantee the paternity of property-heirs and vesting in men the control of female sexuality, became institutionalized, codified, and upheld by the state."[1]

Until the discovery of DNA, men could never be entirely sure that their offspring were really theirs. Controlling women's sexuality and making sure that they did not marry outside the tribal group was therefore crucial to preserve the bloodline. Notions of honor and shame, drummed into young boys and girls, acted as social safeguards. To this day, many arranged marriages are commercial transactions that involve two families exchanging money and goods over the heads of young women, who are themselves viewed as commodities.

"Women's sexuality was designated the property of men, first of the woman's father, then of her husband, and female sexual purity (virginity in particular) became negotiable, economically valuable property," Ahmed wrote.

The Pakistani NGO Shirkat Gah defines crimes committed in the name of honor as

the killing of women to restore male honor and maintain patriarchal structures has been taking place for centuries in lands that were the cradles of world civilisations: in agrarian societies such as China and India (including present day Pakistan), in the tribal Arab Middle East, throughout the lands of the Mediterranean (in Palestine, Lebanon, Turkey, Greece, Morocco, Italy, Spain), in Southern Europe, as well as in Latin American countries across the Atlantic."[2]

Today the link between the desire to keep land within the family and the notion of honor may appear more tenuous than in the past, yet the need to control women often stems from economic as well as moral reasons.

Honor killings tend to occur mainly in the Middle East, in South Asia, and in South America, as well as among migrant communities in Western countries. Until two or three decades ago they were still regularly reported in Mediterranean countries such as Greece, Spain, and Italy.

In the Middle East, the trace of honor can be found in the Code of Hammurabi, circa 1750 B.C., and in Assyrian laws introduced around 1100 B.C. Adulterous couples were punished with death and in some cases, men who committed rape were punished with the rape of their own wives.[3]

The notion that a rape can be erased if the rapist marries his victim still applies in many countries around the world: marital ties somehow restore the social balance upset by out-of-wedlock sexual interaction. Worst still, in the most patriarchal communities, a rape can even now be "compensated" by another sexual assault. A tragic story, which came to light in the eastern province of Van, in Turkey in 2006, demonstrates that this practice is alive.

Twenty-two-year-old Songul, who lived in a remote village near the Iranian border, was raped by a neighbor while her husband was away doing seasonal work. When a relative of his, Bahattin, found out about the rape, he tied Songul in a barn and tortured her for two days for dishonoring her husband, Mehmet, and his family.

Eventually, the village council of elders gathered to discuss how to deal with the matter. As was the case with Rojin, the suffering Songul had experienced at the hands of her rapist was irrelevant. What was important was to redeem her husband's honor.

The elders came up with what they thought was a fair solution: Songul and Mehmet's marriage would be dissolved and the young wife, who had been defiled, would be sent back to her parents' home. To soothe Mehmet's bruised pride, the rapist would give him his 16-year-old daughter in marriage, as compensation for the loss of his wife.

In short, this meant that one man committed the crime, but two women were punished for it. Songul was banished, while the rapist's teenaged daughter was married against her will.

Songul, pregnant from the rape, returned to her father's village, but her brother, rightly fearing for her life, decided to take her to a lawyer. The young woman lodged formal complaints against her rapist and her now ex-husband's relative who had tortured her. The prosecutor who took up her case, perhaps because he wasn't from the region or simply because he lacked sensitivity, failed to understand that she was in danger of being killed for not accepting the villagers' harsh verdict and fighting back in court.

Local women's rights activists sprang into action to protect Songul as well as the teenager who was meant to replace her as Mehmet's bride. They contacted the authorities, but they could find no official willing to respond to their desperate calls over the weekend. Eventually, the head of a local NGO, Zozan Özgökçe, intervened during a live phone-in television program and launched an emotional appeal to save the two women. That night, law enforcement officers took Songul and the rapist's daughter into protective custody and transferred them to a shelter, but the teenager had already been forcibly married to Songul's ex-husband. The men involved in the case were arrested to face prosecution.[4]

The code of honor shows variations from one region to the next, but the overall concept is remarkably similar. In Pakistan, a country where crimes committed in the name of honor are still regularly reported, the practice is thought to have originated in Baluchistan, before being imported to Sindh over the centuries by the Baluchi diaspora.[5]

What is clear is that honor killings have been occurring for centuries and pre-date the arrival of Islam. They are in fact in direct contradiction with the teachings of the Koran. The Muslim holy book takes a dim view of illicit sexual relations and recommends the stoning of adulterers, male and female, but it requires four eye witnesses—a condition that should be almost impossible to meet—to confirm the conviction. Even adultery is not considered an excuse for personal justice: executions of adulterers can only be ordered by a court.

The UN figure of 5,000 provides a vague estimate that only reveals the tip of the iceberg. The patriarchal control exercised over women is pervasive and affects the lives of millions of women around the globe, in many different ways.

Obtaining accurate data is all the more difficult in that there is no universally accepted definition of "honor killings." Human Rights Watch describes crimes committed in the name of honor as

acts of violence, usually murder, committed by male family members against female family members, who are held to have brought dishonor upon the family. A woman can be targeted by (individuals within) her family for a variety of reasons, including: refusing to enter into an arranged marriage, being the victim of a sexual assault, seeking a divorce—even from an abusive husband—or (allegedly) committing adultery. The mere perception that a woman has behaved in a specific way to "dishonor" her family, is sufficient to trigger an attack.[6]

Palestinian-American scholar Lama Abu Odeh[7] describes murders committed in the name of honor as the "killing of a women by her father or brother for engaging in, or being suspected of engaging in, sexual practices before or outside marriage."

Personally, I find this definition too restrictive. In several cases I came across, the sexual element, even as an allegation, was missing altogether. Interpretation may differ from one region to the next, but honor is not only invoked in cases of premeditated ritual killings committed in patriarchal communities by the victim's blood relatives. I found that defiance and disobedience were as common a thread linking the murders as sexual misconduct, and in some cases, women were at risk simply because their existence was socially inconvenient for their male relatives. The "honor" motive was sometimes an afterthought that allowed perpetrators to get away with their crime.

For the purpose of this book, I therefore broadened the scope of my study to look at various forms of discrimination against women that can lead to their death, on the pretext that they have sullied their family's "honor."

In Turkey, where I have lived for over two decades, murders committed as a result of a collective decision taken by the family or by a tribal court are often labeled "customs killings" (töre cinayetleri). Under Turkey's Penal Code, revised in 2005, these are the only crimes committed in the name of honor that call for a mandatory life sentence due to aggravated circumstances.

Also falling under the umbrella of honor killing in the view of many activists—but unfortunately not defined as such under Turkish law—are murders committed by individuals, usually husbands or lovers, who suspect that their partner is involved in an illicit relationship or who refuse to accept that their partner wants to end their relationship. When they strike to express their rage, they too usually claim to have done so to redeem their honor and reputation.

In communities where "ownership" of a woman is seen as passing from her family to her husband when she marries, the spouse, rather than a blood relative, may become the enforcer if she is perceived to have offended the social order. He can also ask his wife's brothers to take action.

The dividing line between "honor killings" and murders known in Western countries as "crimes of passion," committed in a fit of anger or jealousy, becomes very thin in such cases.

I would argue that many crimes labeled domestic murders in the West could easily fit into the broader category of "crimes committed in the name of honor." The discourse and the vocabulary are clearly different: Western men are unlikely to use honor as a defense, but acts of murder committed by male partners are often motivated by a hurt pride or a desire to control a woman who spurned them.

A good example would be the famous case of O.J. Simpson, the famous American footballer, who was acquitted of the double murder of his ex-wife, Nicole Brown Simpson, and her lover, Ronald Goldman, in a controversial trial in 1995 but was later found guilty of their wrongful deaths in a civil court case. During the trial it emerged that O.J. Simpson had often humiliated and pressured his much younger wife, Nicole, publicly. He was known to be overbearing in his relationships with women and was used to calling the shots. When Nicole eventually filed for divorce and started dating other men, he could not accept that she had escaped from his clutches.

Violence against women is a universal scourge, and one that takes many forms according to the local social, cultural, and political environment. In Western societies, we like to think that women are "liberated" and we are quick to spot unfamiliar harmful practices such as honor killings or dowry deaths that take place in foreign cultures. But statistics provide shocking evidence that domestic violence, rapes, and killings are still common and even on the rise in Western societies. The extent of homegrown violence against women in Western democracies is often overlooked.

For instance, the British authorities believe that 10–12 honor killings take place among migrant families in the United Kingdom every year, but up to 120 women are killed every year by their partners or ex-partners in domestic murders.

"Patriarchal violence is universal. It is both Eastern and Western. In the West, where feminist knowledge emerged, anti-feminism continues to be dominant in popular culture," write scholars Shahrzad Mojab and Nahla Abdo. "While identifying male violence as a problem of non-Western societies is a racist claim, it is true that there is an unleashing of male violence in certain parts of the world, especially in North Africa, the Middle East and South Asia."[8]

The main difference between "honor killings" and the "crimes of passion" described in the penal codes of Western democracies—and it is a substantial difference—lies in the social context: domestic murders and crimes of passion are usually received with revulsion, whereas honor killings are still tolerated or even encouraged in some parts of the world.

This latest claim should perhaps be written in the past tense because a growing number of human rights defenders are working to remove this social cover and expose brutal crimes committed in the name of honor for what they really are: the suppression of women's freedom to make their own choices and the ultimate violation of their right to live.

UN data on honor killings can only be seen as a rough estimate, and so also national statistics on honor killings, which are partial at best in the countries where the murders occur.

In Turkey, a police report put at 1,091 the number of crimes committed in the name of honor and customs between 2000 and 2005,[9] but the survey gave no gender distribution of the victims nor did it provide a clear definition of these crimes. The report was also limited to the activities of the police force, which only operates in urban areas. In Turkey, policing of rural areas is the responsibility of the gendarmerie, a semi-military force linked to the Ministry of Interior, whose own data, if it exists, has not been made public.

The Aurat foundation of Pakistan estimated that 1,317 women had fallen victim to violence in 2007. Two hundred and ten of them, as well as 117 men, were accused of being *karo kari,* an expression that means "black man, black woman" and is used to describe couples engaged in illicit relations. A report on Pakistan published by the Convention on the Elimination of All Forms of Discrimination Against Women (CEDAW) in 2005 mentions official figures, quoted by ministers in the Pakistani Senate in July 2004, suggesting that *karo kari* "had claimed the lives of 4,000 men and women in the country during the last six years. From January 1998 to December 2003, the number of women killed in the name of honor was more than double the number of men murdered."[10]

Both "partners-in-sin" are at risk when they are thus labeled in rural Pakistan, but men can often pay compensation and buy their way out of trouble.

In Jordan, some 20 girls are killed every year by their relatives.

In India, too, up to 1,000 honor killings are committed every year and they prevail among Hindus as well as Muslims. Although the traditional Hindu caste system that defined social relations in India has officially been abolished in the country, it still plays a key role in community relations, particularly in the countryside. Honor is invoked to justify murder mainly when strict rules banning relationships between individuals of different social castes are violated. Another, even more common form of violence against women in India is the dowry death. According to the National Crime Records Bureau in India, more than 6,000 women were killed every year between 2001 and 2005 for failing to satisfy their in-laws' demands for dowry funds and assets.[11]

In the broad scope of violence against women, honor killings stand out because they are often carried out by the parents or close relatives of the victims. They are patriarchy's instrument of last resort, a blunt tool wielded not only to punish individuals for perceived infractions of the social code of conduct, but also to send a powerful message to others who might be tempted to stray away from the narrow path laid out by the male elders.

"A woman is like an olive tree. When its branch catches woodworm, it has to be chopped off so that society stays clean and pure," Tarrad Fayiz, a Jordanian tribal leader told a BBC reporter.[12]

Many activists object to the term "honor killing," arguing that putting the two words side by side amounts to accepting and glorifying an interpretation of honor used to police women's behavior and often grossly abused. There is obviously nothing honorable about killing defenseless women.

Finding a suitable term to replace "honor killings" is not easy. "Crimes committed in the name of honor" might be a more adequate description, even if it still refers to the problematic notion of "honor." Whenever "honor" is mentioned in this book as linked to women's behavior, it should be seen as framed by inverted commas: it is not the victims who behave dishonorably, but those who hound and kill them.

It is tempting to dismiss the notion of honor as "a useful fiction in preserving male dominance,"[13] but the concept remains so real to many people around the world that it cannot be rejected outright as meaningless. Gross miscarriages of justice and extrajudicial executions are committed in its name, on the basis of the flimsiest of evidence. It is also used to cover up ordinary murders or justify greed and abuse. But to understand how families can come to kill their daughters, their understanding of honor, however misguided, and the roots of their attachment to it deserve to be examined closely.

* * *

During my visits to rural areas where "honor" still ruled, I often experienced a strange duality. At first glance, the world my interlocutors inhabited appeared very remote from my own: the women I talked to often had little power of decision over their own lives and their fate was largely in the hands of others, while I felt, by and large, free to make my own choices and operate with a large degree of independence.

But their life stories resonated within me at a deeper level, creating a sense of sisterly connection that crossed borders and cultures. Patriarchy, in various forms, is alive in the most developed societies. It does not impose its rule in the same unrelenting way, but it still makes itself felt on a regular basis.

To most Westerners today, honor comes across as a rather old-fashioned word that conjures up images of knights and noblemen throwing down the gauntlet and dueling to death to salvage their pride. Not exactly the stuff of modern life.

But millions of people around the world are still brought up with the notion that honor is a fundamental part of their own identity and the bond that ties their community. For those living in tribal or tight-knit communities, linked by blood ties, honor can at times be unforgiving but it remains a crucial value.

"In its purest and most desirable form, honor is an integral dimension of Eastern culture, where one's honorable deeds are looked on as a valued possession," wrote sociologists Aysan Sev'er and Gökçicek Yurdakul.[14]

But when it is built around the notion that a man's pride and respectability lie in his ability to protect his womenfolk and ensure that they remain chaste, honor can also become a lethal weapon.

The twin concepts of honor and shame (its opposite) exist in all cultures but the communal values that retain a major importance in many developing societies have given way to individualism in the West. Today, in Europe or in the United States, the interests of the extended family rarely trump those of the individual. On the other hand, more people in developed countries suffer from loneliness or feel isolated. And a woman's sexual behavior is still more likely to come under scrutiny and be criticized than a man's.

Peter Mullan's powerful 2002 film, *The Magdalene Sisters*, was a useful reminder that the sexual emancipation of women in western countries was achieved only recently. The movie retraced the true stories of three "fallen" Irish young women—three among thousands who ended up in church-run asylums, condemned by their families to a life of shame and drudgery.

It emerged in the late 1990s that in the course of the 150 years the Magdalene laundries were in operation in Ireland, some 30,000 young Irish women had been locked up in these workhouses, run with an iron hand by unforgiving nuns. Unlike "honor killing" victims, the young women were not murdered, but they were cut off from society, locked up, and effectively buried alive in these bleak institutions. They were required to do hard labor in church-run laundries to expiate their "sins." Some of these young women were deemed too free-spirited for the traditional and religious society they lived in; others had become pregnant out of wedlock and had to be hidden away for fear that they might corrupt the moral fabric of society. The babies they gave birth to were forcibly taken away from them and sent off for adoption. Their fate was, in fact, not very different from Rojin's own.

The fate of these inmates, invisible to the rest of society, had rarely been talked about until several bodies were discovered in 1993 in a former laundry that had been sold to a property developer. After further investigation, the remains of 155 former inmates were found buried in unnamed graves on the site. Forgotten by all, including by their own relatives, they had died within the walls of these institutions. The last Magdalene institution closed down in 1996.

The scandal was a stark reminder that, until recently, some Western European communities, often under the influence of the church, were taking extreme measures against young women perceived as leading a dissolute life. A girl's "bad behavior" did not just affect her own life, but tainted those around her. To prevent the rot from spreading, the offender needed to be isolated, physically and socially.

The shunning of these girls stemmed from a mentality similar to the one that even today condones killing in the name of honor. Heterosexual relations are rarely met with such intolerance in Western societies today, but homosexuality still triggers strong reactions and at times violence from conservative elements in our liberal societies.

In countries where gruesome traditional killings are tolerated, honor occupies such an important place in life that a rich vocabulary is usually available to describe it. In Turkish, for instance, there is a clear distinction between *onur* (close to the Western definition of honor), *şeref* (derived from an achieved status), and *gurur* (closer to pride). *Namus* is the killer: this is the form of honor that is directly linked to women's chastity, and it is the one that affects men through their female relatives.

In Arabic, too, there is a distinction between *sharaf* (social prestige) and *'ird* (linked to women's chastity). In Urdu and Sindhi, languages spoken in Pakistan, honor that comes through chaste behavior also deserves separate terms like *ghairat* and *izzat*.

Honor tends to be a male attribute, while shame belongs to women. This dichotomy has been used throughout the world for centuries to justify male dominance over women: the honor/shame system is an ideology of power.

Male relatives are not the only enforcers of social rules. In many cases, the extended family, women included, is mobilized to protect social mores. If a family is not swift enough to act when its honor is at stake, the wider community will exert pressure, often refusing interaction with members of "the tainted group" to remind them of their traditional duty.

Former UN Special Rapporteur on Violence against Women Radhika Coomaraswamy noted that "in many instances, women and girl children are subjected to violence by their communities because of their sexuality and sexual behaviour. A key component of community identity, and therefore the demarcation of community boundaries, is the preservation of communal honor. Such honor is frequently perceived, by both community and non-community members, as residing in the sexual behaviour of the women of the community. Communities, therefore, 'police' the behaviour of their female members."[15]

Law enforcement officials, when they do bother to investigate these cases, face a challenge to find the real culprits and arrest them. "Honor killings" in their traditional form are a type of organized crime. An entire community is often involved and maintains silence about the events. This unwillingness to speak out may not quite match the omerta, or code of silence, of the Sicilian mafia, but it comes close to it.

Women can be accused of disgracing their family if they do not behave according to the received norms. The honor gained through chaste or modest behavior is not theirs alone to keep: it will be bestowed on the men in their family, and will then trickle down to all members of the group, who will benefit from the reflected glory of belonging to a "respectable" family.

Protecting a girl's virginity until she dutifully marries the groom chosen by her family is a task entrusted to all male members of the clan, especially her brothers. If an illicit affair occurs, the male partner is sometimes killed as well, although in many communities monetary compensation can convince angry relatives to spare a man's life.

Killing a man is more onerous and can trigger blood feuds between families that can last generations. Accepting compensation is therefore a face-saving way to avoid a bloodbath. Another common practice is to hand over a girl from the offending family in compensation. Usually very young, entirely innocent, she, in turn, becomes a victim of the "honor" system.

Most interpretations of honor codes share the common element that they revolve around women. "*Namus* is located between a woman's legs," says Mehmet Faraç bluntly. He is a Turkish journalist and politician who authored a book detailing several murders committed in his native province of Urfa, one of the most conservative areas of Turkey.

Faraç's crude definition comes close to the mark: honor is linked to a woman's reputation for purity and her menfolk's ability to protect it. But illicit relations are not the only trigger for violence—leaving the house without a male kin's permission can lead to neighbors questioning a woman's reputation. Being too feisty and attracting too much attention can also be dangerous.

Some cases are extreme: 16-year-old Hacer was killed by her 15-year-old brother in the Turkish city of Urfa, in March 1994, because a friend had dedicated a song to her on a radio phone-in program. The family ruled that she deserved to die. One husband in Pakistan killed his wife after dreaming during the night that she was having an affair.[16]

In her groundbreaking research on Bedouins in Egypt,[17] anthropologist Lila Abu-Lughod explains that, among the Awlad 'Ali tribespeople she studied, honor "derives from virtues associated with autonomy."[18]

Men have to display independence and self-control in order to gain the respect of their peers. A man who shows too much attachment to one of his wives, for instance, is perceived as weak and unworthy. As Abu-Lughod points out, "women are always dependents" since "Bedouin ideology holds that they are 'ruled' by men and should be obedient."

Modesty and humility then become means of gaining moral worth in the eyes of the community: "those who are coerced into obeying are scorned, but those who voluntarily defer are honorable."

Killing a loved one to defend one's honor may appear to go against every human instinct, but notions of honor and shame, drilled into little boys and girls from a very early age, are often so deeply ingrained that relatives feel that they have no choice. If they hesitate and are reluctant to kill, the community around them will remind them daily of their failings.

Girls naturally learn from a young age to cover their body in loose clothes, to defer to their elders, and to keep their eyes lowered.

In Pakistan, while visiting the Sindhi countryside, I noticed that few little girls were among the young children playing in the dust and chasing each other in the hamlets we visited or drove through. The rare exceptions were usually no older than five years. When I asked why this was the case, I was told that girls usually stayed at home. Their childhood ends when they are barely out of infancy.

Pakistani women's rights activist Nafisa Shah, who is also an elected district official and a member of a prominent family in Sindh, wrote in a thesis focusing on crimes committed in the name of honor in her state[19] that when she visited villages in her region, she was usually given a male escort. Sometimes the escort in question was a five-year-old boy, who would be hard-pressed to provide protection, yet his presence was necessary to preserve the decorum.

Patriarchy is defined as the rule of men, but it co-opts women and children to ensure the implementation of its strict diktat. Coercive methods are used when necessary to guarantee that no one strays.

Crimes are committed in the name of honor in all social classes but poorer folks may feel that they have no options. "Honor is the only possession of the poor. They do not want to lose it," believes Mehmet Faraç. Richer families can find alternatives to killing: a girl who has been "disgraced" can be discreetly sent away before a scandal erupts or money can change hands to find a willing groom. Financial transactions are particularly common to avoid the killing of a man who has transgressed social rules.

"There is an economic dimension to honor crimes. One girl was raped in a poor family. Her brother sold his wife's gold to get her an abortion, but the doctors asked for a higher amount because abortion is illegal. Unable to pay, he bought a pistol instead and shot her with 8 bullets. Rich people can surgically restore the virginity if necessary or go abroad to deliver a child or pay money to buy a husband," lawyer and activist Asma Khader told me when I met her in Amman, Jordan, in 2002. She later became a state minister.

Ms. Khader also pointed out that people living in close proximity in poorer areas made it "easier for secrets to come out." In a big city, families determined not to bow to tradition stood a better chance of doing so, but the activist pointed out that "the pressure exists for all."[20]

What makes "honor" crimes particularly odious is the fact that they are usually committed in cold blood by the very people who should have nurtured and protected the victims: fathers, brothers, cousins, or even mothers.

In this traditional pattern that violates the woman's most basic right to life, the decision is often taken collectively by the tribe or the extended family, and the victim is rarely given a chance to defend herself. Even if she was raped, the suspicion that her behavior must have invited the assault is enough to condemn her.

In many cases, autopsies carried out on the bodies of young victims accused of having an affair reveal that the accused was in fact a virgin.

Guilt does not have to be established to justify execution: being the focus of rumors, even if they are malicious and untrue, is often enough to seal a woman's fate. The entire system rests on the "natural" superiority of men and their right to impose their will on family members. Women marry the candidate chosen by their family and are expected to accept their fate. Girls who show defiance can be beaten into submission.

For every honor murder that is reported, many more are disguised as accidents or suicides, and for every woman who is killed, there are dozens who live in fear and face the constant threat of violence.

Honor killings have survived across continents, through the millennia, because they do not happen in a vacuum: they are the logical conclusion in a social system where women's chastity and obedience are the main currencies and blood ties are usually the social glue holding the community fabric together.

As Nafisa Shah points out, "what we may think is a murder or a crime against the state, in the honor value system is not a crime at all. On the contrary, it is an act of punishing those who violate the honor code."[21]

CHAPTER 3

PINAR

When I turned up, unannounced, at Pınar Kaçmaz's family home in Bismil, in Turkey's mainly Kurdish southeast, the young girl had been dead only three weeks. Her story had made headlines in the media. Captions under a photo showing a young blonde woman reclining on a sofa implied that her unchaste behavior had caused her downfall.

In the picture, Pınar was wearing a red summer dress, slightly see-through, that she had pulled up to mid-thighs. The pose was meant to be sexy and seductive, but with her hair tied back and her round face bare of makeup, the young woman looked too wholesome to be a temptress. The brown tartan pattern on the couch further contributed to creating a homely rather than glamorous atmosphere.

But the photo, innocent as it may have been, was enough to set tongues wagging in her hometown. After her death, some news reports suggested that she had run away and was a prostitute; others that she was working for a model agency. The implication, in both cases, was the same: her behavior had been inappropriate.

When I asked the owner of Diyarbakir's only model agency, the Yıldırım Agency, if Pınar had ever worked for him as media reports alleged, he denied it. He said that she had visited his office seeking work, but he had turned her down. In this conservative part of Turkey, only girls who applied with the consent of their parents were hired, he claimed. But aspiring to become a model may have been sufficient to cause Pınar's death.

The young girl was shot in broad daylight in the city of Diyarbakir on March 22, 2002, as she left the apartment she shared with a friend to buy bread.

It was, in many ways, a double tragedy: her killer was her 15-year-old brother, Erkan. The young boy, influenced by his father, had agreed to help ambush Pınar, but while he was arrested on the spot, their father, Hıdır, who had masterminded the murder, managed to escape.

Hıdır may have thought that he was cleansing his "honor" by having his eldest daughter killed, but he did not have much of a personal reputation to defend. He had earlier killed a man in a row over a gambling debt, his wife told me, and served several years in prison. But even from his cell, he never ceased to be preoccupied with the reputation of his family, egged on by relatives who kept him up to date with the local gossip during prison visits.

In Bismil, Pınar's death was discussed in hushed tones. When a family kills in the name of honor, its decision is usually respected by the community. When we reached the outskirts of town, Hüseyin, the driver who often accompanied me on my expeditions to the region, stopped at a grocery store on the outskirts of town, a simple shack erected next to a muddy wasteland with a limited selection of dusty goods on offer. The grocer, a skinny man in his fifties wearing a skull cap, knew exactly which house we were looking for and gave us directions. He had known Pınar since she was a little girl.

"I feel real pain. I knew the girl. She and my children were friends," he said. "I last saw her at my son's wedding. But she left town a while ago and was working in a textile factory or something. She was a beautiful girl."

The sadness he said he felt was tempered by his belief that the murder was justified. The two feelings were not mutually exclusive for him. "Our traditions are like that. There is no difference between man and woman. If someone goes astray, we have to kill them," he explained. "It's both in our traditions and in our religion. The fear keeps people in check."

I was intrigued by the notion that fear alone kept individuals on the straight and narrow, so I asked him if he considered all people, especially women, as would-be sinners likely to run wild if given half an opportunity. He thought for a few seconds, staring in the distance, before giving me his reply.

"No," he finally answered. "Maybe less than ten out of a hundred would turn bad without the fear, but out of these ten a few may act more cautiously because they are scared."

When we reached the small whitewashed concrete house where Pınar had grown up, a small group of women were chatting in front of it. One of them, a plump lady with a friendly face turned out to be Pınar's mother.

Grief was written all over her face but she invited me in, eager to talk about her daughter. In a small room heated by a wood stove, other women wearing similar baggy pants in colorful patterns were seated cross-legged on cushions: Pınar's toothless grandmother, sitting in the corner, kept shaking her head in denial, still refusing to believe that her granddaughter was dead; the mother's sister-in-law; and a couple of neighbors had also come to pay their condolences and show solidarity.

Many victims' mothers bow to the rule of tradition, but Pınar's mom was not one of them: she was raging against social rules that had taken her daughter away from her. She saw her daughter's untimely death as an injustice and refused to accept it. She was particularly incensed and upset that the media had portrayed her daughter as a girl with loose morals. She described instead a sensitive, supportive daughter who had helped raise her younger siblings.

A portrait of Pınar, looking straight at the camera with intense eyes, hung on the wall. She was pretty, with dark eyebrows contrasting with her blond hair, which appeared dyed. The picture frame had been gaudily decorated with garlands of red plastic flowers, and a miniature Koran hung on a chain from one of its corners. Every time Pınar's mother looked at her daughter's smiling face, a sob would escape from her chest.

The mother of six railed against her good-for-nothing husband, who had caused her endless misery. "He's a useless murderer," she shouted, gold teeth shining in her mouth. "He had no reason to kill her."

Anger would then give way to despair as she raised her hands to the ceiling, imploring Allah for mercy, then lowering them to beat her chest and pull at her hair. "I'm dying, I'm dying, what terrible pain," she wailed, swaying from side to side on her cushion.

After regaining her composure, she explained that Pınar's father had been a difficult husband and a poor father. Hıdır Kaçmaz was a gambler, and years earlier, he had been sentenced to eight years in prison for murder.

His conviction had left the family in dire straits. His wife had three daughters and three sons to support, and she was getting little assistance from his relatives. In Bismil (pop. 70,000), few women work outside the home. In fact, many of the town residents are either unemployed or scratching a living in the fields. Women who work outside the home are usually agricultural laborers toiling on the family land. But the combative woman, determined to provide for her children, braved social convention and took a job as a cleaner at the local hospital. She refused to visit her husband in jail, but his own relatives kept in touch with him and gave her news from time to time.

Money was tight in the Kaçmaz household. As Pınar grew older, she decided to take up a job to improve the family finances. Initially, she worked in a local textile workshop. Then, with her mother's consent, she decided to seek her luck in the regional capital, Diyarbakir, where she could get a better salary. She rented an apartment, which she shared with a friend.

In big Turkish cities like Istanbul or Ankara, many young women have won their independence. Some of them are professionals, who live very much like their counterparts in Western Europe. But in this conservative part of the country, it is still unusual for girls not to be under the supervision of relatives. Pınar's mother, who had heavily relied on her daughter to help run the household in Hıdır's absence, trusted her. Pınar worked hard during the week and came back regularly for the weekend, bearing gifts for her younger siblings and money for the family.

Newspaper reports variously put Pınar's age at 20 or 22 at the time of her death, but her own mother wasn't sure how old she had been. Probably 18, she thought. All she remembered was that she was born at the end of the winter, "around the time when the *soba* (wood stove) is turned off." Families do not always register their children immediately after their birth, and Pınar's exact birth day and year were not known.

In December 2001, Hıdır, benefiting from a partial prison amnesty proclaimed by the Turkish government, was released on parole. His wife initially refused to have anything to do with him, but her father reminded her that it was a woman's duty to keep the family together and he convinced her to allow Hıdır back into the family fold. The newly released convict returned home just in time for the holy month of Ramadan.

The first month was relatively uneventful, but as Hıdır began to interfere and object to Pınar's living arrangements, tension grew in the household. In his view, an unmarried girl should not be away from the family home.

Pınar's mother told me that, anticipating his disapproval, she had obtained a medical certificate showing that her daughter was still a virgin before her husband left prison. She wanted to prove that life in the regional capital had not corrupted the young girl.

"The autopsy produced the same result. She was clean, but his relatives kept telling him his daughter was dirty," Pınar's mother explained. "How could we have survived without working? How would we have gotten bread?"

Rows between the spouses escalated, growing more frequent and more violent. Pınar's mother, who doted on her daughter, stood by her. At one point, Hıdır chased his wife with a knife. Eventually, she decided that enough was enough, and kicked him out of the house.

Hıdır left Bismil and moved to Diyarbakir, staying with relatives who kept reminding him that Pınar was flaunting tradition. He stalked his daughter, following her through the streets of the city. On one occasion, he caught up with her and beat her up. Pınar bravely filed a complaint with the police department and the prosecutor's office.

Policemen were detailed to guard her house, I was told, but it was not clear how committed they were to their task. In any case, they failed to save the young woman. Pınar was hit in broad daylight, at 1 P.M., on her way to the bakery.

For her mother, it was a double blow. Unbeknownst to her, Hıdır had convinced their son Erkan to take an active part in the murder. While his mother was at work at the hospital, the teenager would sneak out and take a bus to Diyarbakir, paying his fare with money his father had provided, to help keep Pınar under constant surveillance.

On the day of the murder, Hıdır and Erkan arrived by taxi accompanied, Pınar's mother claimed, by two more relatives. They intercepted Pınar as she crossed the road, held her, and pumped bullets from two guns into her.

Erkan, paralyzed by the enormity of the crime he had just committed, remained rooted to the spot and was arrested immediately but his father managed to evade justice for a long time. He was only caught 18 months later in Adana, hundreds of miles away from the crime scene.

As the victim's mother recounted the fateful day, her female friends and relatives shed copious tears. "Pınar made me proud every day until she died," her mother told me. "She was so beautiful even in death. She looked like she was smiling," added her 32-year-old sister-in-law. "I don't like seeing dead bodies but when I saw her she looked so peaceful I could even take her in my arms. She was shot in the neck. A bullet hit the jugular."

Not all in the family shared her mother's desire to keep Pınar's memory alive. When the victim's maternal uncle dropped by for a brief visit, he wasn't happy to hear that we were talking about the murder.

"It's all over, why bother talking about it?" he said, obviously irritated.

Pınar's mother shot him angry looks and responded defiantly. "I'll fight for my girl's reputation until I die," she shouted.

Throughout our conversation, she smoked like a chimney. She hardly touched the food—a simple dish of *kısır* (cracked wheat) and lettuce leaves—that the victim's young aunt brought on a tray and placed on the floor in front of her.

"My insides are burning. I can't eat, I can't sleep. I just smoke," the victim's mother moaned.

As we sat eating and talking, Pınar's three youngest siblings—her third-grade brother, who sported a cute spiky haircut, and her two sisters aged 9 and 13—returned from school. They very politely saluted us and immediately sat down to do their homework.

The three of them looked infinitely sad. The 9-year-old girl shot surreptitious glances at Pınar's picture through long eyelashes that matched her dead sister's. Neatly dressed in the old-fashioned blue school apron worn by schoolchildren in Turkey, the children appeared polite and respectful. Homemade embroidery decorated the edges of their white collars. Despite the troubled family circumstances and the poverty that their mother had struggled to overcome, they were clearly loved and well looked after. Their mother had succeeded in giving them a normal life after her husband's murder sentence. Now their lives were once again upside down.

How much did the younger members of the family understand of the tragedy? Pınar had been almost a second mother to them, and they knew that they would never see her again.

The impact of the murder on the family became even clearer when the family's first son, who was a conscript on leave from compulsory military service, joined us. He sat in a corner, silently staring at the floor and refused to participate in our conversation.

Like the women and his other siblings, he had been devastated by his sister's murder. But he appeared to have mixed feelings: he was a young man expected to take responsibility for his female relatives' behavior. Should he have punished Pınar himself?

"I told her people were talking," he answered, shaking his head, when I asked him directly how he felt about his sister's murder. "We warned her."

I suggested that Pınar perhaps thought that she had nothing to worry about because she had a clear conscience, but he shrugged. "People talk," he said.

He had recently visited Erkan in jail and reported that the teenager was full of remorse and haunted by the part that he had played in the murder.

"He cannot sleep. He says a few words then he starts crying," the young man explained. "He hasn't stopped crying since he killed Pınar."

But Pınar's mother could not forgive her teenage boy for shooting her daughter, and she felt that she had lost a son as well as a daughter. She would not visit him in prison, she told me.

"He is no son of mine. He might as well be dead," she said.

*　*　*

After a year and a half on the run, Hıdır Kaçmaz, who had masterminded his daughter's murder, was eventually arrested. On October 4, 2004, the 3rd Criminal Court in Diyarbakir sentenced young Erkan to 11 years and 8 months of imprisonment, taking into account that Pınar's decision to live alone in Diyarbakir against the wishes of the male members of the family constituted "light provocation." The sentence was further reduced due to his young age, and he was released after serving three and a half years.

The verdict was more severe for his father, Hıdır Kaçmaz, although "light provocation" was also considered a mitigating factor in his case. He was eventually sentenced to 20 years in prison, of which, under the Turkish system, he was expected to serve only six years.

In 2006, I happened to drive through Bismil shortly after reading in the newspaper that Erkan had been released. I did not want to visit Pınar's family home again and reopen old wounds, but I did stop at a café and ask if the young man was still in town.

By coincidence, I came across a young teacher who had served a short prison sentence for a political offence and had been Erkan's cellmate. He told me that Pınar's brother had left the region upon his release and settled in the Aegean city of Izmir in the hope of leaving the past behind. Erkan was profoundly repentant for his actions, he said, and kept talking about his sister during his incarceration. He would forever regret having followed his father's orders, but unlike the sister he had slain, he at least survived and was able to make a new start in new surroundings.

CHAPTER 4

BORN UNEQUAL

Honor crimes take place against a background of widespread prejudice and unequal treatment vis-à-vis girls. The arrival of a baby boy is usually a cause for lavish celebrations, but female newborns rarely elicit such enthusiasm.

"Discrimination starts the day a girl is born," says Pakistani religious scholar Riffat Hassan. "Women themselves put so little worth on their own life, on protecting their daughters. They often show very little compassion for other women."[1]

Variations of this attitude persist in most countries where the concepts of honor and male superiority are deeply entrenched, although this mentality is sometimes eroded by higher levels of income and education.

I experienced this myself when I gave birth to my second daughter, Amanda, in Istanbul in 1989. The nurses assumed I was disappointed not to have a boy. They were almost apologetic when they brought me my newborn baby girl. "You'll see, girls look after their mother much better," they consoled me. "Boys aren't as useful." I told them I was delighted with my first daughter and not the least bit worried about having a second girl, but I could not shake their conviction that I would have preferred a son.

As the girl child grows up, the gap with her male siblings widens. Boys are often fed the best morsels at the table and they get plenty of maternal attention, while the girls are expected to help perform household chores from a very young age. Mothers and female kin often reinforce the boys' sense of superiority by treating them like little princes.

The clear division of gender roles enforced from early childhood often sets the stage for honor crimes in the more traditional communities. Men are expected to dominate and protect the women, who should submit to their will and follow them unquestioningly. Male supremacy is easily enforced, particularly in rural regions, where women have little education and no independent means of survival. They are at the mercy of their menfolk.

But men and women do share a common burden, although they may not perceive it as such: they all owe allegiance to the family, the community, or the tribe first and foremost, and the collective interest of the group tends to take precedence over their personal wishes. Men enjoy greater power and may eventually find themselves at the top of their social pyramid, but their freedom is circumscribed by what is perceived to be the common good. Despite their greater level of independence, boys too are expected not to question their elders' decisions. The father will often decide what job a boy will do and who he will marry. Society also demands that young males display macho attitudes, and one of the boys' main tasks is to ensure that their sisters remain untouched until they marry.

Being at the bottom of the social ladder, young girls are conditioned from early childhood to adopt a modest attitude and do what they are told. Mothers and female relatives play an important role in relaying the message that obedience and chastity are primordial. This belief can become so ingrained that when their reputation is called into question, some girls share the community's shame and accept their punishment even if they had done nothing to deserve it. It is when they are young and considered sexually attractive that discrimination against women is at its worst.

Roweida, a 17-year-old Jordanian, who was shot three times by her father after confessing to having an affair, believed that she deserved to die. "He shouldn't have let me live," she told NY Times reporter Douglas Jehl, who interviewed her in a Jordanian prison where she was held in protective custody. "A girl who commits a sin deserves to die."[2]

A young female lawyer I met in the conservative Turkish city of Urfa, said to be the birthplace of Prophet Abraham, told me that being stared at in the street or whistled at provoked strong feelings of shame in her.

"The *töre* (traditional customs) is something we all carry inside us. I also tell my younger sisters not to wear revealing clothes," she explained to me. "I tell them, because whenever anything happens to me, whenever I experience any kind of sexual harassment, it bothers me for days. It is partly because an injustice committed against me is also committed against my mother and my father."[3]

Too many women come to view coercion and domestic violence, frequently used to ensure compliance, as a normal part of life. A study conducted in 2004 by Hacettepe University in Ankara, Turkey, showed that 39.2 percent of Turkish women believed that a husband has the right to beat his wife. This perception was, however, spread very unevenly across society: while only 8.8 percent of educated women justified domestic violence, 62.1 percent of uneducated women were resigned to it.[4]

Another study published three years later suggested, however, that women were becoming more aware of their rights and were less willing to accept abuse as an unavoidable fate, perhaps because of increased media coverage: nine out of ten women in a poll of 1,800 married women across Turkey stated clearly that violence was never justified, and as many wanted abusive husbands punished by the courts.[5]

The concept of honor remains widespread across Turkey, but murders commandeered by the family appear more common among people from the southeast region, where tribal links remain strong. While female illiteracy in western and central Turkey was 15.5 percent, in the eastern provinces over 40 percent of women could neither read nor write and were therefore more vulnerable.[6] But it is also in this part of the country, torn by conflict for many years, that women are the most vocal and active against patriarchal tradition.

* * *

The conservative mentality that finds it most extreme expression in honor killings comes in different shades. Thus in most of the countries where some women are still killed for overstepping social boundaries, others may live a life as independent as their Western counterparts. The wide avenues of Islamabad and the fragrant gardens that give the Pakistani capital an atmosphere of sleepy suburbia reflect little of the violence many women in the country are subjected to or indeed the general level of insecurity in the country.

The same dichotomy exists in Turkey, especially in big cities like Istanbul, where some women can live an independent life, occupy managerial positions at work, and go out with their friends at night, while others living a short distance down the road are barely allowed out of their home alone.

Traditional perceptions of women's role in society—primarily as wives and mothers—are inherently paradoxical: women are discriminated against, yet they are a family's most prized "possession."

"Women carry a heavy responsibility. There is a contradiction: women are considered to be worth nothing at all, they don't have a voice in the society, yet men pay huge prices to marry them," explains Turkish journalist Mehmet Faraç. "They are an investment: they produce children regularly, they look after the house, they cook for guests. But if they make the smallest mistake, they are killed. A woman can cook a meal for her brother, and be killed by him two hours later."

This duality is hard to understand. It is due in part to the fact that in the most patriarchal quarters, a woman is perceived as an asset, a commodity. But unlike land, gold, or material goods, she is also viewed as a ticking sexual time bomb, ready to explode and cause chaos in the community from puberty to menopause. "Essentially, the worth of a community is vested in its land and its women, and notions of shame and honor came to be linked to these possessions: men would kill to protect their land and they would kill to protect their women. And they would kill the women if the strict code governing sexual relationships was violated,"[7] Pakistani activist Rabia Ali wrote.

The social system is built around women's ability to reproduce and the need to control it. Not always valued as individuals, women play a crucial role as mothers.

At birth, a girl belongs to her father and his family; when she marries, "property rights" are in effect transferred to the husband and his family, although in some communities the girl's birth family retains a degree of control over her until she dies.

Today, few Western brides object to being "given away" at the altar by their father: it is a symbolic gesture that has lost most of its meaning since women are, by and large, free to choose their spouses. But what we see as a quaint tradition of transferring responsibility from the father to the husband is still a shift of ownership in more traditional communities, where women literally change hands when they marry, in the way slaves used to be sold to new owners.

The new proprietor expects his wife to be pure when she comes to him. Ensuring the purity of the bloodline appears to be the main reason why virginity is still considered paramount in many rural and conservative societies.

The father of psychoanalysis, Sigmund Freud, had another explanation: in articles on the psychology of love, he explained that "virginity is buried in the most primitive recesses of human memory, and that it is a manifestation of men's fear of women, a fear arising in the first place from her crushing superiority—only she could create life in and through blood—and in the second place from their suspicion that women, behind their veil of obedience, would be plotting their revenge."[8]

Indeed the cult of virginity is not limited to communities ruled by a code of honor. Although sexual purity has lost a lot of its importance in Western countries in recent decades, thanks to the women's liberation movement, we do not have to look back very far to remember that the white dress was a symbol of chastity that could only be worn if the girl's hymen was intact.

When Princess Diana was first introduced to the world as a prospective bride before her 1981 marriage to the heir of the British throne, for instance, the media made much of her innocence, which made her a suitable royal consort. By the time Diana's son William married in 2011, the purity of his bride-to-be was no longer a concern. In the United States, virginity has made a comeback with the rising influence of the Christian right and has developed into a movement among teenagers that bucks the trend of sexual freedom to promote abstinence before marriage.

But if it is largely a matter of personal choice for American teenagers, virginity remains a girl's—and her family's—most valued possession in many conservative or rural societies, where displaying a bloodied sheet is still common after the wedding night to prove that the groom's family has acquired a "clean" girl. Failure to produce the telltale sign that a hymen has been breached can lead to the rejection of the bride and her subsequent death at the hand of her angered groom or her own family, despite medical evidence that not all girls are born with a hymen or that it can be broken accidentally during childhood.

In Turkey, virginity was much debated in the late 1990s after five teenage girls living in a state orphanage attempted to commit suicide by taking rat poison and jumping into a deep water tank. The head of the institution had ordered them to submit to virginity tests after they returned late to their dormitories. The minister in charge of Women and Family Affairs at the time, Ms. Işilay Saygın, caused outrage when she defended the decision to check the chastity of girls in state care as a useful deterrent to immoral behavior.

"Girls of 12 or 13 are falling pregnant," the minister explained, boasting during an interview that she herself was still a virgin. "If girls commit suicide because of the virginity tests, they would have committed suicide anyway. It is not that important." Her spokesman later tried to put a more positive spin on her declarations, claiming that the tests were necessary to allow girls to "clear their name." In fact, many newspaper readers probably agreed with her views.

A survey of 118 Turkish forensic specialists, carried out in 1998, found that 5,901 virginity examinations had been performed in the previous 12 months, of which 1,856 were listed for "social reasons."[9]

The results of such tests can ring the death toll for young women, and Turkish feminists fought hard to ban virginity checks and to amend a whole range of legal provisions discriminatory to women.

Convincing politicians that an entire category of crimes, such as assaults against women and their bodies, should not be listed as "crimes against public morality" but as "crimes against individuals" proved a challenge. But the women's movement actively lobbied for change and won the battle. In 2005, a new Penal Code entered into force in Turkey that marked a fundamental shift in the legal approach to women. The activists could not, however, prevent the inclusion of an article giving judges the right to order virginity tests in special circumstances, such as rape, without requiring the consent of the woman concerned.

Because of conservative social perceptions, arbitrary rulings on girls' alleged impurity are rarely disputed, sometimes with devastating consequences. Some cases reported in the media are particularly tragic. Seventeen-year-old Çiğdem Kaya came from a tiny Turkish village in the arid mountain scenery near the Iranian border. Her father had gone to France as a migrant worker, and left his own father in charge of his family. When the local *muhtar*'s son asked for Çiğdem's hand in marriage, her grandfather could not turn down the proposal, which came from a local dignitary. He knew, however, that the prospective groom had already sent two girls back to their parents alleging that they were not virgins. One of the girls had subsequently "disappeared."

Shortly after Çiğdem got married, she, too, was sent back to her relatives. Her husband, who alleged she was not a virgin, never explained why he waited several days before raising his objection. If her virginity was really the issue, should he not have made his doubts clear immediately after the wedding night? Or was it his own inability to fulfill marital duties that he was trying to cover up?

Whatever the reason behind his decision to reject a third wife, gossip began to spread in the village. Çiğdem was said to have lost her virginity after being raped by her grandfather. To escape the rumor mill, the family members packed their bags and moved to Istanbul, at the other end of the country. But they settled in a district where others from their region also lived and the whispers followed them.

One day, according to media reports, Çiğdem's grandfather announced that he was taking the young woman to the doctor to establish the truth. She followed him willingly, confident that the doctor would confirm her innocence. But the old man returned alone at the end of the day. It is unclear if he or other relatives killed Çiğdem, but her body was later found; she had been strangulated. Çiğdem was only vindicated postmortem, when the autopsy confirmed that allegations against her had been wrong all along.[10]

Aside from securing a guarantee of paternity, some researchers suggest that men also want to ensure that the womb in which their seed is deposited has not been polluted by foreign elements.

The woman, in this case, is not seen as the cocreator of her child, but merely as a receptacle for the man's seed. Sociologist Carol Delaney, who carried out field research in the early 1980s in a village of Anatolia, noted that "a woman's value in a (Turkish) village society depends, therefore, not only on her fertility, which is a generalized medium of nurture that any woman can provide, but more importantly on her ability to guarantee the legitimacy of a man's seed."[11] Similar perceptions may apply to other traditional societies.

Marriage within the family—or endogamy—remains the norm rather than the exception in many developing countries. In a landmark book published in the 1960s, French anthropologist Germaine Tillion, who lived for many years in the North African Maghreb, questioned the origin of this tradition. Strong taboos, often assorted with legal prohibitions, are attached to the union of close kin in many parts of the globe, she pointed out, but such unions remain the marriages of choice in many patriarchal communities.[12] This is still the case in several countries where honor killings occur today.

Tillion's explanation was that endogamy was favored as a way of preventing the division of family assets. A girl's father will often give priority to his own brother's son as a prospective groom, but more distant relatives are also deemed suitable as long as it all remains in the family.

In close-knit communities, finding a partner outside the community is not always tolerated, although males are more likely to be allowed to marry "foreigners." A bride from outside the community would automatically become part of the clan when she marries. Losing a girl to an outsider is much more controversial, and many girls have paid with their life for daring to fall in love with men rejected by their family.

Twenty-four-year-old Rabiya, whose case I detail later in the book, was killed in the Harran plain near Sanliurfa, Turkey, because she had eloped with a man she loved. Her suitor had asked for her hand in marriage, but he was turned down.

"Her father refused, he didn't want to give her to a foreigner," her uncle Halil Konak, who served a five-year prison term for her murder, explained to me when I met him at his home shortly after his release. When I naively asked him which country the foreigner came from, Konak told me that he was from the nearby city of Urfa, located less than 30 kilometers away from their village. He was a local boy, but he was not part of their community.

On the surface at least, Freud's theory that discrimination against women is due to a belief in their "crushing superiority" appears irrelevant in communities based on male dominance. But female sexuality does inspire fear.

Here again, patriarchal perceptions of women are paradoxical: they are seen as vulnerable creatures, eternal children in need of protection and constant supervision, but they are also believed to be endowed with a rampant sexuality that threatens the social order.

Seclusion of women, still enforced in some traditional countries, has come to be identified with Islam and the Koran in most Westerners' view. But the roots of segregation and indeed the veil that many Muslim women wear, pre-date Islam.

The harem is not a Muslim invention: in the early Christian era, Byzantine and other women of the eastern Mediterranean "were not supposed to be seen in public and were kept 'cloistered as prisoners' "; they were always supposed to be covered, "the veil or its absence marking the distinction between the 'honest' woman and the prostitute."[13] According to the famous Greek philosopher Aristotle, women, lacking a crucial appendage, were merely imperfect men, "as it were an impotent male, for it is through a certain incapacity that the female is female."

Over the centuries, religious beliefs have merged with ancient traditions. Radical Muslims who want to keep women locked indoors or hidden under a burqa at all times would be hard-pressed to find texts justifying these customs in the Koran, but they have come to believe that there is a religious justification for keeping women secluded and in a subservient position.

"The religious right discourse gives men more means and avenues of satisfying desires—if heterosexual. Polygyny frequently becomes an unbridled right of Muslim men—in some cases (like Nigeria) almost an obligation," wrote social anthropologist Ayesha M. Imam. "The right to marry girl children is defended and promoted as men's right and the prevention of immorality. There is increasingly a lack of concern for the consent of the bride to marriage."[14]

As a result, girls are often married off at a young age before their sexual urges lead them astray and create *fitna* (chaos) in the community. Unlike Christian culture, which largely ignored women's sexuality, at least until the feminist revolution of the 60s, in Muslim societies women are thought by many "to have greater potential for sexual desire and pleasure, nine times that of men."[15]

This view is epitomized in the classical work of Muslim scholar Imam Ghazali (eleventh-twelfth century). According to Fatima Mernissi, Ghazali "saw civilization as struggling to contain women's destructive, all-absorbing power," and he believed that keeping this overwhelming energy under check was the man's job, who had to increase or decrease sexual intercourse according to the woman's need in order to "secure her virtue," and thereby, protect other men from falling prey to her urges.[16]

Christianity and Judaism, of course, also have mixed feelings about women's sexuality. As religious scholar Karen Armstrong puts it, "all religions have had a problem with women and sex—and Christianity more than most."[17]

The myth of Eve, the temptress, remains a powerful example of religious misogyny. "The writing of such church fathers as Augustine, Origen and Tertullian, for example, reflect the concept of the female as inferior, secondary, defined entirely by her biology, and useless to man—and worse, as causing sexual temptation, corruption, and evil. Augustine, pondering the mystery of why God had created woman, considered that he had created her neither as man's companion, for another man would have filled this role better, nor as his helper, for again another man would have been more appropriate. He concluded, 'I fail to see what use women can be to man... if one excludes the function of bearing children.' "[18]

Islam, in contrast to Christianity, sees sexuality as a positive force. Within the confines of marriage, men and women are allowed and even encouraged to enjoy a healthy sex life. In fact, the Koran considers it sufficient grounds for divorce, for women as well as for men, if a partner is unwilling or unable to provide sexual services over a prolonged period.

The reality in Muslim countries today is somewhat different. The Koran, as written by Prophet Mohammed, granted women rights that were considered revolutionary at the time. But just as was the case with Christianity, which became increasingly misogynistic over the centuries until modern societies loosened the moral straitjacket, the basic principle of gender equality and the right of a woman to enjoy her sexuality were whittled down to almost nothing in many Muslim countries.

Germaine Tillion has argued that it was precisely because the Koran brought a "feminist" revolution and particularly granted women a right to a share of inheritance—which Western women did not enjoy until the nineteenth century, as Karen Armstrong points out—that patriarchy retaliated with segregation and veiling to prevent family assets from being divided. Women are only entitled to half the share of men according to the Muslim holy book, but, Tillion underlined, they are given independent control of their dowry and inheritance while their husbands are obliged to fulfill all their needs, no matter how personally wealthy the women are.[19]

The Koran's attitude to women was broad-minded in its historical context, but the window it opened for women closed gradually as interpretation of the religious texts grew more patriarchal. Enjoyment of marital sex has in some cases also partly succumbed to the assault of traditional social mores. Girls, brought up with the notion that sex equals shame, and that any interaction with a man is a threat to their life, may not be in the best frame of mind to enjoy a healthy sex life when they get married, particularly if their partner was imposed upon them.

Common trends can easily be identified, but not all traditional societies interpret gender roles in the same manner. In the Western Sahara, administered by Morocco since 1975, women have a powerful position in society. Their private life is not policed by the wider community. If a man beats his wife, he has to throw a second wedding, with all the gifts of camel and jewelry that entails, to obtain her pardon. Saharawi women, who can marry for love, can divorce their husband easily, and when they do, they throw a party, which can last up to three days, to show that they are free. This gives a chance to men who are interested in them to bring presents and court them.[20]

Even in stricter communities, the extended family can also be a protective cocoon, but the safety it offers can be wrested away in an instant if social mores are thought to have been violated. "With regard to women's rights, the term community is a Janus-faced concept. On the one hand, the community is often the site for the denial of women's rights... On the other hand, the community is often a nurturing space, which provides women with social support and solidarity, especially when they are seeking redress from the State," wrote

Radhika Coomaraswamy, UN Special Rapporteur on Violence against Women.[21]

The extended family or the tribe, at times, leaves little space for the development of an intimate relationship between spouses beyond sexual intercourse, but it also fosters strong ties among family members and between members of the same gender.

The family offers the best and the worst: it is a source of warmth and support but it can also be stifling and controlling—as thousands of honor killings and cases of abuse attest.

In the course of my visits to rural areas, I was often struck by the communal sharing of chores among women. I remember a trip to the Harran plain, south of Urfa, where I had gone to see the curious conical mud houses that are typical of this region that borders Syria.

I came across a group of four or five giggly young women, who were sharing a few jokes and playfully teasing each other while looking after their children. There were enough noisy kids around them to fill an entire classroom, but there was no way of matching each child to its mother. Child rearing was too some extent a collective activity.

In villages where I discussed issues of honor and patriarchy with local people, women always questioned me about my own life. Was I married? Did I have children? I encountered disbelief and pity on many occasions when I revealed that I was divorced and was bringing up two daughters on my own. How could I live without the protection of a man? My female interlocutors thought life had dealt me a cruel blow. There was nothing I could say to convince them that I enjoyed my independence and felt no need of male protection.

For people born in these tight communities, the extended family or the tribe is a world in itself, one that they rarely wish to leave or that keeps pulling them back when they do. In several instances, young women who had run away with a lover returned to their families when the relationship turned sour, knowing they were facing certain death. They felt they could not survive outside the group.

These strong ties can make it more difficult to help potential honor killing victims: leaving the community may save their life, but alienation is a lifelong burden, a sense of permanent uprooting, that only the very strong can bear.

Women's living conditions and mobility within the community improve as they get older. Domestic violence and other repressive practices are inflicted primarily when women are in their prime, because of the sexual threat they represent in the eyes of the society.

By the time women and men who had felt repressed by their elders when they were young reach middle age and they could use their increased power within the community to make the lives of the younger generation easier, the incentive to promote change has disappeared. By then, they have climbed the rungs of the social ladder and the system works in their favor. Their turn has come to enjoy the privileges of age. The hierarchical structure of the family, which gives older members great influence, carries within it the seeds of its own preservation.

Once they are past their reproductive years, women often become powerful within the extended family and the wider community, particularly if they have successfully borne sons. The clever matriarch who saved Rojin's life is a good example of how a woman exercises influence in the family: Zekiye used her power skillfully, deferring to her menfolk, while discreetly steering them toward the right decision. They were convinced that the choice was theirs, when in reality, she was the one who had planted the ideas in their minds.

Not all women reach such a position. Some of them have their spirits crushed by years of drudgery and cannot enjoy the safety of their later years. And those who come to wield influence within the family do not always exercise it as benignly as Zekiye did. Far from defending the rights of younger women, many older women become instead fierce defenders of the status quo and enforcers on behalf of their sons. Whether they protect the patriarchal system either out of fear, out of the need to be seen as valuable members of the social group, or simply because they enjoy bossing others around, these women contribute to the survival of patriarchal abuse.

Oppressed by their husband's relatives when they entered the family, the shy young brides can become tyrannical mothers-in-law a couple of decades later, instilling fear in the young women who threaten the special bond that unites them with their sons.

The social mechanisms that lead to honor killings are often set in motion by the malicious gossip spread by women, who are well aware it can be lethal. Older women sometimes take an active part in murders committed in the name of honor, or encourage the males in their family to display their manliness.

Traditions, of course, do not stand still. No society today can claim to be unaffected by the winds of globalization. Television and soap operas are now reaching the most remote villages, showing women a way of life very different from their own.

Rapid social change can be perceived as a threat, leading to greater repression. To defenders of patriarchy, Western imports like television represent a danger. Activist Nafisa Shah describes how in her extended family, in the Sindh province of Pakistan, men would gather in the courtyard in front of a TV screen when episodes of Baywatch were being broadcast, while indoors, women had to watch dreary documentaries chosen by their menfolk for their "suitability."[22]

When I visited the province in 2003, I asked a local colleague if this was common practice. Much to my surprise, he did not dismiss the anecdote as being an extreme example of controlling behavior. Instead, he replied very seriously. "Well, we can't allow women to watch anything on TV, can we?"

The rapid pace of modernization also creates new tensions between generations. Traditional parents are finding hard to control daughters who demand more independence. Political considerations and conflicts also affect women's role in society.

Sociologist Deniz Kandiyoti explains that "on the one hand nationalist movements invite women to participate more fully in collective life by interpolating them as 'national' actors: mothers, educators, workers, and even fighters. On the other hand, they reaffirm the boundaries of culturally acceptable feminine conduct and exert pressure on women to articulate their gender interests within the terms set by nationalist discourse."[23]

In Iraq, for instance, violence against women—domestic violence, abductions, honor killings, and threats against students in universities—has increased dramatically since the U.S. invasion in 2003, largely due to the growing influence of extremist religious groups. Even in the northern part of the country, in Iraqi Kurdistan, a region that has been relatively stable, honor killings are rife and the practice of female genital mutilation has become more widespread, affecting thousands of young girls, since the first Gulf War. The fight for women's rights is usually seen as an unwelcome and a frivolous distraction when more "serious" national struggles have to be won.

Despite these monumental obstacles, in all countries where honor-based crimes are still common, awareness is rising that they represent major violations of human rights. Pressure from the outside world has little to do with it: within the cultures that have maintained these practices, progressive women and men are fighting to eradicate their most brutal aspects, often risking their lives to draw attention to the plight of the fair sex. It is largely thanks to their efforts that the practice of honor killing is now challenged in most countries where it still occurs.

CHAPTER 5

NASREEN*

In a shelter in Islamabad, thousands of miles away from the English city of Birmingham where she was born and brought up, I met 16-year-old Nasreen. Her story was one that has become increasingly familiar to the British authorities, who rescue dozens of UK passport holders forced into marriage abroad every year. In 2008, the British High Commission in Islamabad repatriated no less than 131 young women. Many others, either less lucky or less brave, do not escape the fate their families have planned for them.

When I met her in August 2003, Nasreen was hours away from being flown back to the United Kingdom from Peshawar with a ticket purchased by British officials. Her pout was that of a defiant teenager attempting to appear tough and careless, but her eyes betrayed the helplessness and vulnerability of a child.

Born in the United Kingdom, she looked like many of her British peers. Her hair, turned red by henna, was gelled to her head and contrasted with a skin so pale that it did not betray her subcontinental origins. Eyebrows plucked into thin arches drew attention to large greenish brown eyes, which looked immensely sad. Like many girls of Asian origin living in Western countries, Nasreen had a foot in each culture. Often, it meant she was torn between the two. She wanted to have the same freedom as her English classmates, but her strict parents expected her to adopt the dutiful attitude that befits a traditional Pakistani girl.

Her father, a taxi driver, had moved to Britain when he was a child, but he had remained true to tradition and had chosen a wife from his homeland. Aside from Nasreen and her three siblings, he also had two older children from a previous marriage.

As Nasreen reached puberty and became more independent, relations with her parents deteriorated. She alluded to crises within her family, but revealed few details, except the belief that her parents "hated everything I did: the way I dressed, everything."

"From the time I was little, I wanted a different life," she said. "I had lots of friends at school, but I was never allowed to see them outside the house. All my friends looked forward to the school holidays, but for me it meant staying at home the whole time." At the same time, she had a strong attachment to her family, even if the ties were strained. She found comfort unloading her burden in conversations with a cousin who was in a situation similar to hers.

"We used to talk a lot," she explained. "I ran away from home a few times and went to friends' houses, but the police always brought me back."

Pakistan was a foreign land that Nasreen had rarely visited until she was in her teens. A couple of years before I met her in Islamabad, she had paid one traumatic visit to her country of origin and ended up staying an entire year.

The journey was meant to be a brief holiday to visit relatives, but shortly after the family's arrival, Nasreen's older sister Aisha was forcibly married to a relative. "They told her, 'get married, then you will be able to go back to England,' " Nasreen explained.

Aisha was shocked but she saw no way out. She dutifully complied with her parents' wishes and married the selected groom. Aisha was kept in Pakistan until she became pregnant and her marriage was safely cemented. Her sister Nasreen stayed with her. Their parents assumed, rightly, that the baby would keep Aisha on the straight and narrow. Once a contented mother, she would accept her fate and bring her husband to the United Kingdom. "My sister is fine now, but she feels more Pakistani than I do," explained Nasreen. "She is back in Britain with her baby daughter. Her husband is still in Pakistan, and she has applied for him to migrate to Britain."

When the girls' mother suggested another vacation in Pakistan two years later, Nasreen was understandably suspicious and refused point-blank to accompany her. The mother enlisted the help of a trusted uncle and asked him to intercede. The relative talked at length to the girl's parents. It is not clear if he was convinced of their good faith or complicit in the deception, but he urged Nasreen to accompany her mother. "I only came because mom swore on the Koran, in front of my uncle, that she would not get me married," said Nasreen.

As she was recounting this episode, the teenager was shaking her head, bewildered. She was still unwilling to accept that her mother had lied, therefore betraying both her daughter and her faith.

Once they arrived in their home city of Mirpur, in Pakistani Kashmir, Nasreen was told that the family had decided that she would marry her father's young cousin.

"Mum said, 'if you get married you can leave the next day,' " the teenager explained, "but I knew she had told my Auntie that they wanted to keep me here for 6 or 7 years."

Nasreen was shocked: she'd had plenty of rows with her strict and austere dad in the past and didn't expect him to understand her. But she thought her mother was on her side and would defend her interests. "After she kept me and my sister here for a year, mom begged me to trust her again," she explained. "Then she betrayed me again. Everything mom and dad do, they do together."

Nasreen put up such fierce resistance that her father flew in from England and used strong-arm tactics to break her down. "When I refused to get married, he got very angry and very violent," she said. "He was not normally a violent man."

Not everybody in her extended family approved of the plan to marry her off against her will, but her young relatives respected the family hierarchy and were not in a position to interfere. "My cousins offered to help me, but I didn't want to get them into trouble," Nasreen said.

Help came, unexpectedly, from sympathetic neighbors, expatriate Pakistanis who had recently returned from the United States. Nasreen befriended their daughter, a girl of her age, who sympathized with her plight and mentioned it to her less traditional father. Through them, Nasreen obtained the phone number of the British High Commission in Islamabad. She was under almost constant watch, but she took advantage of a moment of inattention while others were eating to place a call for help.

"In such cases, we first lodge a complaint with the authorities, stating that a girl is illegally confined. The court then asks her to be presented at a hearing," Khaleda Salimi, who ran the NGO in charge of the shelter, told me. "Policemen are sent to the house where the girl is held. We then file a petition for divorce if the marriage has taken place. Sometimes we fly them out of the country first, and they file from England."

Not all rescue operations are successful. In some cases, families manage to snatch the girls back. Victims of forced marriages or potential brides who had been rescued were initially housed at the Marriott

Hotel in Islamabad until they boarded their flight, but the hotel became known as the place of sanctuary used by the British High Commission and in at least one case, relatives turned up hoping to kidnap the young woman.

Discreet safe houses were later set up in the city to shelter potential victims until they could leave Pakistani territory. The young women often remain at risk of kidnapping or killing, even after they have returned to Britain. "One girl stayed with us then went back to England," Khaleda Salimi told me. "Her family negotiated with the High Commission, and told them the girl would be fine with them. But they brought her back to Pakistan, and killed her here."

Two days after Nasreen phoned the High Commission, embassy officials accompanied by Pakistani policemen turned up at her relatives' door. The police officers were doing their duty, but they made their disapproval clear to Nasreen: in their view, young girls should stay with their parents and obey them. "Why do you want to leave? Be a good girl!" one of them told Nasreen. "Why don't you want to get married?"

Nasreen acknowledged that she hesitated for a brief moment. Freedom was within reach, but she also knew that it would mean a complete break from her past, from her family, and from the life that she had known. "One of my uncles was shouting 'you can't go!' " she explained. "I didn't know what to do. I started backing away from the car, but my cousins from the UK were clapping. They told me 'if you don't leave now, you'll never get out.' "

This ambivalence is not unusual. Potential brides sometimes abandon their bid to freedom at the last minute, when they realize that it would mean lifelong estrangement from their family and loved ones. Leaving their parents behind is never an easy option. "When girls first arrive, they are overwhelmed with guilt at the thought of disobeying their parents," said Khaleda Salimi. "They feel shame and they are afraid of death."

Nasreen was obviously relieved her nightmare was over, but she too had mixed feelings. She faced an uncertain future. "I need time to get over all this. I want to be kept away from them all, at least for a while," she told me. "I hope to go to college." She paused for a while, her shoulders hunched under the weight of her sorrow. "I left," she finally whispered.

Throughout our conversation, she had been restless, shifting uncomfortably on her chair. Her primary concern now was not for herself, but for her younger sister, who was 11. The two of them were very close, she said. Her younger sibling looked up to her, and as she entered puberty, she counted on Nasreen's support.

"My brother, who is fifteen, will be fine; he knows his rights. But my little sister, she needs me; she can't live without me," she said. "I told her 'whatever happens, don't go to Pakistan.' " Nasreen was worried that after her desertion, her parents would try to get their youngest daughter married at an even earlier age to avoid a similar conflict.

As I stepped out of the room, I looked back. Nasreen hadn't moved from her chair. She was still sitting at the table, staring vacantly into the distance.

A few hours later, she would be taking a big step into the unknown. The British authorities would look after her. She would probably be relocated to another city and be placed in a social institution until she finished school. Her physical needs would be taken care of, but she would carry for the rest of her life the scars of the emotional wounds inflicted by her own parents.

In 2005, the British Foreign Office and the Home Office jointly set up a Forced Marriage Unit, specifically to deal with cases like Nasreen's, mostly in Pakistan, Bangladesh, and India. Two years later, the British Parliament adopted the Forced Marriage Bill, giving courts wide discretion to issue orders protecting anyone at risk of being married against their will. The British authorities receive up to 1,600 reports of forced marriages every year. The legislation caused quite a controversy before it was eventually adopted. The line that separates an arranged marriage from a forced one is sometimes very thin and some Britons of Asian origin initially feared that racism would interfere with proper implementation of the law. But the legislation eventually won the support of immigrant women's associations, which welcomed its adoption.

CHAPTER 6

HARMFUL PRACTICES

Honor killings are the most powerful weapon in the arsenal of patriarchy, deployed when all other measures of coercion and repression have failed. But these brutal crimes do not happen in a vacuum.

In communities where honor is a value defined through women, murders are at the extreme end of a wide spectrum of discriminatory practices. These include forced marriage, underage marriage, betrothal at birth, and bride exchanges. In some areas, girls are offered in compensation for a murder victim or to settle the score between two clans involved in a dispute or they can be sold to older men as the second, third, or fourth wife.

Domestic violence at the hand of parents, brothers, husband, or in-laws often provides a familiar backdrop. Not all women suffer abuse—the majority of women, let's not forget it, do live in happy family environments—but pressure, psychological or physical, is accepted as the norm in many communities. In Turkey, a popular saying, still heard these days, warns that "he who doesn't beat his daughter will beat his knee (in regret)." Unless daughters are coerced into submission from the start, many believe, they may prove troublesome later on.

A young lawyer I met a few years ago in Urfa, a conservative Turkish city said to be the birthplace of Prophet Abraham, told me that she expected to be married off in the very near future. Despite having attained a level of education far higher than her parents', she still accepted that her father would decide when and who she should marry. She was in her late 20s and enjoyed her work, but she knew that her life could change radically any day.

I asked how she defined a good marriage and what she hoped for. "A good marriage is one in which there isn't much violence," she told me. She was placing the bar very low, and considered herself lucky to have graduated from university with a law degree and to have attained a degree of independence.

In the Sindhi city of Larkana in Pakistan, the hometown of politician Benazir Bhutto, who was murdered on December 27, 2007, I had a brief encounter with a man detained at one of a handful of police stations in the country set up specifically during Bhutto's tenure as prime minister to handle cases involving women.

The man, held on suspicion of raping his 12-year-old daughter, was locked up behind thick iron bars in a bare concrete room that opened onto the courtyard of the police station. He was apparently destitute, wearing dirty rags, and looked utterly defeated by life. Gripping the bars that held him captive, he was pleading to be let out. A heavy moustache that seemed too big for his scrawny face partly hid his rotten teeth. He told me that he had fathered seven girls and one boy.

While pleading innocence, he was also raging against his wife. She had concocted the accusation of incest, he said, because she objected to his decision to sell their daughter. How could she thwart his plans?

"I've already sold two daughters. I was going to sell this one for 30,000 rupees (roughly 520 dollars at the time)," he told me.

Under the deal that he had concluded with the buyer, he explained, his daughter's first female child would be handed over to him, to be sold as well: his grandchild was, in effect, enslaved before she was even conceived. Marriage transactions involving unborn or very young children are called *pait likkhi* in Sindh. It applied, in this particular case, because the prospective husband could not pay the "full price" for his bride.

The father was happy with the terms of the deal: he would have one less mouth to feed; he would get what, for him, was a handsome sum of money and the prospect of further income in the future.

His wife apparently disagreed. She had already witnessed the sale of two of her daughters, and she hoped to spare this one, who had barely reached puberty.

"She never listens to me, and my children don't follow me. They follow their mother," he raged from his cell. "She is a bad woman, it's all her fault."

I asked him if he had thought of his daughter's feelings. Had he considered the possibility that she didn't want to be sold? He just shrugged and said,

"She's a girl. It's her fate."

Officers at the police station had not yet determined whether he was guilty of incest. Nor could they tell me what would happen to his wife and daughter if he was released.

Few fathers, of course, disregard their children's feelings to such an extent, but in this particular man's world, a woman was little more than a slave to be used and abused at will. Clearly impoverished, he may not have enjoyed a status much above theirs, but he was in a position to make decisions that impacted their fate.

Incest is a largely unspoken problem in rural communities where large families share close quarters. Young girls can fall prey to their teenage siblings, who often sleep feet away from them. Cousins, uncles, or even fathers can also be involved, and at times, the family turns a blind eye as long as the girl's virginity is left intact. If the girl becomes pregnant, however, the situation changes drastically and the family can even resort to killing to cover up the abuse.

This was the case of Kifaya, a 16-year-old Jordanian girl, whose case in 1994 was documented by Jordanian journalist Rana Husseini, who became a prominent activist in the fight against honor killings in her country.

She reported that Kifaya, raped by her younger brother, was married off to hide the incestuous assault. Six months later, her new husband decided to send her back to her relatives. Her 32-year-old brother, Khalid, decided that he could not face the shame of having his sister rejected by her husband, and stabbed her to death. At his trial, Khalid received a seven and a half year sentence for the premeditated murder, which was later reduced to one year. Mahmoud, the young brother, was sentenced to 13 years in prison for the rape and attempted murder of his sister.

It is important to underline, once more, that killing is not a solution favored by all or even most parents when a potentially embarrassing situation arises in tight-knit communities. Most families are reluctant to kill and will go out of their way to find other solutions. When they do commit murder, it is often under intense communal pressure. A hurriedly arranged wedding to hide a young woman's pregnancy is a possible alternative to maintain social status. In Rojin's case, for instance, achieving this outcome involved offering money to a man with limited resources to encourage him to accept a girl who was no longer considered prime marriage-material.

Marrying a pregnant girl before signs of her "disgrace" are apparent is of course not a custom limited to the Middle East and the subcontinent: the term "shotgun wedding" originated in the early years of the

American West. Men who had impregnated young girls were quite literally forced at gunpoint to tie the knot to restore the young woman's reputation and that of her family.

As mentioned earlier, the legal code of dozens of countries around the world contain clauses that allow men who have sexually assaulted a woman to get off with a lenient sentence, or no conviction at all, if they marry their victim and therefore restore her reputation.

This rule was hotly debated in Turkey in 2003 and 2004, while parliament was working on a new penal code to replace criminal laws dating back to 1926. Under pressure from women's groups, which formed a very efficient lobbying platform, many legal articles affecting women were liberalized and the article allowing a rapist to get a suspended sentenced was scrapped in the Penal Code introduced in 2005.

While parliament was drafting the new legislation, a heated media debate revealed how deeply entrenched patriarchal roots still were. In October 2003, Dr. Doğan Soyaslan, a law school professor who was at the time advising the Justice Ministry, provoked angry reactions from women's groups when he defended the practice of marrying a victim to her rapist during a television interview.

"Nobody wants to marry someone who is not a virgin," the professor claimed. "Those who say otherwise are liars. If her virginity is broken, she must marry him."

Guaranteeing social peace and maintaining respectability at all costs was, in his eyes and those of many traditionalists, far more important than providing a victim with a secure and loving environment.

In March 2003, Turkish newspapers had reported the case of a 17-year-old girl raped by her 72-year-old Koran teacher. Tried in the Anatolian city of Sivas, the old man, a widower with six children, was given a suspended sentence because he agreed to marry his victim.[1]

He claimed that before he engaged in sexual intercourse with his teenaged pupil, the two had contracted a religious marriage. A friend of his, a plumber, officiated. When the assault was revealed, he clinched a deal with the girl's family, which was keen to avoid social disgrace, and he was allowed to marry her officially.

To make matter worse, the judge ruled that the two would have to be married for a minimum of five years. In case of divorce, the rapist would have to serve his sentence. But, the media asked, who was being punished in this case: the elderly rapist or his teenaged victim, who found herself married to a man old enough to be her grandfather?

Forced marriages—distinct from arranged marriages conducted with the consent of the bride—are the source of countless personal tragedies that often pave the way for honor killings. In eastern rural cultures, when parents decide that it is time for their daughter to get married, priority is often given to her first cousin—her father's brother's son—as a prospective groom, but other close relatives are also considered suitable candidates.

Once the would-be husband has been selected, the reputation of the family is engaged and the marriage has to go ahead. Girls can be killed for refusing the man that their father has chosen, for opting to marry the man of their choice against their family's will, or for running away from an abusive relationship that they had never wanted.

"The biggest problem is that parents force their children into marriages they don't want," Turkish journalist Mehmet Yıldırım, who covered numerous cases of honor killings in the conservative city of Urfa, told me. "This is a recipe for disaster and will eventually push women to make some mistake."

Yıldırım, a jovial, barrel-shaped man who looked a bit like a friendly squirrel with full cheeks and prominent teeth, was familiar with local customs. In this region, many people still feel an allegiance to a tribe, be it ethnic Turkish, Kurdish, or Arab. He knew that the elders' judgment could be harsh.

"Here there is no mercy: we kill," he said. "The strangest thing is that the women know it and yet they run away."[2]

Nineteen-year-old Gönül Aslan,[3] who was the daughter of a civil servant from Urfa province, had a narrow escape after she was thrown into the Euphrates River in southeastern Turkey in 1998. Gönül had grown up in the more liberal atmosphere of the Mediterranean city of Antalya, where her father was posted. But she was forced against her will into a religious marriage that was never legalized with a man from a conservative district of Urfa province. The young woman chose to escape with a man she loved and wanted to marry.

On the run for a few days, the lovers made the fateful decision to return and confront their families, hoping to get permission to marry legally. But Gönül's father, shocked by his daughter's "dishonorable conduct," convened a family council to discuss the situation. Male relatives were called in from other towns to join in the decision. Eventually, they decided that Gönül would be returned to her husband and he would have to dispose of her.

Bundled into a car, the young woman was taken to the banks of the Euphrates River on a cold February day in 1998. With the help of her uncles, her husband strangled her with a scarf before throwing her unconscious into the Euphrates. Fortunately, the ice cold water brought Gönül back to consciousness and she managed to swim to the shore and seek help.

Following her miraculous escape, her husband, Sakip Aslan, her father and her uncles were arrested and initially sentenced to 16 years of imprisonment for attempted murder. But due to "mitigating circumstances" and "good behavior" during the trial and the fact that the men had acted under "extreme provocation," the judges later reduced the sentences to four years and five months and then decided to release the convicts, since they had already served a few months in jail.

Gönül disappeared and is living in hiding. She got a second chance and hopefully leads a normal life somewhere in Turkey, but it is significant that her tormenters got away with their attempted murder very lightly.

* * *

Statutes of limitation don't apply to honor killings. Long-running grudges can even survive in a Western environment, where one would expect community pressure to be diluted by the more liberal environment of the host society. In some cases, hanging on to anachronistic traditions becomes a way for migrants to preserve their identity, even if their traditional perceptions are often at odds with the rapidly changing social environment in the country of origin.

Jack and Zena Briggs, a British couple, had been on the run in the United Kingdom for 16 years by the time they publicly testified at a Metropolitan Police conference on honor killings in London in October 2004. With the help of the authorities, they had changed their identities twice and had to move on 30 occasions to evade the wrath of Zena's relatives.

Petite and pretty, Zena, whose family is of Pakistani origin, was 21 and Jack was 30 when they met in the summer of 1992. Jack was a working-class man from Yorkshire in north England. Zena, from a well-to-do family, had been promised since infancy to a compatriot.

After the couple eloped in January 1993, Zena's brothers turned up at Jack's mother's house, threatened her, and announced that they intended to kill her son. They even introduced her to his would-be killer. Jack's sister also received calls warning that she and her children would be burned in their beds. The British police took the threats seriously and entered them into a witness protection program.

At the time they appeared at the police gathering, Jack and Zena still feared being recognized in public. Zena's brothers had warned them that they were ready to spend any amount of money and sell their belongings if necessary to track them down. They even hired bounty hunters to look for them.

As Jack told me after his presentation, more than a decade after they had eloped, he and his wife had no way of knowing if the danger had receded. The security forces still believed them to be under threat. Jack and Zena had no choice but to remain on guard constantly. They had avoided buying furniture and accumulating possessions during their years of married life, knowing that they might have to leave them all behind to flee again if they were spotted by potential hit men.[4]

Eventually, the pressure of living under cover proved too strong. While Zena, acting upon advice from the police, slowly began to resume a more normal life, Jack struggled to adjust and the two drifted apart. In 2009, they separated, although both continue to work actively against honor killings.[5]

Forced marriages are not limited to Muslim and South Asian communities. They occur in many different cultures. In October 2003, the European Parliament demanded action after a 12-year-old Gypsy "princess" from Romania tried to escape during a lavish marriage ceremony to seal her union with a 15-year-old bridegroom. Family members said that she had been promised in marriage to the young man for the price of 500 gold coins when she was only seven.

The reluctant bride was caught by her relatives and dragged back to the altar. The ceremony went ahead, with the bride looking sad and sullen in front of hundreds of guests, even though the minimum age for marriage is 16 in Romania. The groom's family later displayed the bloodied sheet to prove that the union had been consummated. But the news articles generated by the bride's resistance reached the European Union, which intervened and demanded that the Romanian authorities take the girl into care.[6]

While this may be a relatively rare case in Europe, girls are still routinely married off against their will around the globe, at puberty or even before. A study conducted in 2009 by Turkey's Parliamentary Commission on Equal Opportunities for Women and Men revealed that 30 percent of marriages involved partners between 12 and 19.[7]

The exchange of brides, called *berdel* in the Turkish southeast and *watta-satta* in Pakistan, is a variant of forced marriage, more complex and doubly damaging because the fates of two women are at stake.

It involves the exchange of girls of "similar value" and allows two families to avoid paying a bride price. It is extremely unfair to the couples involved, and particularly to the brides, who have little choice in the matter. If one of the marriages fails, the other has to be dissolved as well to maintain the social equilibrium.

In 2006, a 21-year-old Turkish mother, Şahe Fidan, killed herself, three years into an unhappy marriage that was the result of such an exchange. After yet another violent argument with her husband, she had returned to her parents' home but her family had rejected her plea to let her stay. "In our family, a married woman only leaves her husband's house as a corpse," they told her. A few days later, the young woman tied her baby to her back before using a rope to hang herself from the bathroom ceiling.[8]

Kareena*, whom I met at the Dastak women's shelter run by lawyer Hana Jilani and her colleagues in Lahore, Pakistan, was also a victim of the *watta-satta* tradition. This 28-year-old mother of three told me that her marriage had been relatively happy. But when her brother, who had chosen a bride from her husband's extended family, decided to divorce his wife, Kareena's in-laws kicked her out at once. Her husband claimed that he loved her, but was too weak to stand up to family pressure.

Expelled from the marital home in Faisalabad, the young woman asked her parents to take her back but they, too, rejected her. "They wanted me to return to my husband, but he did not want me," Kareena explained.

When her father eventually visited her in Lahore and told her that she could return to the fold of her own family, Kareena was suspicious. A relative later confirmed that her family had in fact planned to kill her as soon as she came back.

When I met her in August 2003, she had been at the shelter for four months. Her divorce had been finalized, and her husband had already remarried.

For a brief period, she had managed to maintain contact with her 14-year-old son through his school, but when her former in-laws found out, they moved the young boy to another establishment. Discreetly wiping away her tears, Kareena told me that her chances of ever being reunited with her children were very slim.

Her case is by no means uncommon. Sitting next to her in a room crammed full of bunk beds in the Lahore shelter was 35-year-old Sumera* from Mianwali, who shared a similar fate. She too had been exchanged in a *watta-satta* agreement while still in her teens, and thrown out on the street when her brother decided to swap his wife for another woman. "We won't keep you," her husband told her. She managed to take her youngest child with her—a toddler who was fast asleep, spread-eagled on the hard concrete floor while we were talking—but she had not seen her four other children. She had contacted her husband three weeks earlier and pleaded with him to take her back, but she had received no response.

Another practice sometimes found alongside forced marriages and bride exchanges is the tradition of giving girls in compensation to prevent a feud erupting between two families. Land disputes, men eloping with girls without the consent of their families, or other rows can result in decisions, sanctioned by elders, to give compensation in kind to bury the hatchet.

The girls or women thus transferred are rarely embraced into the fold of the opposing families. They often end up bearing the burden of the families' hostility for the rest of their lives. A UN Population Fund report on compensation marriage in Pakistan quotes such a victim, who was handed over at the age of one. "Everyday they beat me for petty issues apparently in revenge for the murder," Zainab Bibi told the researchers.[9]

The Fund warned in 2008 that the practice appeared to be on the increase in countries where families commonly marry off adolescent girls. In Northern Iraq, the agency said, "parents will often sell girls into marriages to offset family debts, or to compensate another family for the murder of one of their male members by the girl's father, brother or uncle. Again, though forced marriages are illegal in the country, the law is not enforced. And with the ever-increasing level of violence in Iraq, more young girls are being forced into marriages with insurgents from various factions."[10]

News articles about the subcontinent and the Middle East are also replete with examples of such transactions conducted on the bodies of women or even infant girls.

A correspondent for the British newspaper *The Guardian* reported, for example, in April 2005 that a village court awarded a two-year-old girl in compensation to a 40-year-old man in the southern Punjab region of Pakistan, in a practice known as *vanni*. The toddler's uncle was said to have committed adultery. He was found guilty by the elders, who ordered him to pay the wronged husband 230,000 rupees (3,900 dollars) in compensation and to give his niece in marriage to him when she reached her 14th birthday.[11]

The law in Pakistan prevents marriages of girls under 16 and boys under 18, but it is often ignored. Giving girl children in compensation to settle disputes is also common in the Northwest Frontier Province, where it is known as *swara*, as well as in neighboring Afghanistan.

Although it violates civil law, the practice continues to blight young girls' lives. Women and female children continue to pay for the sins of their male relatives. As Amnesty International mentioned in a report on Afghanistan, "there is no legal recourse and few advocates lobbying to end the practice."[12] In the case of the two-year-old, the Pakistani authorities got involved to block the marriage, or more accurately, the transaction.

But many equally outrageous transfers have been allowed to take place and other cases go unreported. In another *jirga* (tribal court) ruling in 2004, seven women were ordered to divorce their husbands in order to end a feud between two clans. The women were the principal victims but the couples' 25 children also paid a high price when they were handed to their fathers.

Examples like these, each more shocking than the next, still abound throughout the Middle East and the subcontinent, even if awareness that they constitute human rights violations has grown considerably.[13]

In 2008, two warring clans made headlines in Pakistan with a dispute that began when a dog owned by the Chakrani clan was shot for overstepping its boundaries and straying close to a well belonging to the Qalandaris. A donkey was then killed in retaliation and the feud escalated until 19 people had been killed. In June 2008, after a tribal chieftain intervened to bring the two families together, the Chakranis agreed to pay financial compensation and to hand over 15 girls aged between three and ten. In an angry editorial that condemned the "medieval mindset that dominates many sections of our society," the Pakistani newspaper *Dawn* described the deal as "barbarity in the name of tradition."[14]

While it is traditional in many patriarchal communities to marry girls to close relatives, parents will in some case marry their daughters to outsiders against payment of a sum of money or another girl. The younger and prettier the girl, the higher the price she is likely to fetch.

Zita* was a good-looking 20-year-old, dressed in a lilac shalwar kameez, whom I met during my visit to the Dastak shelter in Lahore in 2003. She played nervously with her fingers, keeping her head lowered and avoided my eyes while telling me her sad story. At the age of 14, she was sold by her father to an elderly man. She told me that her mother was so upset about the marriage that she died of depression within 15 days.

Zita's husband, possessive, jealous, and constantly fearful that she would leave him for someone younger, kept her isolated from the rest of his family. He beat her regularly and never gave her any money. She stayed with him for five years and gave birth to a daughter and a son, who were aged four and two, respectively, at the time I interviewed her.

Eventually, Zita could no longer take the abuse and she left, seeking refuge at Dastak. After three months at the safe house, she moved to her uncle's house, but her stay was brief. Although he had offered to look after her, he was in fact exploiting her and using her as a maid. She returned to the shelter and filed for divorce.

Her husband visited her a few times and tried to engineer reconciliation, but he never brought the children. He was using them as a bait to entice her to come back to him. "If you loved them, you wouldn't have left," he told her.

Zita had no hope of ever getting custody: her husband had made clear he would never give up the children. Losing their children is a high price to pay, but it is a choice many women have to make when they escape an abusive relationship in Pakistan. Patriarchal mores require wives to submit to their husbands, even if it means putting up with daily physical and emotional abuse.

In neighboring India also, many women's freedom is circumscribed by patriarchal practices. Crimes are committed in the name of honor in many rural areas, most of them linked to an outlawed and obsolete caste system that continues to overshadow many people's lives. When a girl from a higher caste marries or falls in love with a boy from a lower social rank, her caste members may seek revenge, sometimes in a particularly gruesome way.

Geeta Devi, a 20-year-old Rajput woman from the northern Indian state of Punjab had to watch while her husband, Jasbeer, 22, from the Jat caste, had his hands and legs chopped off by her fellow caste members. The incident took place in broad daylight in July 2003, in the market town of Hoshiarpur, two months after the two young people had married. Three of the four perpetrators were arrested, while one escaped. "As I am one of the eyewitnesses, I am receiving threatening calls from the fourth killer who is absconding. The other three have been arrested," Geeta told a gathering of the All India Democratic Women's Association (AIDWA), which has been working to increase awareness of honor killings in India. "My life is in danger. The members of my Rajput community can kill me anytime."[15]

According to figures cited by AIDWA in 2004, murders of men and women committed in the name of saving the honor of the community, caste, or family "account for up to 10 percent of all killings in the northern states of Punjab and Haryana." Similar murders were on the rise in Uttar Pradesh, where in the worst affected district, Muzaffarnagar, "thirteen cases of honor killings were reported during the first nine months of 2003, up from ten in 2002. Some thirty-five couples were declared missing during this period, according to a report by the organization."[16]

None of the women mentioned in this chapter had violated any law or committed any crime. Nor had they been unfaithful or sexually promiscuous. Yet all of them faced the threat of death at the hands of their own community, either because they had been rejected by their spouse, they had refused the imposition of a partner, or they had fled abuse.

Traditionalists frequently refer to the need to preserve public morality when they seek to justify the violence. But these cases show that interpretations of what constitutes honor stretch well beyond notions of chastity and propriety, targeting women—and more rarely men—who have in no way strayed away from traditional sexual mores.

CHAPTER 7

ZAHIDA

When I visited the Women's Crisis Centre in 2003, it was run by NGOs but funded by Pakistan's Ministry of Women Development. It was located in a leafy suburb of the Pakistani capital, overrun with colorful vegetation. The quiet atmosphere in the sleepy neighborhood felt in sharp contrast with the violent stories that the activists running the Centre heard every day.

At the Women's Crisis Centre, lawyers, psychologists, and other volunteers dispensed advice and help to abused women, while an elderly female attendant with a kindly face and a dazzling smile served tea and sympathy.

Anjum, the woman in charge when I visited, had encountered numerous stories of torture, brutality, and murder. She showed me stomach-churning pictures of an 18-year-old, disfigured by acid. I instinctively flinched and turned my head, but she insisted: "Don't be frightened. Look at what he did to her."

The face and upper body of young Zarina were barely identifiable as belonging to a living human being: her eyelids had been welded shut by the acid, while one of her eyes and her nose had melted. Her lipless mouth reminded me of the painting "The Scream" by Edvard Munch. Yet Zarina had survived her deep burns and was still alive, lying in hospital after undergoing numerous surgical procedures that had restored her ability to breathe through her nostrils and eat again.

In a matter-of-fact way, with the calm of someone who has seen many tragedies, Anjum narrated Zarina's story. The attack took place in July 2002 during a hot summer night when the young woman's husband was asleep in the courtyard. Family honor, even in its most patriarchal interpretation, was not involved. It was a story of revenge and hurt male pride.

Zarina was in bed inside the house, with her six-month-old baby girl resting next to her, when a wealthy neighbor whose advances she had rejected sneaked into the house in the dead of night and poured acid over her face and body. Zarina woke up screaming, feeling her body on fire. A few drops had also fallen on her sleeping baby, who suffered burns.

The perpetrator was later arrested and charged with attempted murder, but he had achieved his goal: Zarina's life was irremediably destroyed. In a few seconds, the dark-eyed beauty shown in an old photograph was turned into a grotesque and frightening figure.

Zarina was not alone. In rural regions, acid, used to soak seeds, is cheap and easy to obtain. A report published by the Human Rights Commission of Pakistan noted that "particularly alarming was the soaring rate of cases of mutilation by the pouring of acid over women, in a crime that acted to scar them permanently, both physically and emotionally."

During our conversation, Anjum mentioned another tragic case of a woman sadistically tortured by her husband, allegedly for tarnishing his honor. Anjum knew her well, having provided legal and moral support to her after the attack, and she offered to arrange a meeting.

The attack on Zahida Parveen, which took place on December 20, 1998, was so savage that even in a country largely immune to violence against women, it made headlines. The young woman later featured in a moving television documentary produced by National Geographic, "Honor among Men: The Killing of Women in Pakistan," which highlighted her courage. Frail-looking, Zahida proved that she had plenty of inner strength. Refusing to bow to pressure, she fought in court to have her attacker convicted.

Zahida was three months pregnant when her husband, Mehmood Iqbal, a barber, set upon her, in an unprovoked and apparently uncharacteristic fit of jealousy, accusing her of having an affair.

Despite her protests of innocence, he tied her up, gagged her to make sure that she could not call for help, and hung her upside down from the rafters. He then proceeded to beat her with an axe handle, breaking her ribs and bruising her entire body. Using a razor, the tool of his trade, he cut off her long plait and slashed off her ears and nose before gouging out her eyes with a metal rod, cutting through the eyelids. But his anger was not yet spent, and he also clipped off the tip of her tongue.

Zahida mercifully passed out while she was being tortured, but she regained consciousness after he severed the rope that supported her and left her for dead, crumpled in a pool of blood on the ground. For hours, she lay there drifting in and out of consciousness.

I wanted to travel to the village of Sukho, 40 minutes away from Rawalpindi to visit Zahida in her place of residence, but Anjum told me that she would probably prefer to meet me in the city. Her notoriety had upset some of her fellow villagers, and receiving foreign visitors would only attract unwelcome attention. Zahida traveled once a month to Islamabad with her brother to collect a small pension that allowed her to survive financially, I was told, and I would be able to meet her during one of her visits.

Several days later, I turned up at the Centre at the appointed time, a bit nervous about my meeting with Zahida. I always feel uncomfortable, a ghoulish voyeur, when witnessing human misery, but the urge to tell the story usually gets the upper hand.

When I arrived with my friend and translator Masooma, the 32-year-old Zahida was entering the building. Her brother, a handsome young man sporting a short beard, was guiding her with a light hand on her elbow. Trotting behind them was a serious-looking little girl with short hair and intense dark eyes, wearing a bright orange dress.

Zahida's youngest daughter was born in July 1999, six months after the attack. Like her mother, she had proved resilient, emerging miraculously intact after experiencing the brutality of the attack from inside the womb.

Tiny and bird-like, Zahida was not much bigger than a child. She had wanted her suffering to serve as an example, to protect others from experiencing the same fate. She boldly took the witness stand and testified against her husband.

Despite her blindness, Zahida obviously cared about her appearance: on the day we met, she was wearing a bright blue shalwar kameez decorated with large white flowers and kept pulling at her clothes with a small bony hand to check they were properly adjusted. Her narrow feet, constantly in movement, betrayed her restlessness.

Tehmina Daultana, then Minister of Social Affairs, had heard about Zahida's ordeal as she visited the hospital where the young woman was recovering from her injuries. She was instrumental in getting Mehmood arrested and tried.

Zahida's shocking story, published in the Western press, caught the eye of Pakistani-born Dr Nasim Ashraf. The physician, who divided his time between Maryland and Pakistan, arranged for plastic surgeons in the United States to operate on Zahida in 2001 and restore her lost features. The young woman traveled to Washington, accompanied by her brother Shakir, and National Geographic television recorded her progress in the course of her treatment.

"This woman did more for me than a mother would. She took such good care of us while we were in America that we didn't feel we were in a different country," Zahida said, turning her sightless eyes toward Ashraf's wife, Aseela, who was sitting with us.

I had watched the documentary, which ended on a note of hope as a beaming Zahida flew home, obviously happy to be reunited with her children and relatives. Her eyelids had been reconstructed quite successfully with skin grafted from her stomach. Fake eyeballs had been fitted into her empty sockets, while prosthetic ears and a nose covered the gaping cavities carved by her husband's knife.

But the return to reality had been no fairy tale. By the time I met Zahida, five years after the attack, the broad smile was no longer forthcoming. Once the initial flurry of media attention died down, the extent of her losses became evident as the young woman resumed life in her village and struggled to adapt to her new circumstances.

By the time I interviewed her, she rarely wore her glass eyes. Her eye sockets were prone to infection in the dusty and humid environment of Pakistan, and she needed frequent doses of antibiotics to ward off disease. A white Band-Aid stretched across the bridge of her nose, holding her prosthesis in place.

She looked uncomfortable, and it becomes clear that she no longer welcomed publicity. "The media played a bad role, we feel embarrassed," explained her brother, who chaperoned her. "People in the village taunt us."

The attention her case received had alienated Zahida from her community. In rural Pakistan, women are expected to keep a low profile. Neighbors assumed that she was wealthy because she had appeared on television, when in fact she was just surviving. Some ill-intentioned villagers had even suggested that she was only pretending to be blind.

Despite her wariness, Zahida kindly answered my questions. I asked her what might have triggered her husband's sudden rage, but she could offer no explanation. He was a quiet man, prone to long silences, she said, and nothing in his behavior prior to the attack suggested that he was capable of such barbarity.

"I don't know what was in his heart. Occasionally he got a bit upset, but nothing to predict what he did later," she said.

Mehmood Iqbal was Zahida's second husband. She had married at the age of 16 and had a son from her first husband, who died of a heart attack before her baby was born. She hadn't planned on remarrying, but Iqbal had approached her family and her mother arranged the match.

Aside from one incident when he slapped her, Zahida said that her husband was neither violent nor particularly difficult. He was also nice to her son, who was only one-year-old when they married. At the time Mehmood lost control and proceeded to torture his wife, the couple already had one daughter and Zahida was expecting the little girl who was flashing me a flirty smile while hugging her mom's leg.

"It was Ramadan and he had just returned from praying at the mosque," Zahida explained. "He told me to get inside the house. I thought he wanted to have intimate relations and I said 'not now because the children are sleeping', but he grabbed my hair, pulled me inside and bolted the door."

Mehmood had apparently become convinced that the child she was carrying was not his. He later claimed that he had stopped in a village on his way to a friend's house and had seen Zahida in bed with another man. His claim was clearly unconvincing. After inflicting his savage "punishment" and leaving his wife bloodied and mutilated on the floor, he ran away with their baby daughter.

"He did it because of suspicion. He said I was a bad character," Zahida said.

When Zahida's young son woke up and found his disfigured mother unconscious on the floor, he screamed, prompting her to regain consciousness and cry for help. Villagers on their way to the mosque for morning prayers came to her rescue. They too were horrified when they saw the gaping holes the knife had left on her face. "Even my children were scared of me," Zahida explained.

Mehmood, by then, was on the run. He had dropped their baby daughter at his sister's house before taking refuge in a mullah's house. It took a while for the authorities to convince him to surrender and hand over their daughter.

I asked Zahida if her husband had intended to kill her. "I'm already dead. What else could he have done to me?" she asked, opening her hands in a helpless gesture. "Maybe it was just because of the baby. He believed it wasn't his. I don't know why he did it. There is nothing left in life for me. I just try to survive and live my days."

Interviewed at Rawalpindi prison by National Geographic reporter Michael Davie, Mehmood Iqbal was quite unrepentant. Wearing a white skullcap over his shaved head and sporting a long dark beard, he talked on camera about the terrible mutilations he had inflicted on his wife. He didn't think his 14-year sentence—five for attempted murder, three for cutting off Zaheeda's nose, three for removing her eyes, and 18 months each for her ears and for her tongue—was deserved because his actions were motivated by honor.

"I cut her ears off because she would never listen to anything I said. She would listen to others, even all the men she slept with," he explained calmly, before adding that he "took her eyes out because she would see things that I didn't approve of."

It is hard to understand how a man can cause such suffering to a woman who has borne him children and kept house for him day after day. Fantasies, suspicion, and odd notions of honor, it seems, can turn men into psychopaths. "The worst thing was," Iqbal told National Geographic, "I really cared for her and loved her."

Amazingly, Aseela Ashraf told me, Mehmood was still pestering his wife and asking her to take him back. He probably hoped to get out of jail if she pardoned him. But for Zahida, there was no going back: she had filed for divorce and expressed bitterness that the court had not handed down a heavier sentence on Mehmood.

"My husband is now working as a barber in jail. He's having a good time. He is happy," she told me. "He should be made to suffer like I have."

Her brother was furious too. "This man should have been hanged. If I didn't have a wife and children to look after, I would have killed him for what he did to my sister."

Back at the village, Zahida was doing her best to look after her children. Within the confines of her home, she could operate quite well despite her blindness. "I'm so used to my house that I don't feel blind at home. I just make sure that one of the kids is there to watch the fire," she explained.

But her mother, who lived with her, was now old and ill and could no longer go out to fetch water. Nobody in her family was really willing or able to take care of Zahida and her children. Her life was bleak, despite the support of the Women's Crisis Centre and other activists who had taken an interest in her case.

Illiterate and blind, there was little that she could do to improve her lot. The pension that she collected monthly from a trust set up by her Pakistani-American friends was just sufficient to cover basic expenses and ensure that her children could attend school. All she could hope was that her children, her daughters in particular, would have a better future.

CHAPTER 8

CRUEL AND UNUSUAL

Zahida survived her ordeal, but she ended up scarred and blind. It is sadly not rare for noses to be chopped off or facial features destroyed with acid in the name of honor. The disfigurement symbolizes the victims' loss of face in the eyes of the community.

Such crimes frequently carry a ritualistic element. "Once the violation is made public, the male members of the family must take immediate action. The family's honor is normally purged in public to restore the social status of the family, tribe or clan," wrote Fadia Faqir about crimes committed in the name of honor in Jordan.[1]

In Pakistan, axes and other sharp implements have often been used to kill *kari*, women accused of illicit affairs. Their lovers, real or alleged, can sometimes get out of trouble by paying compensation or offering girls from their family in compensation. When men are killed, they rarely suffer the kind of painful and cruel deaths that are often associated with honor killings.

"The weapon of choice for the murder of a condemned woman is the axe; often slaughtered like an animal, she must die a thousand deaths before her executioners are done. (The man, if he is killed at all, is usually shot). The different rituals for honor killings that still prevail faithfully replicate the practices that were recorded nearly two hundred years ago," writes Shirkat Gah activist Rabia Ali. She also explains that in Kandhkot and other areas of Sindh province, "the *kari* is dressed in bridal red and henna is applied to her hands. At dawn, the time for the morning *fajr* prayers, she is dragged to the banks of the river where she is hacked to death with an axe. In some areas, the woman is taken to the top of a hill and her neck is broken."

Her report mentions the case of a woman who, after being kidnapped, was brought back to her brother and son who, it turned out, were not relieved to have found her alive, but intended instead to punish her for the harm they felt had been done to their reputation. "Before killing her, they cropped her hair, cut off her nose and her ears, broke her teeth with the handle of an axe, and poured a liquid disinfectant down her throat. Then they finished her off with an axe."[2]

Although honor killings continue to be defined as a response to a social transgression that a woman has committed, in many of the cases I have come across or read about, the alleged violation is one that was perpetrated upon the victim, in which she played no active role.

"*Karo kari* murders have been committed on the strangest of pretexts. In a case that took place some years ago, an expatriate wrote a letter to his family and asked them to convey his salaams to a cousin. The woman was declared *kari* and murdered," wrote Sindhi politician and women's rights activist Nafisa Shah, who cited an even more bizarre instance, reported by a primary school teacher in Jacobabad: "A man dreamt his wife was a *kari* and killed her on waking up," he says.[3]

Just like Zahida Parveen, Zainab Noor, whose case made the headlines in Pakistan in 1994 for the sophisticated level of sadism it involved, had committed no wrong. She had been married to her first cousin, Mohammad Qari Sharif, an Islamic cleric at the local mosque in their village of the NWFP, in a *watta-satta* (bride exchange). The marriage went sour from the start because the parallel union that should have brought Zainab's brother together with her husband's sister never materialized. Zainab frequently experienced domestic violence at the hands of her resentful husband. When he heard that she had complained to neighbors about the constant abuse, he planned a particularly barbaric form of punishment.

In February 1994, he inserted metal rods into her private parts and connected them to electricity, destroying her vagina, rectum, and bladder. Despite undergoing reconstructive surgery in London, Zainab Noor was left permanently impaired and will have to use colostomy and urine-collection bags for the rest of her life.

When she bravely filed a case against Qari Sharif in Rawalpindi, with the help of activist Shahnaz Bukhari, her husband was initially convicted to ten years of imprisonment and a fine of 210,000 rupees for each of the three major organs that he had destroyed. Against medical evidence, he had claimed that Zainab had suffered burns when she tripped on a stove. On appeal, the three ten-year terms were reduced to one by the Lahore High Court, and he left prison in 2001 after a foundation settled the fine on his behalf.[4] But in February 2002, in response to Zainab Noor's challenge, the Supreme Court ruled that he should be rearrested and serve another 20 years, because the physical damage his wife had incurred was caused by two separate rods inserted into her private parts and therefore two separate injuries.[5]

Another Pakistani woman, Mussarat Shaheen, also survived a particularly vicious attack. She was left in a critical condition after her brother-in-law, claiming that she had a liaison with a local villager, cut off her legs after first dipping them in boiling oil with the help of his mother and a friend. The young woman had reportedly been frequently abused by her in-laws, who also stole the money that her husband, who was working abroad, was sending her. Her brother-in-law had apparently proposed to Mussarat's sister, who turned him down. He and his mother, offended by the rejection, directed their wrath at the young woman living under their roof.[6]

In June 2001, activist Ansar Burney, chairman of the Ansar Burney Welfare Trust, wrote to then President Pervez Musharraf to draw his attention to a particularly awful murder that had taken place in Khanpur Mehar in Sindh. A 21-year-old woman, Ajeeban, was wrongly accused of adultery. Her husband first shot her in the legs, leaving her seriously wounded. Her uncle, consulted about what to do, advised against taking her to hospital to avoid possible punishment. Instead, the two men dug a grave in front of the injured women, who was crying and claiming her innocence. Relatives who were present could not come to her rescue. Eyewitnesses explained that when she heard her baby crying, Ajeeban crawled toward it and nursed it one last time. When the grave was ready to receive her, her husband snatched the infant from her breast and shot her dead, before burying her without any ritual.[7]

Women accused of having shamed their families remain disgraced even in death. "Her body does not get the ritual bath or the shroud; no funeral prayers are recited over her; and she is interred in an unmarked grave in a graveyard reserved only for women like her," wrote Rabia Ali. In many places, however, her bludgeoned body is simply dumped into a river.[8]

Although the Pakistani media is doing a better job of reporting honor killings and human rights activists are keeping the issue on the agenda, attacks continue, some of them involving such cruelty and sadism that they defy comprehension.

* * *

In Turkey, as in Pakistan, families rarely claim the bodies of honor killing victims. While elaborate forms of physical cruelty appear rarer—victims tend to be disposed of in the most expedient way—the lengthy period that can elapse between the time when a woman is declared disgraced by her relatives and her actual death constitutes a form of mental torture. Like a prisoner on death row, a potential victim can live for weeks, if not months, with the knowledge that she will soon be killed.

Before they threw 15-year-old Naime Sulman off a highway bridge near Istanbul in June 2000, her brothers drove for hours with their victim sitting in the back seat of their car, in search of a suitable spot for her execution. They drove to Sapanca Lake, 100 kilometers from the sprawling Turkish metropolis, hoping to abandon her corpse in an orchard or a wooded area.

The teenager, from a southeastern family, had run away from the marital home in the Aegean town of Aydin one year after being forcibly married to a man 20 years her senior. When police officers found her in the Mediterranean resort of Antalya, hundreds of miles from her birthplace, Naime should have been placed under state protection. Instead, the policemen dutifully returned her to her family, as tradition dictates, ignoring the danger she faced or the fact that her parents had unlawfully married her off when she was underage.

"By running away from her husband, our sister had done wrong according to our *töre* (customs). When the three of us took Naime into the car, she understood that she was going to die," one of her brothers testified after his arrest. The brothers first toured a wooded area where unidentified bodies had been found in the past, but declared it unsuitable for their purposes. They then returned to Istanbul and opted to throw Naime off a highway viaduct. "We pulled to the side. Our little brother stayed in the car. With Ismail, we took Naime out of the car. We came to the fence and looked down. Naime said: 'I know you're going to kill me.' She had one last request from us: '*Abi* (big brother), please blindfold me before pushing me.' We looked around but we couldn't find anything to cover her eyes with. She just put her hands in front of her eyes."[9]

Lawyer Vildan Yirmibeşoğlu, one of the pioneers of the struggle against honor killings in Turkey, conducted a survey among 560 people of different levels of education in eight provinces of east and southeast Anatolia. She found that women were mainly killed after being raped (23.57 percent). Other motives invoked included adultery (22 percent), pregnancy outside wedlock (18 percent), and "going astray" (16 percent).[10]

The notion of going astray is of course wide open to interpretation, as was demonstrated by the case of 18-year-old Halime from the Kurdish city of Batman. She was killed by her 27-year-old brother, who pulled out a gun and shot her in the course of an argument triggered by her wearing trousers at a family wedding. In an attempt to hide his involvement, he then threw her, injured and unconscious, from the roof of their one-storey house, He later drove her to hospital, claiming that she had tried to commit suicide. Halime succumbed to her injuries in hospital in the regional capital, Diyarbakir.[11]

In Turkey, as in Pakistan, cutting implements are the most commonly used weapons in crimes of honor, but instead of the axe used to dismember victims in Pakistan, would-be Turkish murderers favour wielding a knife and cutting their victim's throat.

Seventeen-year-old Sevda Gök was executed in this fashion by her 14-year-old cousin in 1996 shortly after the midday prayers, in the middle of the marketplace in the conservative city of Sanliurfa. The perpetrator complained that she had gone to the cinema and was meeting men in cafes. None of the dozens of people who were streaming out of the mosque at the time of the attack were willing to testify against her teenage murderer, who ended up serving only 34 months in jail. He expressed no remorse for his crime.

Shooting a victim or drowning her in a well or a river were other convenient methods listed in the survey. Şeyhmüslüm Çam, for his part, chose to feed his 16-year-old daughter Ayşegül meat *pide*—a flat and elongated type of bread commonly consumed in Turkey with a variety of toppings—spiked with rat poison when he found out that she was pregnant as a result of a two-year illicit relationship with a 36-year-old man.[12]

Palestinian academic Nadera Shalhoub-Kevorkian spent years studying what she terms "femicide" in Palestinian society. The cases she surveyed involved stabbing, decapitation, strangulation, suffocation, and striking with a rock as killing methods.[13]

* * *

Claiming responsibility for a murder committed in the name of honor or making the deed public was traditionally an intrinsic part of reinstating a family whose reputation had been tarnished in the eyes of the community. But few regions have remained entirely untouched by media condemnation of honor-based violence and the rising chorus of protest coming from human rights activists. Making the death appear like an accident or a suicide is an increasingly popular option, particularly in countries like Turkey, where legislative changes have increased the possibility that perpetrators will face stiff sentences and be jailed for lengthy terms.

This flexibility in the face of changing mores may not be new: patriarchal traditions have always cleverly adapted to survive. Although many of the harmful practices used against women pre-date Islam and conflict with its religious principles, perpetrators continue to wrap themselves in the mantle of religion. In some regions, they benefit from the support of clerics who have a particularly narrow-minded and misogynist interpretation of the principles of Islam.

Anthropologist Germaine Tillion, who wrote about honor-based crimes in the early 1960s when they still took place all around the Mediterranean, explained how they were carried out in Sicily. Then, as today, "tradition" showed a great deal of pragmatism when confronted with an evolving legal environment.

... among Christians of Sicily—fervent Christians—the brother of noble ladies suspected of adultery would have them respectfully strangled in front of him in the presence of an aumonier. Murders of this type go back, it is true, three or four centuries, but it is only the external form of the execution that has changed: these days Sicilians prefer to use the revolver, and it is the husband who officiates because the crime can therefore be labelled in the "passion crime" category, and it is then possible to make an arrangement with the Christian-democratic justice; in the rural areas of Greece and Lebanon, in a similar case, the head of family remains usually quite faithful to the knife, and young modern village girls can therefore be—must be—Christianly stabbed by their own father, or better still, by their elder brother. [14]

In Turkey, suicides of young girls have reached alarming levels in some parts. The numbers were in sufficiently sharp contrast with the gender balance of suicide statistics around the world to justify an exploratory mission by the UN Special Rapporteur on Violence against Women, Yakın Ertürk, who visited the mainly Kurdish southeast provinces of her country of origin in May 2006 to investigate an epidemic of suicides among young women. She could not come to the absolute conclusion that they were homicides but, she wrote in her report, "there are reasonable grounds to assume that some of the recorded suicides are indeed disguised murders. In other cases, family members appear to have instigated the suicide."

Other attempts have been made to elucidate why so many young women are taking their own lives. A research into 134 cases of female suicides, carried out in 2003 in the same region of Turkey by Dr. Aytekin Sır of Dicle University, concluded that most of them were in fact murders. While around the world, men are more likely to commit suicide, in Turkey's east and southeast provinces, he found a female suicide rate that was double that of men. "They put rat poison in front of her, or they hang her. This passes for suicide,"[15] explained Dr. Sır.

Family pressure is in some cases sufficient to incite girls to take their own lives since they too have internalized the honor/shame concept from an early age and they may want to spare their families further grief.

When a young woman called Sevide Uyanık died on December 30, 2002, in the southeast town of Batman, aged 24, her death was initially ruled a suicide by hanging. But a postmortem revealed that she had received two Kalashnikov bullets, one in the chest, and one under the chin. It was also determined that she had given birth in the days preceding her death.

The young woman was a second wife, which meant that her marriage was not legal but had received the sanction of a cleric and was therefore socially acceptable. When her husband was jailed for smuggling, his first, and only legal, wife arranged for Sevide to move to his brother's house. Shortly after the young woman died, the body of a three-day-old baby was dug up from a nearby field. Her husband's brother and his son were arrested for her murder but it was unclear whether either of them had fathered the infant.[16]

Nebahat Akkoç, the activist who brought honor killings to the attention of a wider audience in Turkey and founded Ka-Mer, the first support association for female victims of violence in the region, is in no doubt that many suicides are in fact hidden murders.

Many of these cases don't look like suicides, but like murders. In many cases, the family or the members of the tribe who have condemned a girl to death for tarnishing their honor put pressure on her, saying 'instead of forcing us to kill you, commit suicide.' If you look at cases of girls either jumping from the balcony or drinking poison. Did she jump or was she pushed? Did she voluntarily drink poison or was she poisoned? We have serious suspicions about this."

Based on interviews that members of her association carried out with 1,800 women who applied for support at the Kamer center, the well-known activist reckoned that 1 percent of the women who requested assistance from her center felt under constant threat. About 7 percent of the applicants felt so pressured by their entourage that they were genuinely considering putting an end to their lives.[17]

Even when girls really do kill themselves, it is often a form of murder by proxy. Fifteen-year-old Gülhan Sarıkaya was two months pregnant when she shot herself with a hunting gun in the eastern province of Van. She had been forcibly married, or was sold, to a 45-year-old with 11 children, whose wife had abandoned him. Tradition had denied her a chance of preventing the wedding. Eventually, she saw suicide as the only way out.

In her conclusion, UN Rapporteur Yakın Ertürk recommended that the authorities investigate all apparent suicides thoroughly. She suggested in particular that they perform a "psychological autopsy" by carrying out interviews with friends and relatives of the victim, whenever there was indication that the "suicide" might involve others. The process would help determine the victim's psychological state at the time of her death. She also urged the authorities to make use of Article 84 of the Turkish Penal Code, which covers "instigation to commit suicide," to ensure that those who pressure women into killing themselves get suitably punished.

* * *

In Pakistan, too, human rights activists believe that an increasing number of *karo kari* murders or other honor killings are now disguised to avoid censure and possible legal implications.

"Methods of killing are changing because of resistance and media interest. Now we see more deaths with fertilizers and pesticides, which are defined as 'accidents'," Sohail Akbar Warraich from the NGO Shirkat Gah told me in Lahore in 2003. "People have become very clever; they plan carefully to exploit the legal loopholes. How do you explain bullets through clothes when people were allegedly caught naked? An intended injury is almost always different from accidental one. Medical reports can show the difference. But usually there is precise planning over time. Bodies are found in mysterious circumstances. It usually means that the perpetrators have worked for six months to think of a clever way to do it. Every third murder has a reference to honor—even thirty-year-old feuds."

In Pakistan, kerosene stoves, commonly used in rural areas, are suspiciously prone to explosion and an inordinate number of women suffer severe "kitchen accidents" that maim them or provoke extensive burns that eventually kill them. Some women douse themselves with kerosene as a way to kill themselves, a tragically common and particularly painful form of suicide common in the subcontinent, but many others are burnt by husbands and relatives.

The Islamabad-based Progressive Women's Association founded by Shahnaz Bukhari recorded 7,500 burn cases between 1994 and 2005 in the Islamabad area alone. Although only a tenth of a percent of the women survived, the perpetrators were convicted only in four percent of the cases.[18] Most of the women were aged between 18 and 35, and almost a third were pregnant, when they died.

A similar trend has been observed in Iraqi Kurdistan. A December 2006 report published by women's rights organization Asuda warned that such stove "accidents" were increasing at an alarming rate. In the first six months of 2007, the Women's Union of Kurdistan counted 95 cases, an increase of 15 percent on the previous year.[19] As honor-based violence comes under increased scrutiny, methods are evolving. But traditional perceptions continue to weigh heavily on many young women's lives.

CHAPTER 9

ŞEMSE

It was Christmas day 2002, and a bitter wind was blowing in Diyarbakir, the unofficial capital of Turkey's southeast. I had flown in from Istanbul the day before, after celebrating an early Christmas with my daughters, who were spending the holiday with their father. The trip had involved a lengthy wait at the airport. Most flights had been cancelled due to poor weather conditions. All of eastern Turkey was under a thick blanket of snow.

Toward the evening, the blizzard abated long enough for the flight to take off. I am not a confident flyer, and I was somewhat apprehensive, aware that the airport, under military control, did not have sophisticated radar equipment. My concerns, it turned out, were not entirely unfounded. Three weeks later, the same plane crashed as it approached the runway to land in Diyarbakir, killing 75 people on board.

But that day I was lucky. By the time we touched down, snow ploughs had already cleared the main streets. The next morning, the roads leading out of the city were practicable as well, although icy patches still shone here and there. Hüseyin, the driver who frequently accompanied me on my forays in the region, picked me up from the hotel, undaunted by the weather conditions. We set off at cautious speed toward the Syrian border. We were heading for the village of Yalımköy, on the outskirts of Mardin, where only weeks earlier, on November 21, a particularly gruesome execution had been reported.

According to media reports, Halil Acil, 55 years old, married and a father of four, had been having an affair with his 34-year-old neighbor Şemse. When she became pregnant, Halil tried to regularize their situation by taking her as his second wife. Polygamy has been illegal in Turkey since 1926, but it still subsists in rural areas and the authorities turn a blind eye. In fact, some conservative members of parliament are rumored to have more than one spouse.

The community, which does not tolerate sexual interaction outside wedlock, accepts these marriages as long as they have been blessed by an imam. Şemse's bulging stomach, however, was proof that she had been intimate with Halil long before their union had received the religious seal of approval. For some of her relatives, her expanding girth was an unacceptable source of shame.

The two lovers, alerted by a member of the clan that the young woman's family had met and ruled that they should be killed, tried to escape across the fields, accompanied by Halil's 13-year-old son, Erdal. But their pursuers caught up with them as they reached the main road and set upon them with stones and knives. Halil, stabbed, succumbed to his attackers' blows immediately. Şemse was left for dead.

Erdal, who was the only witness to the savage assault, ran to the town to seek help. Rescuers found Şemse unconscious, but still breathing. She was rapidly transferred to the university hospital in Diyarbakir, some 90 kilometers away, where surgeons operated on her brain.

Activists from the Kamer women's center in Diyarbakir are at the forefront of the fight against honor killings and domestic violence in this part of Turkey. As soon as they heard of the attack, they stepped in to ensure that Şemse, who was in a deep coma after her surgical intervention, would get the best treatment. They visited her daily in hospital, and raised funds to pay for the costly medications that helped keep her alive. Their efforts were rewarded with death threats from the young woman's relatives, who were bold enough to turn up at the hospital to ask how long she would take to die. They did not want her to recover.

When I visited Şemse in the intensive care unit of Diyarbakir university hospital, her head, which had been shaved for surgery, was covered with short, dark fuzz, growing in all directions. Kamer activists had taken photos of her in that state so that they could have an ID card issued in Şemse's name, needed for her to get access to treatment and medication. It turned out to have been the only photo ever taken of Şemse.

She had tubes coming out of her nose and although she was comatose, she appeared restless. Behind her closed eyelids, her eyes were rolling in their sockets as if intense activity was taking place in her brain. Was she having a nightmare, perhaps reliving the savage attack, or was her brain working hard to rebuild broken connections? She did not seem to respond to external stimuli, but the Kamer representatives who sat with her for long hours, telling her stories, told me that she occasionally opened her eyes and listened intently to what they were saying. Once a tear was even seen rolling down her cheek, I was told.

Despite their support and the dedication of the doctors trying to save her and the unborn child that was the source of her troubles, Şemse suffered a miscarriage in February 2003. Her body was getting weaker or perhaps, as her regular visitors suggested, she had lost the will to live after her miscarriage. She never regained consciousness and eventually died on June 7, 2003.

* * *

I did not expect a warm reception in Yalimköy. The brutal stoning of Halil Acil and Şemse Allak had attracted unwelcome local media attention, and the villagers were wary of strangers.

The office of the *muhtar* was located in an unfinished single-storey house on the side of the road, a small concrete cube that would have suited a hardware depot more than an official building. Inside, I found a few people huddled in near total darkness around a wood stove, in a sparsely furnished room, during an electricity cut. Not much state money had been lavished on this office and the place was largely bare.

Despite the biting cold, the woman who greeted me was cheerful. She explained that she was an employee of the municipality, who had been transferred to this remote outpost seven years earlier. "I am the only 'foreigner' in the village, the rest are all related," she said of the 4,000 residents of Yalimköy. "You won't find many willing to talk about the incident."

I sat down and accepted the traditional glass of tea. I was particularly glad of the offer. The roaring stove only heated a limited area and the room was glacial. Little clouds of vapor formed in the air as we talked. I knew that getting people to open up and share their impressions about the tragedy would take time, and a lot of tea would be consumed. I am not particularly fond of this beverage, but I usually end up drinking gallons of it out of politeness when I travel around Turkey. No conversation can take place until tea has been poured and drunk.

As expected, no one admitted to having seen the attack and no one was willing to give information about the people involved. "If I told you anything, I would be in danger," a young man who only gave his name as Mehmet explained reluctantly. "Besides how can I talk about something I have not witnessed personally."

I gamely continued chatting, talking about the weather, politics, and the depressed economy in this part of the country, before gradually a few details began to emerge about the lethal attack. It was clear that the incident had been much discussed behind closed doors. Slowly, Şemse's life story began to take shape.

In this region where young girls often wed first cousins or close relatives shortly after puberty, it was unusual for the young woman to remain single until she was in her 30s. Villagers explained that her father was a widower, who had kept his daughter by his side to look after him, thus depriving her of a chance to marry and have children.

How Şemse and Halil's relationship developed remains unclear. The two lovers took their secret to the grave. Some people suggested Halil had raped Şemse; others that it had been a consensual affair and the two were in love.

When trying to piece together events that led to an honor killing, forming a complete picture is often difficult. Gray areas often subsist. Even after a victim is killed, her or his family members will still spin a tale that will shine a more positive light on their own position. Some wanted to believe that Şemse had been forced to have sex with Halil. Others saw her as a "fallen" woman, who had seduced him. Whether or not her pregnancy was a result of a rape or a love story, in many people's eyes, her relatives had been justified in killing her.

Halil was also a victim, but no amount of spin could reduce his role to that of a passive player. He had either raped Şemse or committed adultery. A man straying away from the marital bed may be viewed with relative leniency, but the pregnancy was too visible a sign to be easily overlooked. The only way for his relatives to exonerate him was to claim that the baby was not his.

What is certain is that Şemse and Halil ran away together, and they were still side by side when their assailants caught up with them. This would suggest that the two shared a bond and were most likely in a relationship.

A few days before the events, Şemse's relatives had taken her to the hospital for a checkup. They must have suspected that she was pregnant because money is not often spent on visits to the doctor. The medical test must have confirmed their worst fears.

The young woman's family approached Halil and convinced him to take his lover as a second wife. Local rumors suggested that he had later changed his mind and sent her back to her family, but Mardin's police chief, Orhan Kaya, told me that Halil's invalid wife herself had visited Şemse's father and formally invited the young woman to move in with her family as a *kuma* (concubine or second wife).

Although the civil code gives Turkish women equality with their husband, many marriages are only conducted before an imam and never officially recorded. In the eyes of the local population, the religious ceremony is the one that really counts, but unregistered spouses, whether an only wife or a *kuma,* do not benefit from the protection of the law in case of divorce.

In the *muhtar*'s office, my reluctant interlocutors were willing to concede that the attack on Şemse and Halil was "bad business," but they did not overtly condemn the crime. The female civil servant, the only outsider, did not seem particularly shocked either. In the seven years that she had spent in this village, she had obviously become accustomed to local traditions. She did however offer the opinion that stoning was an unnecessarily barbaric method. "It would have been better if they had shot her," she said.

The *muhtar,* Celal Başçi, was out of town when I visited, but one of the men sitting by the stove turned out to be his brother. He offered to make contact and I got a chance to speak to headman on the telephone. Başci was unhappy with the publicity generated by the case. The stoning had cast his village in a bad light, he complained. The attack had wrongly been described as a stoning, and it was bad for tourism. "This story has been much exaggerated," he deplored.

The police chief for Mardin province was more forthcoming and condemned the attack unequivocally. "This is beyond acceptable human behavior; it must not be allowed to happen," Orhan Kaya said. One of Şemse's brothers, who was physically handicapped, confessed and said that he had been the main assailant, but the police did not take him seriously. "We dismissed his confession. He was obviously not the one who did it," Kaya said.

Families often designate a minor to carry out the violent deed, knowing that an underage murderer will get a more lenient sentence. In this particular instance, Şemse's relatives may have felt that an invalid family member would attract the judges' sympathy. Since the good of the community rather than that of the individual is taken into consideration, sacrificing a handicapped and less productive member of the family by sending him to jail would lessen the burden on the family group.

Police officers are not always very zealous in their pursuit of perpetrators of honor killings, but in Şemse's case, women's rights activists saluted the attitude of the security forces. Police officers even took it upon themselves to organize a funeral for Halil, whose body had not been claimed by his family as is usually the case when honor is at stake. As a result of their investigation, seven of Şemse's relatives were arrested, including her own brother.

* * *

Halil had a sister living in the nearby town of Mardin, I was told by one of the villagers in Yalimköy. Perhaps she could shed some light on the tragedy. We neither had her exact name nor her address, but news of the attack had traveled throughout the town. Although Mardin is a fairly large provincial capital with 80,000 inhabitants, the first people we stopped on the street were able to guide us to her house.

We were led through a maze of narrow alleys in this stunningly beautiful town of beige stone houses, then had to climb a few steep and icy steps before reaching her house.

She opened the door, her head wrapped in the traditional white scarf worn by Kurdish women and dressed in a voluminous flowery skirt that doubled her already impressive girth. Halise welcomed us in and gave us her own version of the story. "Şemse's father offered her to my brother," she said. According to her, Halil had returned the young woman to her family when he discovered that she was pregnant. "I cannot believe the baby was his; he was a good man," she explained as tears rolled down her cheeks. Other relatives, sitting cross-legged on cushions lined up against the wall, opined: Halil could not possibly be the father. Besides, he was ill and impotent, they said, apparently ignoring the fact that he had fathered several children.

Halise admitted that she knew nothing about her brother's relationship with Şemse until she received a phone call from a relative in Istanbul, tipping her off that an honor killing was imminent. The "jungle telegraph" had rapidly spread the news throughout the extended family.

Halise dispatched her son-in-law by car to her brother's house to warn him of the impending danger. When the young man arrived, Halil and Şemse had already been alerted and had fled. He collected Halil's first wife and her daughters, and brought them to Halise's house in Mardin, where they were gathered when the news came that Halil had been killed and Şemse mortally wounded.

* * *

Halise was quite adamant that her family would pursue the case through the courts as plaintiffs. "We cannot let Halil's death go unpunished," she said. But on February 12, the local daily *Özgür Gündem* reported that a female mediator, close to the pro-Kurdish party DEHAP, now disbanded, and distantly related to both the Allak and the Açil clans, had flown in from Brussels and successfully convinced them to drop the matter. The article praised the families for sorting out their dispute in a civilized way and averting a blood feud. Şemse's uncle Xelef Allak was even quoted as saying that Halil's death was an "accident."

The implication of his comment was that Şemse had been the intended target. If the young woman had been the only victim, mediation between the two families may not even have been needed: women are more easily expendable.

Representatives of DEHAP were present at a traditional peace banquet later organized by the two extended families in Istanbul to formally bury the hatchet and close the matter. The savage attack had cost the lives of Şemse, her unborn child and Halil, but a good meal and a few handshakes were all it took for their relatives to move on and forget their grief.

The case did proceed through the courts, but without the testimony of Halil's son Erdal, who was the only witness to the crime, the prosecution's position was weakened.

In June 2006, a criminal court in Mardin sentenced Şemse's brother Mehmet Emin Allak to a total of 20 years, eight months, and ten days of imprisonment for the two murders. Şemse's cousin Rıdvan Allak received a 17-year sentence, while his brother Emrullah Allak was condemned to 12 years and six months of imprisonment, but was released for time served. Several other members of the family were acquitted.

* * *

Şemse's body remained unclaimed at the morgue of Dicle University Hospital for 15 days. Women's rights activists, who had remained by the young woman's side as she fought for survival, continued to support her after her death. On June 20, 2006, a small funeral procession of some 50 women and municipality officials accompanied Şemse on her last journey. Her female companions broke with Muslim tradition by carrying the body of the deceased themselves and reading the funeral prayers at the graveside. These rituals are normally performed by men. Şemse was buried in a section of the cemetery reserved for unclaimed or unnamed dead.

Şemse and Halil's violent deaths became one of the first honor crimes to be intensely debated in Turkey. The crime grabbed headlines and was even discussed in parliament. Şemse's life story became the subject of a play, widely performed across the country, but her senseless murder was not an isolated incident and many other women have since suffered a similar fate.

CHAPTER 10

PERPETRATORS

I hadn't expected to share a cup of coffee with a murderer when I headed down to the southern Turkish city of Şanlıurfa in 2002. Many of Turkey's honor killings have occurred in this conservative and still largely tribal region inhabited by ethnic Turks, Arabs, and Kurds. According to a parliamentary subcommission formed in 2009 to investigate child marriages, this region also has the highest incidence of teenage marriages in Turkey.

Cab drivers are often a journalist's best friends, and it was a fortuitous conversation with one of them that led me to the small village of Kisas, in the Harran plain, where Halil Konak lived.

This part of Mesopotamia was, in the distant past, a booming commercial and religious center. According to the Bible, Abraham stopped in Harran on the way from Ur to Canaan. Abraham's pool and the fat carp that lazily swim in it are a major tourist attraction in Urfa. Harran is also connected to the Original Sin: Adam and Eve are said to have first stepped foot here after being expelled from Eden.

In more recent times, this flat expanse of land adjacent to the Syrian border was largely arid until Turkey built the massive Atatürk Dam in the 1980s to harness the waters of the Euphrates River. Thanks to an extensive network of irrigation channels, cotton and wheat now grow in abundance and the region has become more prosperous.

Fifty-five-year-old Halil Konak had been released from prison only days before I met him. He had served a five-year sentence for the murder of his niece Rabiya. I explained the purpose of my research, expecting him to show me the door but, much to my surprise, he agreed to talk to me and invited me onto his property.

We sat outdoors in the courtyard of his small farm, drinking Nescafe oddly prepared with milk rather than water. The conversation turned out to be surprisingly frank, given the circumstances.

Halil was a matter-of-fact killer, an unremarkable middle-aged man sporting a thick moustache and glasses. Nothing in his demeanor identified him as a murderer. He expressed no anger, and was neither boastful nor repentant about his actions. He felt that he had performed a duty that needed to be done: nothing more, nothing less. And he was prepared to do it all over again, if necessary.

"Killing is not something that everyone can do," he acknowledged, with a hint of pride, as we sipped our drinks. He explained that he had become the designated assassin after Rabiya's brother, chosen to carry out the communal decision to kill, had proved incapable of fulfilling his mission. "Her brother agreed with the decision to kill," Halil said, "but he couldn't do it." I detected a slight note of contempt in his conclusion. After Rabiya's brother lost his nerves, the family needed another executioner and Halil accepted the mandate.

Twenty-four-year-old Rabiya had to die, her relatives believed, because she had fallen in love with a man unwelcome by her family. Her suitor, respectful of tradition, had duly approached her parents to ask for her hand in marriage, but he was turned down.

"I never saw him and I don't even know his name," Halil said. "From what I heard they loved each other, but he'd been married and divorced twice, I think, and he was around 40 years old." He wasn't actually sure about the personal details of the potential groom, but of one thing he was certain: the man was an outsider, from the city, and therefore was unsuitable.

Disappointed, the two lovers decided to elope. It was a decision that sealed Rabiya's fate. Even more important than the relationship itself was the fact that she had defied her father's order. This could not be tolerated.

The young woman's death could perhaps have been averted if the local police had not joined in the search for the two lovers. Rabiya was, after all, an adult. But police officers had located the young couple in the city of Urfa, and escorted the young woman back to her family. In several other cases of women's deaths in Turkey, law enforcement agencies—the police, the gendarmerie, or even courts—have failed to provide protection and indirectly become accomplices.

Halil confirmed that the police had played a key role. "They were found together in Eyübiye near the police building," he said. "The girl was returned to her father, and the boy was released."

The police officers must have known Rabiya was in danger. As a grown-up, she should have been free to make her own choices, but the mentality that gives males in a family full power over their female relatives also prevailed in local law enforcement.

Male members of the family spent time carefully planning the execution: they wanted to disguise the murder and pretend it was an accident. According to their plan, Halil's tractor was meant to "accidentally" collide with a car in which Rabiya was sitting, squashing the vehicle and its passenger. But things did not exactly go according to plan: the collision damaged the car but it did not kill the girl.

"The tractor went over the car, but the girl didn't die," Halil explained. "She was injured, but she managed to open the door and she ran out, screaming."

Rabiya sprinted to save her life, screaming loudly, with her relatives in hot pursuit. It wasn't long until they caught up with her. The young woman never stood a chance.

As Halil drove his tractor forward, two relatives grabbed Rabiya and threw her under the advancing wheels, which crushed her body. She died instantly, on August 24, 1995.

Halik Konak's dispassionate account left me with a sense of unreality. In the courtyard where we were sitting, hens were running in the dirt, clucking as they herded their chicks. Occasionally, we heard peals of laughter from barefoot children playing nearby, and goats kept a close eye on us while chewing scraps of food. This serene bucolic scene was entirely at odds with the violence of Rabiya's untimely death. Here we were, soaking in the sun while discussing unimaginable violence.

"There never was another solution. According to the *töre* (customs), this is the way. It had to be done," Halil explained with a slight shrug. "If we hadn't killed her, we couldn't have sat on the village council. We would have had to leave all our wealth, our fields and move away. Tradition demanded that we save ourselves."

Rabiya's life for a seat on the village council: the exchange hardly seemed fair, but Halil was in no doubt that it was adequate justification for his actions.

Killing his niece was not a task Halil had particularly relished. At no point during our exchange did I detect any sign of passion in him. He was simply convinced that her trespass could not go unpunished. His main concern was to avoid creating a precedent by allowing a woman to defy her elders. Instilling fear in other female members of the family was the main motive behind the murder.

"Our story was shown on television in Germany, and my married daughter who lives there watched it on the news with her friends. She was very scared," he said, with obvious satisfaction. "The impact of the killing on the women of our family will last at least fifty years. They'll know that disobeying means death."

I asked Halil if it didn't bother him that fear rather than love dominated his relationship with his five daughters and two sons.

"Children have no right to speak," he told me, making it quite clear that he ruled over the fate of his adult sons as well as his daughters. "It's not a matter of love. The father has his own duty, the children have theirs. My son has a shop but I run it," he said. "If he has new ideas or wants to sell something different, he has to come to me with his proposal and I decide. I own the capital."

Halil knew all about family hierarchy. As a youngster, he had been at the receiving end of it. When he was only 14, his father suddenly decided to pull him out of school to get him married to his cousin.

"I was married at fourteen to this woman," he said, pointing dismissively to his wife, a large woman, prematurely aged, who was sitting stone-faced a few feet away from us during our entire conversation. She was folding laundry with fingers thickened by years of hard domestic labor.

Halil was direct, and showed the same disregard for his spouse's feelings as he had for his children's when he explained how they had come to marry.

"She is my cousin and she is ten years older than me," Halil explained. "I was in middle school and I hoped to study. I didn't even know what husband and wife do together," he said, clearly referring to sexual intercourse. "One day, my father pulled me out of school and told me to get married. I was clever and I wanted to continue studying but I had no choice. I'm now fifty-five and I've been married for more than forty years."

Halil Konak would probably have agreed with the views expressed by academic Amir Hossein Kordvani in an essay on hegemonic masculinity and violence against women: "Senior men of a family have authority over everyone else in that family including younger men and women, who are in turn subject to a form of control and subordination. Senior men, it is believed, make reasonable and rational decisions with the good of the kin in mind." Women, on the other hand, are considered "weak and emotional, and thus incapable of making any important decision on their own."[1]

The 15 men who sat on the family council and imposed a verdict of death on Rabiya had wanted to inflict the same punishment on her lover, but the young man disappeared after he was released by the police and Rabiya's relatives did not bother to go after him.

Killing a man is always riskier than killing a girl: a murder can ignite feuds between clans that can last generations and claim many lives.

Rabiya's family could have demanded financial compensation instead. "The boy's family could have given money in exchange for his life," Konak said. "One man's life is worth a lot of money, and a girl's life is worth nothing."

The family felt, however, that Rabiya's death had brought them the closure they sought and there was no need to pursue the matter further. "We didn't ask for any money," Halil said.

I tried to draw Halil's wife into our conversation. Wearing a flowery skirt and a loose top over a shapeless body, she looked a generation older than her husband and had so far kept utterly silent and expressionless. She looked defeated by life—resigned. When I asked her what she thought of Rabiya's death and her husband's arrest, she just shrugged. "How would I know?" She had learned the family lesson. A woman is not expected to question the men's judgment. She had no opinion of her own, or at least none that she was prepared to share publicly.

Halil acknowledged that times were changing. "My father used to live in a mud house. I built a concrete one," he said. "I can send my daughter to town on the bus, and maybe her children will be free to meet friends on their own," he said. But for the time being, maintaining the family's reputation at all costs was still an obligation for the inhabitants of this region, and Halil stood firmly by his decision to punish his niece.

"I killed Rabiya and served my time. You may be right to challenge my actions according to your customs, but I'm right according to mine and I'm not bound by the law," Halil told me. "If a similar thing happened again, God forbid, I'd do it again."

*   *   *

In another village of the Harran plain, just a few kilometers away from Halil Konak's house, I visited Hamza Tumbul.

He, too, had recently been freed after spending two years in prison for his part in the attempted murder of his 14-year-old daughter, Azize. Two of his sons were still in jail, serving longer sentences for shooting dead their neighbor's 19-year-old son, who had seduced Azize and left her pregnant.

The day after Hamza's sons shot the teenaged boy in the city of Şanlıurfa, they had turned their attention to their sister. She, too, had been sentenced to die by the family council.

Azize was lured to a meeting in the fields by her own sister. When she arrived at the isolated site, she was grabbed by her brothers and thrown into one of the irrigation canals that crisscross the plain and bring water from the nearby dam to the parched land.

Dragged by the current for nearly a mile, Azize, who couldn't swim, would have drowned if her long flowing dress had not caught on to a metal pole protruding from a bridge. Farmers tilling the fields spotted her bright red headscarf and pulled her out of the water.

At the police station, Azize filed a complaint against her brothers and was whisked away by the social services, to be looked after in a shelter in an undisclosed part of the country until her 18th birthday. There, she would give birth to her child and would have a chance to complete her education or at least acquire marketable skills.

Interviewed shortly after the events by Amberin Zaman, a reporter for *The Los Angeles Times* and *The Economist,* Azize's mother, Ferdi, expressed little compassion for her daughter.

"That stupid child shamed our entire family," she said. "We could not show our faces to the neighbors, not even to the shopkeepers, and now all our men are in jail. We must find her, not to harm her, but to make her change her testimony."

Nine members of Azize's family, including her father and the two brothers who shot the teenage Lothario who had impregnated their sister, faced charges.

Fortunately, this time the authorities were not fooled by the mother's claim that the family only wanted Azize to drop the charges. Her brothers, brought back to the scene of their attempted crime for a reconstruction, showed no sign of repentance and only expressed regrets that they had failed to accomplish their mission. "We apologize to our tribe for failing to kill Azize," they said.

Unlike Halil Konak, who had spoken calmly and openly about Rabiya's murder, Hamza Tumbul wanted to erase the entire episode from his memory and would not talk about it.

Born in 1931, he had a total of 20 children with his two wives, ten of them girls. Looking after his offspring was not his main preoccupation: he was obsessed with two race horses he had recently acquired. The two lean thoroughbreds could be seen grazing in a rough patch of shrub-covered land, which seemed an unlikely paddock for the elegant animals. They competed regularly at the local track, but the relentless summer heat in this part of the country kept the racing season short.

We sat on the floor for the inevitable cup of tea that accompanies all discussions in Turkey. Hamza, short and rotund, sat cross-legged: his heels showed deep cracks and he hadn't shaved for several days.

He called for the beverage to be served, and a tiny little girl with a dirty face and grubby feet walked into the room. She turned out to be his five-year-old granddaughter. Hamza's gruff mien visibly softened when he saw her. He asked her to serve tea to the visitors.

She disappeared, soon to return carrying a tray far too big and heavy for her. She held it aloft with the earnestness of a child proud to be entrusted with a task normally reserved for adults. She expertly flipped off her slippers before stepping onto the carpet barefoot and kneeling on the floor to pour the hot tea.

At five, she had already acquired the deference that was expected of her gender. It was still tempered by a childish mischievous smile, but she would probably grow up under the same pressure that had caused her young aunt's tragedy.

I tried to get Hamza Tumbul to talk about his daughter Azize and the incidents that had led to his incarceration. But unlike Halil Konak, he had put them behind him and was unwilling to revive the past. "Here it is the way. People have their fate written on their forehead. A girl talks to a boy and we have to strike. There is no escape," Hamza sighed. "I have ten girls. Boys have to come and ask for their hand first. That is our way."

He then redirected the conversation to his favorite topic, pointing at photos of his horses proudly pinned on the wall and praising their performance on the race track. Hamza Tumbul had nothing more to say about his lost daughter.

* * *

The two men I met that day in Urfa province were both middle-aged, but many perpetrators of honor killings are much younger.

In Turkey's mainly Kurdish southeast, the decision to kill is often a collective one. "The *aile meclisi* (family council) is composed of the grandfather, the father, the *amca* (father's brothers), the *dayı* (mother's brothers)," explains author Mehmet Faraç. "They meet to decide whether or not to kill the girl, who will do it and how it will be done."

The task of killing is often entrusted to a young member of the family, in the hope that judges will be lenient toward an underage killer. "The perpetrator is also a victim," believes Faraç. "The pressure on the family is intense. Neighbors won't say hello, they won't trade with members of the group and they won't marry their other daughters until the deed has been done. Perpetrators are encouraged to act."

Hot-blooded young males can be eager to prove their virility. "Killing is sometimes seen as a rite of passage into manhood," explains Leyla Pervizat, a Turkish researcher who wrote a PhD thesis based on

300 crimes committed in the name of honor in Turkey. "Underage boys are sometimes forced to kill, but they take great pride in it. In prison they are treated like heroes."

Pressure from peers in the community, as well as relatives, can be a powerful trigger. Mustafa, a 14-year-old Turk stabbed his 32-year-old mother to death in Adana on the eve of Mothers' Day in 2001. The young boy said that he was constantly taunted by his friends with allegations that his divorced mother was a prostitute.

The victim's younger sister, who was living with Mustafa and his mom, protested that the allegations were totally groundless. "Honor was just a pretext," she said. "My sister was killed because she wouldn't reconcile with her husband." The teenager first lunged at his mother with a knife while she was asleep. "She still managed to run outside and he stabbed her in the back," his aunt, the victim's sister, told reporters. He shouted at me, "Auntie, stay away or I'll kill you too."[2]

Mustafa continued hitting his mother until she was lifeless, all the while crying, "Mother, forgive me." His father, who had been jailed the year before after inflicting seven knife wounds on his wife, was arrested on suspicion of inciting his son to commit the murder.[3]

Many murders are committed by young men, but there is no evidence that the sense of injury men experience when social mores are allegedly violated diminishes with age. Seventy-five-year-old Abdullah Taşkiran shot his 45-year-old son, Muzaffer, and his 17-year-old granddaughter, Gayime, with a hunting rifle in May 2004 in the eastern Turkish province of Erzurum because the young woman, who was unmarried, had just given birth. The grandfather also tried to strangle the baby Gayime had hidden in a closet, but neighbors, attracted to the scene by the sound of gunfire, intervened and saved the infant. "This is an ugly event," Taşkiran told police officers, referring to Gayime's pregnancy. "I cleaned up my family's honor. I'm unrepentant. When they told me my granddaughter had been raped by someone from a nearby village, my eyes went blind."

*   *   *

Girls and women are the primary victims of honor-based violence, but no discussion of honor crimes would be complete without acknowledging the role played by members of their own gender in many of these tragedies.

Amnesty International rightly pointed out in its 2002 Pakistan report that "women, too, have to some extent internalized norms of 'honor' and are known to have approved of or assisted in killings of other women in the context of 'honor.' "[4]

The role of women in keeping harmful practices alive is undoubtedly one of the most perplexing, and distressing, aspects of the honor system: although patriarchal rules are designed to serve the needs of men first and foremost, women are often patriarchy's most enthusiastic agents.

"What drives women, generation after generation, to perpetuate the vicious cycle that made their own lives miserable as they grew up?" wondered journalist Alam Fareena in a *Guardian* article published in 2004.[5] It is indeed hard to understand how a woman who is not a sociopath can be driven to participate in or approve the cold-blooded murder of her own daughter, a child she has carried for nine months and nurtured through childhood and adolescence?

Several tentative answers to this question have been put forward. Sometimes, mothers or female relatives are simply trying to protect their own lives and their own positions within the community. Challenging the established order would be futile, as well as dangerous, and they feel that by going along with it, they are at least granted a small share of power.

Others probably make the rational decision to sacrifice one individual member of the family in order to protect the rest of their children, as well as the honor of the extended clan.

Once women have reached middle age and have borne children, especially boys, their sex appeal, it appears, is no longer perceived as a potential threat to social peace and they often enjoy a degree of influence within the family. But this power is still bestowed and mitigated by men. Imposing matriarchs may rule over the younger generation with an iron fist, often making life a misery for their daughters-in-law, but they still owe their position largely to their children and in particular to their sons.

The temptation to use their newfound influence is great and many wield it to deny younger women the freedom that had eluded them in their youth. Small communities are tightly knit, but within the confines of the extended family, feelings of jealousy are often rife.

Whatever the reason, women do at times play an active role in the killings. More often, they are indirect but crucial participants. Malicious gossip can be the trigger for honor killings and women play an important role by keeping the rumor mill running. Occasionally, mothers or other female relatives take it upon themselves to commit the murder or they are accomplices involved in its planning.

In February 2009, a 42-year-old mother of four was arrested in the Turkish city of Adana for the murder of her 18-year-old daughter, Meryem. The teenager had been found with a T-shirt tightly bound around her neck and her family alleged suicide. Bruises on her face, however, led investigators to suspect a homicide. They were able to link the murder to Meryem's mother, Irep, who confessed after traces of her daughter's skin were found under her fingernails.

Her daughter had been running around with a married man and had been exchanging text messages with him on her telephone, Irep claimed. She gave a factual and an unemotional account of the murder, which was particularly chilling.

"My daughter couldn't live with this stain on her honor. She knew she had to die and she was ready. She even said, 'I'll jump into the river to kill myself,' " Irep claimed. She was concerned that her daughter's body might never be recovered and no prayers would therefore be held. She chose instead to murder her at home.

The killing took place on Meryem's birthday. After celebrating the auspicious event, the two women retreated to the bedroom where the teenager was fed rat poison and several of the pills prescribed to her father for a heart condition. "We waited a few hours," explained the mother, apparently emotionless. "When she didn't die, I suffocated her. First I pressed a pillow onto her face. Then to make sure she was dead, I clamped my hand tightly across her face."

"If her father had heard that she had been with a married man, he would have had a heart attack," Irep said to justify the murder. She was also concerned that her daughter's alleged misbehavior would affect the entire neighborhood and lead to the disintegration of the alleged lover's family. Preserving the family unit at all costs, no matter how unhappy the partners may be, is a recurrent theme in honor-based communities.[6]

Although it is rarer for female relatives to take an active part in murder, this case is by no means unique.

A 16-year-old Palestinian girl, Salwar, engaged to be married, was killed by her own sister after she allegedly confessed to being pregnant. The young woman put heavy pouches of detergent into a plastic bag and laid it on Salwar's face, with several pillows to increase its impact, while she was sleeping. She held it down until Salwar had stopped breathing. She later claimed that she had tried to stop her sister from snoring. Charges of intentional murder were reduced to involuntary manslaughter. She was eventually sentenced to one year of imprisonment, but was released after payment of a fine.[7]

In the Aegean city of Izmir, in western Turkey, three sisters joined forces to get rid of their sister-in-law, a mother of three, in January 2000. The perpetrators' brother had disappeared several months before the murder and was believed by the authorities to have joined the Kurdish PKK guerrillas, fighting government forces in the mountainous area separating Turkey from northern Iraq. Local gossip suggested that in his absence, his 26-year-old wife had developed relations with other men. When confronted by her three sisters-in-law, Nezahat Aksoy got angry and told them to mind their own business.

Nezahat's murder was a joint venture: "Veysiye (aged 30) picked up a stone in front of the house and hit her on the head. I stabbed her a few times and I strangled her with a rope," 31-year-old Songül, the oldest of the three sisters, told the judge. "In order to stop her from crying out, Nuriye (aged 24) pressed a pillow on her face. At night, we wrapped her body in a carpet and threw it in an empty plot of land. We've cleansed our honor. We do not regret it." The trial was suspended until the court could determine if the victim had been a registered prostitute, as if this would have justified the decision to kill her.[8]

The case of 14-year-old Elife Atılgan, from Kahramanmaraş in Turkey, illustrates the conflicting emotions that some mothers experience when honor issues are involved. Elife left a note stating, "No one is responsible for my suicide," before she hanged herself with a clothes line in August 2002. At the time of her death she was eight months pregnant, after being raped by her cousin. Summoned by the young girl's parents, the alleged rapist denied having intercourse with the teenager. In fact, DNA tests on Elife's unborn child later confirmed her version of events.

A police investigation into the young girl's death revealed that her mother, 36-year-old Naciye, had handed a rope to the victim's 17-year-old brother, Tufan, asking him to do the necessary to ensure that his sister died. In his court testimony, Tufan explained that he had brought a stool and tied a noose around Elife's neck before leaving the room. When he returned an hour later, her body was hanging from the ceiling. The family's honor had been redeemed.

In February 2003, a court sentenced Elife's mother to life imprisonment, while Tufan received a 30-year sentence for his part in the murder/suicide.

A few days after the verdict was announced, Naciye killed herself in her prison cell, following her daughter into the grave. Was it the prospect of a lengthy detention that convinced her to take her life or remorse over the role that she played in killing her daughter? No one will ever know. One thing is certain: Elife's death, far from saving her family, had in fact destroyed it.[9]

* * *

The late Kurdish filmmaker Yılmaz Güney masterfully illustrated both the mercilessness of the community's response to violations of social mores and the internal struggle of the designated killer in his film *Yol* (The Road), which won the Palme d'Or at the Cannes Film Festival in 1982.

The movie focuses on five convicts on temporary leave from their Turkish prison. One of them, Seyit, is told that his wife, Zine, has become a prostitute. Her relatives have already ruled that she must die, but they have kept her chained in a barn for eight months, waiting for her husband, the "injured party," to return and execute her.

Yılmaz Güney, who was himself jailed for murder, partly directed his movie from prison. Memorable scenes show Zine, struggling, and failing, to keep up with her husband and their son as they progress through thigh-deep snow. Against a background of relentless whiteness, the camera wordlessly captures Seyit's conflicted feelings, a mix of hate and love, and eventually reluctant compassion as he tries but fails to save his wife from freezing to death.

For all the men and women who choose to perpetuate the practice of honor killings, there are plenty of others who do their best to resist community pressure.

They are not always moved by a deep-seated belief that making women bear the weight of a family's honor is wrong. Sometimes they choose not to act out of self-preservation.

A 21-year-old Istanbul management student, identified only as F.A., expressed his concern, through the media, that family pressure might turn him into a murderer, and would have a negative impact on his own life and his plan to pursue his studies. His sister had been abducted in March 2004 by a neighbor, Mehmet Doğan, after her family had turned down his marriage proposal. The girl's family ruled that the kidnapper should be killed and, as brother of the kidnap victim, F.A. had been entrusted with the task. He urged the authorities to step up their investigation and find his sister and her abductor before their relatives discovered their hiding place. "I want the authorities to find them before we do. If we find them, blood will flow," he told the Turkish media. "Either I'll kill them or they'll kill me."

The abductor's family knew where he was hiding, and F.A.'s sister had called the house once asking to be rescued. F.A. said that he didn't want to be "part of this savagery and go the jail," although he admitted that he may be forced to. "Otherwise we won't be able to be part of the community anymore and we won't be able to look our elders in the face."

Compassion for his sister, however, appeared to play little part in his reluctance to take action. He was, above all, thinking about himself. "In order not to kill my sister, I pray that she commits suicide. I want to continue my education; it's the only chance I have not to go to jail," he explained.[10]

Social changes and better awareness of human rights have led a growing number of young men to question the tradition of killing in the name of honor. Another reluctant perpetrator who made a passionate plea for help was 28-year-old Erşan Baran, from the oil town of Batman in southeast Turkey.

He had returned home from work one evening and found that his wife had left home without warning, leaving their one-year-old daughter asleep in her cot. The next day, his mother-in-law called and told him that her daughter no longer wanted to live with him and he should leave her alone. It turned out that she had run away with a construction engineer and moved to the Aegean city of Izmir.

The family council met and decided that Erşan, the oldest of nine children, should kill his wife. The young man was also asked to hand over his daughter, who would be raised by his own mother.

But the young man wanted to divorce his wife, not kill her, and he was determined to look after his little girl himself.

For two months, he resisted the family pressure. Eventually, he fled to the nearby town of Silopi, the last Turkish outpost before the Iraqi border crossing. "I stayed in Silopi for eight months. I managed to survive by working as a truck driver. I was comfortable because my family didn't know where I was," he told *Milliyet* newspaper, calling on the authorities to help him. "But one day, my father and my brother found me. My father approached me and pulled out a gun: 'Either you kill your wife and cleanse our honor or we'll kill you,' he threatened. I came to Istanbul."

The young father had been hiding in the sprawling metropolis for a month by the time he made his emotional plea through the media. He was running out of money, he had no place to stay, and he hoped that the local government or a charitable organization would help him support his daughter. All he wanted was to secure a modest existence for himself and his daughter, Didem. He didn't want to become a killer.

But while the authorities were ready to settle his daughter into a state institution, they could not offer him protection.

The young man later moved to the Turkish capital to keep ahead of his pursuers, all of them members of his own family.[11] By then, he was in despair. "I'm in danger, I do not want to kill," he told the authorities. "But if the state does not help me, I may have to kill myself, my child, or my wife. I will commit murder under duress. But when I surrender and appear in front of a court, I will tell them that the state institutions have ignored me. I am sick and tired of fearing death whenever I'm in the street and walking with my head bowed," he was quoted as saying in *Sabah* newspaper.[12]

Another young father, from the Turkish town of Adana, also turned to the media to highlight his plight in 2009. He and his wife had moved with their five-year-old son to the Aegean city of Izmir, hoping to find work but as soon as they were settled, his wife took her belongings and left them. Şeymus returned to his native city and filed for divorce, but his father-in-law, from the conservative town of Viranşehir, further east, put pressure on him to find and kill his absconding wife.

The young man then lodged another complaint, alleging that his in-laws were inciting him to commit murder. He also mentioned that he was receiving threats for refusing to comply with their demands and feared for his own life.[13]

Some do bow to tradition, but end up regretting their actions for the rest of their lives. Savaş Yüksel and his relatives who lived in a suburb of Istanbul, had, quite literally, got away with murder. In 2001, they had reported the disappearance of his younger sister Çimen, then aged 17. The police found no trace of the young woman and the case was closed.

Eight years later, in November 2009, Savaş confessed to the police that his sister was not missing: she had been murdered by her family for "wandering with boys." "I see my sister in my dreams every night. I can't sleep. We, her family, murdered her," Savaş told investigators. The decision was made by the young girl's brothers and the job of killing her was given to the youngest, Izzet, who strangled her with a length of cable while she slept. Following Savaş's confession, charges were brought against the victim's parents, her three brothers, and her sister.[14]

Cenap Şimşek, from the town of Birecik in Turkey's Sanlıurfa province, resisted his relatives' call to kill, but he could not live with himself. The family council had sent him to Istanbul to execute his 26-year-old sister, Evrim Sarıçiçekler. The daughter of a relatively well-off engineer, she had married a man from a modest background—a *kebabcı* (kebab shop worker)—against the wishes of her family.

She knew she was at risk and frequently told her neighbors that "one cannot escape from tradition. I only have a few months left, but I'm happy." Cenap traveled to Istanbul in December 2004, with the intention of killing the young couple. But after seeing how happy they were together, he could not bring himself to fulfill his mandate and returned home. The shame of not being "man enough" for the job eventually broke him. Under pressure from the extended clan, the 29-year-old committed suicide.

Another family member completed his mission: in February 2006, neighbors of Evrim and her husband, Selahattin, in Istanbul, worried that they had not seen the young couple for a few days, alerted the police. When the officers opened the door, they found the two young people's bodies. They had both been shot in the head the previous day.[15] According to some newspaper reports, Evrim was four months pregnant at the time of her death. Her brother Cenap had spared her, but his attempt to save her had proved futile.

CHAPTER 11

BERFIN*

I met Berfin at a conference on honor killings organized by the Swedish government outside Stockholm, where she had come to testify about her extraordinary ordeal. She was accompanied by Dr. Nazand Begikhani, a London-based Kurdish rights activist, who had played an important role in her rescue.

Nothing in Berfin's demeanor or in her fresh face, free of makeup, betrayed the long ordeal that she had experienced. At 37, she had the lithe body of a young girl and thick light-brown hair that made her look years younger than she really was. She spoke in a low voice, and only the intensity of her tone and the nervous movements of her fingers gave a hint of her inner turmoil.

Berfin was a Kurd from northern Iraq, a region that has experienced much upheaval in the past few decades. Kurds do not have their own country: they are divided between Iraq, Iran, Turkey, and Syria, and they have all experienced oppression to varying degrees over the years in their respective areas. Iraq's dictator Saddam Hussein waged a ruthless war against Kurdish resistance fighters, known as *peshmergas* (literally those who defy death), who were seeking more autonomy from the Baghdad government. Kurdish civilians too were targeted.

A vicious military campaign known as *Anfal* (the word means spoils of war, and comes from a verse in the Koran) led to the destruction of some 4,000 villages and claimed 100,000 to 150,000 victims, mostly male, between 1986 and 1988. It culminated in the gassing of Kurdish civilians in the town of Halabja in March 1988, which killed up to 5,000 town residents and injured thousands more.

Although it is in a process of rapid transformation, Kurdish society remains very tribal. The U.S. invasion in 2003 and subsequent occupation did not cause as much unrest in the north of Iraq as it did in the rest of the country. In fact, Iraqi Kurds were able, to a large extent, to consolidate their quasi-autonomous status.

The two main Kurdish political factions—the Kurdistan Democratic Party (KDP), led by Masoud Barzani, and the Patriotic Union of Kurdistan (PUK), founded by Jalal Talabani, who is now Iraq's president—have acted in concert in the past few years and the Kurdish enclave in northern Iraq has been relatively peaceful. But as recently as in the 1990s, their rivalry triggered lethal clashes.

Against this backdrop of violence, Kurdish women have been trying to gain more autonomy for themselves. Activists have become more vocal in their demands, but honor killings and other forms of gender violence, including female circumcision, are still rife in this patriarchal region.

Like many girls growing up in Iraqi Kurdistan, Berfin was expected to submit to her male relatives' will and accept the fate that they had chosen for her. "I have been oppressed since the age of six," she said, stating a simple fact. "My father had banished my mother and her four children, including myself, and remarried. It was only when I reached fifteen that I realized how bad he was."

Berfin had little contact with her father during most of her childhood, but he reappeared in her life when she was a teenager, to demand that she marry one of her cousins.

Powerless to resist, Berfin complied with her father's wishes but from the beginning her marriage was a disaster. "My husband treated me very badly. He always accused me of loving someone else. I kept telling him I was only fifteen and hadn't had time or an opportunity to love anyone else," Berfin explained.

Unconvinced, her husband regularly subjected her to beatings and abuse, psychological as well as physical. The ill-treatment did not stop after the births of their three children. He took pleasure in humiliating and hurting her. "At one point, he kicked me so hard that he fractured my spine. I had to be taken to Baghdad for an operation and spent three months in hospital," the young woman recounted. "I accepted it all because of my children."

No matter how much she tried to anticipate his wishes, hoping for some peace at home, Berfin was never able to keep her husband satisfied. Rows were frequent and violent. One evening, he returned around dinnertime, and without warning, kicked her out of the marital home. "I had nowhere to go, so I returned to my family in

Koisanjak." The young woman didn't expect to be received with open arms: women are meant to stay with their husbands come what may. If a marriage fails or they are rejected, their own families often see it as a matter of honor that they failed to perform their duties as wives. "My father and my brother insulted me and blamed me for the breakup of my marriage," she said. "During the seven months I stayed with them, I didn't see my children at all. They had stayed with my husband. My husband's relatives came several times to negotiate my return."

Berfin missed her children dreadfully, but she wasn't prepared to return and face more abuse. She decided instead to file a court request to gain access to her three children. This proved to be one step too far for her relatives, who were still hoping that the spouses would end their feud and resume marital life.

That Berfin was living apart from her husband was shameful enough; turning to the courts to settle a marital dispute would expose the family to public scrutiny. "One member of my family pulled out a gun and threatened to kill me if I went to court. Then the head of the tribe came to my house, and told me to return to my husband," she said. "I told him I would only return if he agreed not to beat and insult me."

Women are not supposed to stand tall and talk back, let alone dictate the terms in their marriage. "The man got angry, dragged me by the hair to the middle of the room, in front of the men of my family, and he started insulting me. 'How dare you impose conditions, you are shameless.' He beat me, he hit my head on the floor and kicked my back in front of my brother, my husband, my father, and all the men in the family," Berfin explained quietly. "I was so shocked that I wet myself in front of them all." When her sister heard her cries of pain and humiliation, she rushed into the room. She and two other female relatives escorted Berfin out of the room.

In the end, the family opted not to send her back to her husband's house. But this decision did not mean they accepted the breakup of her marriage and would offer her permanent shelter. On the contrary, they had realized that she would not bow to their demands and had devised a different plan: they were trying to convince her younger brother, who was only 17, to kill her. "Every night, the men would gather in our house. I knew they were planning my death, but I didn't know what to do," Berfin said, revealing little about the emotions that she must have experienced at the time.

One evening, her father asked her to help him prepare for evening prayers. Suddenly, she heard shots outside the house. Whenever anything unusual happened, Berfin's father always rushed to the window. This time, he ignored the sounds and continued to pray. "I asked him what was going on," she said. "He told me to go out and find out."

As Berfin opened the door, she saw her brother waving a gun and advancing toward her. "I was so shocked I couldn't move. I just put up my hands and couldn't say anything," she says. "He shot me three times in the stomach. Another shot broke my hip. As I tried to run away, he shot me one more time and I fell."

From her position on the ground, Berfin, still conscious, could see her brother running away. Her older sister, furious, ran into the house and confronted their father. "Why are you doing this to my sister?" she asked.

Meanwhile, more shots were heard. "My mother had rushed to my side," Berfin told me. "I only realized I was injured when I saw her bloody hands pulling at her white hair. I wanted to survive, mainly for her sake."

Later, Berfin learned that her family had told her husband that she was having an affair. She stressed that the entire story was fabricated.

On the day of the attack, her husband had been tasked with attacking her alleged lover, while her brother's assignment was to shoot her dead. She didn't know what had happened to the man who got caught up in her family drama; like her, he was an innocent victim. She didn't have a boyfriend. "I believe he was wounded, but survived," she said, repeating again that there had been no relationship between them.

Honor killings may be widely tolerated in traditional communities, but there are often individuals who object to the tradition. Berfin's brother-in-law was a decent man who disapproved of the practice, and he acted swiftly to save her life. He wrapped her in a blanket and tried to take her to hospital, but was stopped by local *peshmergas,* who apparently sided with Berfin's relatives and would not allow any car to provide transportation.

Eventually local policemen turned up and transferred the injured woman to hospital. There, her brother-in-law instructed the doctors and the staff to tell callers that she and her alleged lover had both died. But Berfin's injuries were too severe to be treated locally. She was taken to Suleymaniye, the nearest city, by ambulance. "I underwent several operations on my stomach," the young woman said.

News did eventually leak out that Berfin had survived the attack. Her relatives came to the hospital several times, hoping to finish her off but hospital officials were aware of the danger. Guards posted at the front door checked visitors. During visiting hours, Berfin was moved to a room out of sight.

When Berfin was well enough to leave the hospital where she had spent three months recovering from her injuries, she was first transferred to a protected center for mentally distressed women in Suleymaniye. Conditions were miserable there, she said, and she became so depressed that she thought of returning home to face the wrath of her relatives or of committing suicide. Thoughts of her children kept her alive.

Back at the family home, her sister and sister-in-law were both under severe pressure and they were unable to come and visit her. Berfin felt totally hopeless until she met Runak Raouf, a rights activist who ran a legal center for women and decided to help her. "She was like a mother to me," remembered Berfin. "I was unable to work and she looked after me for a year."

Aware that Berfin would never be safe in Iraqi Kurdistan, the Kurdish Women's Action against Honor Killings (KWAHK), an NGO that has been actively working in Kurdistan and in Western Europe to promote awareness of traditional practices and improve protection for potential victims, contacted several European governments to get the young woman accepted as a refugee. Eventually, thanks to the help of Kurdish NGOs in Germany, which actively lobbied for her, Berfin was granted a visa. In 2000, her friends from the Kurdish network arranged for her to leave Kurdistan discreetly. She was ready to start a new page, but her children were still in Iraq.

In Germany, Berfin was granted asylum and a lawyer assigned to her case put her in touch with a German nongovernmental association, which helped her settle into her new life. To avoid putting her in harm's way, they deliberately chose a town that had few Kurdish migrants. Initially, Berfin lived with the fear of being discovered, but gradually she began to relax and enjoy her new life. "I no longer feel in danger," she told me.

Although the young Kurdish refugee could appreciate her newfound freedom, there was not a day when she did not think of the children she had left behind. She received news occasionally through her brother-in-law, who wrote her letters, always stressing that she must not return: in Kurdistan, she still risked being killed.

The children led quite a chaotic life, she learned. When they stayed with their father, her eldest daughter cooked and took over household chores. Sometimes they were looked after by his sister or his mother. The children were also missing her, but they had learned to keep their emotions hidden from their relatives. It turned out that when her daughter had tearfully enquired about her mother, shortly after Berfin was expelled by her husband, the little girl was hit by her cousin who told her: "Don't cry, your mother has dishonored our family." As the eldest, Berfin's daughter was aware of the contempt others felt for her mother. She rarely ventured out of the house in order to avoid facing the taunts of her cousins and her peers.

After the shooting incident, the children initially thought Berfin had died. Their grandmother eventually took pity on them and secretly told them that their mother had in fact survived. The children kept hoping that they would one day be reunited.

To make this possible, KWAHK negotiated with the children's father. One of the organization's founders met him in Iraqi Kurdistan. He had limited resources and found it hard to look after the children. After months of hesitation, he finally agreed to let them go to Germany, where they would have a much better life.

In 2003, the children were brought to the Turkish capital, Ankara, where they were finally reunited with their mother, who had not seen them for five years. At the time, the two girls were aged 12 and 7, while the little boy was 10.

In the black-and-white photos taken as she first embraced her children, Berfin looked very different from the young woman I met. The happiness that shone on her face could not hide the toll the events of the previous five years had taken on her: deep lines were etched into her face, and she looked like an older woman carrying the weight of the world on her shoulders.

Eighteen months later, it was a rejuvenated Berfin, who told her story in Stockholm. That day, she was marking the 6th anniversary of her shooting, a day that had changed her life. "I was shot on December 7, 1998, but I survived. It is like a new birthday for me," she explained, pulling out a box of chocolates and passing it around the table.

Berfin's three children were still undergoing therapy in Germany, but they had adapted well to their new life and already spoke the local language. Hardship had forced them to mature quickly, but they were still young enough to put the past behind them, with the love and support of their mother. They had a chance to lead normal lives.

Berfin too was recovering. Her broken hip had almost entirely healed, and she described her current life as happy. She maintained contact with a few supportive relatives in Kurdistan, mainly her mother and her sister. The children had no contact with their father and remained full of anger against the relatives who had plotted their mother's death and mistreated her.

Berfin agreed to go public and tell her life story in Stockholm in the hope that her ordeal might help others. She was visibly moved by the support that she received from the dozens of conference delegates, who had gathered to discuss ways of providing better protection for other women victims of extreme patriarchal violence. "Being here has made me aware that I'm not alone," she said, her eyes welling up. "Other women are fighting for our rights."

CHAPTER 12

RELIGION, TRADITION AND PATRIARCHY

Articles in Western publications often describe honor killings as an "Islamic tradition." Summary executions of women carried out in the name of honor are often given a religious cover, but the practice predates the advent of Islam and is found in other cultures. Around the Mediterranean, honor killings featured in countries like Greece, Spain, and Italy until a few decades ago. They have now largely disappeared but some cases are still reported in South America.

In Beirut in 2002, I met Rafif Sida Sidawi from the Lebanese Council to Resist Violence against Women. Lebanon is an interesting country because several religions coexist within its small confines stretched along the eastern Mediterranean coast.[1] Lebanon's religious faiths have not always lived in harmony: the country was torn apart by a civil war that lasted 15 years and was further inflamed by outside involvement. As if political violence had not exacted a heavy enough toll, honor crimes were still reported in most of Lebanon's communities, whether Christian or Muslim.

"Attitudes are similar in all religions. Despite modernisation, there are still many honor killings. These are social issues, linked to traditions that are similar in all religious communities," Rafif Sida Sidawi told me. She explained that each of the country's 17 religious communities is ruled by its own personal status legislation. "In all of them, there is no equality between men and women, and women are discriminated against in case of divorce," she said. "Divorce is particularly difficult to obtain in Christian communities. Muslim men can still divorce their wives without the wives' approval." The minimum age for marriage for girls is nine among Shiites, 15 among the Druzes, and 14 for Eastern Catholics.

Another interesting example is Albania, where the Code of Leke Dukagjini, also known as the Kanun, was introduced in the fifteenth century, before Islam took hold in the country.

The Kanun, which still retains some influence in the north of the country, essentially codified the patriarchal order, regulating family law, marriage, inheritance as well as blood feuds. A woman was considered "a sack, made to endure" and she could be shot for adultery and for inhospitality, "both considered acts of infidelity."[2] In 2001, *The Boston Globe* reported the killing of 20-year-old Haxhere, the day after her wedding on October 7, 2001, because the newlyweds had failed to produce the bloody sheet expected by the community as proof of the bride's virginity. The groom summarily sent his bride back to her family home where, after an altercation, she was shot seven times in the chest by her 28-year-old brother.[3] Her murder showed that old perceptions were still claiming lives in the rapidly changing environment after the fall of the Communist regime.

Rejecting the "Islamic practice" label too often attached to the practice of honor killings should not, however, obscure the fact that a narrow-minded interpretation of Islam plays a part in many of the cases that are still regularly reported around the world. Against a backdrop of growing Islamic radicalism, which has turned into a political as well as a religious movement, women in several Muslim countries, perceived to embody the culture and the national honor, are facing new challenges, in addition to traditional perceptions.

Increased tension between the West and developing countries has made nationalists and religious fundamentalists even more reluctant to accept any hint of "Westernization" in their own cultures.

"Unable to come to grips with modernity as a whole, many Muslim societies make a sharp distinction between two aspects of it," writes theologian Riffat Hassan. "The first—generally referred to as "modernization" and largely approved—is identified with science, technology, and a better standard of life. The second—generally referred to as 'Westernization' and largely disapproved—is identified with emblems of 'mass' Western culture such as promiscuity, break up of family and community, latchkey kids, and drug and alcohol abuse. What is of importance to note here, is that an emancipated Muslim woman is seen by many Muslims as a symbol not of 'modernization' but of 'Westernization.' "[4]

In Iraq, for instance, honor killings are said to be on the rise in the Shia-militia controlled south as a side effect of the U.S.-led intervention that toppled Saddam Hussein's government. In November 2008, the UK-based *The Guardian* newspaper reported that 81 women had been killed since the beginning of the year for allegedly bringing shame to their family. This marked a 47 percent increase on the previous year.[5] Hitmen were willing to carry out the executions for fees of only 100 dollars.

In Chechnya, where an uneasy normalization has taken hold after years of brutal conflict with Russia, the current Ramzan Kadyrov, a close ally of Russian Prime Minister Vladimir Putin, openly condoned honor killings after the bodies of seven women, who had been shot dead, allegedly by relatives, were found in 2009. "If a woman runs around and if a man runs around with her, both of them are killed," the flamboyant 32-year-old leader said, claiming that the victims had "loose morals."

A polygamist himself, Kadyrov also encouraged his compatriots to take a second wife. His public endorsement was seen by some as a cynical attempt to boost his position and block the advance of an Islamist opposition. But every time, honor-based "values" are so publicly praised, women see their mobility in the public sphere restricted a bit further.[6]

Anti-Western sentiment, further fuelled by growing prejudice against Muslims in the West after the 9/11 attacks, has also severely undermined efforts to improve women's rights in the developing world. Female activists in Muslim countries risk being accused of selling out to Western values and promoting immorality, while in the West, a backlash against migrants is turning the spotlight on the negative aspects of foreign cultures at the expense of the larger picture.

Migrants who have failed to integrate and adopt local values are singled out for media attention, while the silent law-abiding majority, which successfully adapts to the host nation while retaining its cultural identity, is barely noticed.

A Gallup Coexist survey conducted in 2009 showed, for instance, that Muslims in Europe were in fact better integrated and had embraced the nations where they live far better than was generally acknowledged. The poll, however, also showed that while Muslim migrants fit in relatively well, the general public still harbored suspicions about them. In the United States and Canada, the general level of tolerance and integration was higher than in Europe.[7]

That more attention is paid to the situation of women is of course a positive development. The widespread discrimination and the violence many of them are exposed to worldwide were until recently neglected not only by governments but also by human rights organizations.

But to address the serious issue of gender equality in Muslim countries with any chance of improving the gender balance, it is important to place these problems in the right context. Is Islam itself the root cause of women's stifled lifestyles or is religion merely offering a convenient cover for patriarchal practices? Are interpretations of religious principles stretched to justify existing patriarchal practices or is the root of the problem in the religious texts themselves?

The Koran, believed by Muslims to have been revealed by Allah to the Prophet Mohammad over several years in the seventh century, contains several verses that do not stand up to standards of gender equality in the twenty-first century. The problem stems less from the Koran itself, which introduced revolutionary new rights for women at the time it was initially inscribed on leaves and tablets, but rather from the way it became interpreted through an increasingly rigid and narrow lens in the years, decades, and centuries after the passing of the Prophet.

"The Koran teaches that men and women have exactly the same responsibilities and duties, and gives women rights of inheritance and divorce that we would not enjoy in the west until the nineteenth century," wrote religious expert and best-selling author Karen Armstrong.[8] "There is nothing in the Koran about the veiling of all women and their confinement in harems. This practice came into Islam some three or four generations after the Prophet, under the influence of the Greek Christians of Byzantium, who had long covered and secluded their women in this way."

Many Westerners today forget that Christianity and Judaism were also born in the Middle East. The three "religions of the book" share many characteristics. In fact, the Koran acknowledges both the Bible and the Torah as being brought by the same God, and it borrows stories from them.

Numerous passages in the Bible and the Torah also reflect a mentality sharply at odds with today's reality. All three religions, for instance, struggle to accommodate women's sexuality. Islam fares rather better than Christianity, since it at least acknowledges a women's right to enjoy sex, as long as it takes place within marriage.

Condemning Islam itself for honor killings ignores the fact that these crimes were committed long before the religion came along. The Koran is strict on adultery, but it does not condone vigilante justice.

The interpretation of the religious texts became increasingly male oriented in the decades following Mohammad's death. Modern principles of human rights today do not condone the marriage of underage girls. Prophet Mohammad wed Aisha, who became his favorite wife, when she was only nine years old. Nor is polygamy tolerated in the same way it was in the days when the Muslim Holy book was written, although it is still common in many countries.

But it is really in the Hadiths—the sayings of the Prophet collected long after his death—that the most discriminatory material is to be found. Some of the statements attributed to Mohammad, of dubious veracity, are far more patriarchal in spirit than the Koran itself. For instance, it was more than 25 years after the Prophet's death that the Hadith stating that those who let themselves be led by a woman will be defeated was issued. It was probably not a coincidence that Abu Bakra, the Prophet's follower, only remembered it after Mohammad's widow Aisha led insurgents in a revolt against the Caliph Ali, one of the Prophet's successors.

Christianity, in many ways, followed a similar trend. The Old Testament, parts of which are similar to the Jewish Torah, reflects the patriarchal and tribal mentality that still subsists in some parts of the Middle East. The Biblical verse in Leviticus 20:10, for instance, "And the man that committeth adultery with another man's wife, even he that committed adultery with his neighbour's wife, the adulterer and the adulteress shall surely be put to death," bears strong similarities with the Koranic provision that married men and women who commit adultery should be killed. According to the Muslim Holy Book, unmarried people found guilty of unlawful intercourse are to be given 100 lashes each, if four witnesses can be produced to attest to their sin.

Honor killings are mentioned in the Old Testament. If a man accuses his bride of not being a virgin and her parents, by producing the sheet bloodied during the wedding night, can prove that she was, the man will be fined and he will have to keep the girl as his wife. If however, proof of her virginity cannot be provided, "she shall be brought to the door of her father's house and there the men of the town shall stone her to death. She has done a disgraceful thing in Israel by being promiscuous while still in her father's house. You must purge the evil from among you."[9]

Misogyny also spread to the New Testament and the sayings of the church fathers. As was the case in Islam, the message of Christianity was egalitarian in spirit but it, too, fell prey to an increasingly narrow interpretation. Passages attributed to St-Paul, but probably written long after his death, suggest women should remain silent in churches.

The antifemale trend continued in the following centuries: Martin Luther abandoned priesthood to marry, but he believed women should be confined to the home "as a nail driven into the wall."

He saw the pain of childbirth as a punishment for the crime of Eve. "If they become tired or even die, that does not matter. Let them die in childbirth, that's why they are there."

St Thomas Aquinas, for his part, described women as biologically flawed, "defective and misbegotten."[10] In short, chauvinism is not the prerogative of Muslims.

All three religions punished adultery. The Koran places the burden of proof on the accuser, for anyone who alleges that adultery has taken place, but cannot back this claim with four witnesses, faces a similar whipping. Even if witnesses are found, only a Sharia court is authorized to make a ruling.

In practice, the safeguards that should protect women from wrongful allegations and evil gossip are rarely respected because patriarchal values have overridden the more compassionate aspects of religion. The infamous execution that took place in Saudi Arabia of 1977 when Princess Mish'al, a member of the Royal Family, was beheaded for trying to escape with a Lebanese man she hoped to marry was, for instance, in direct contravention of Islamic law, even if the Wahhabi state used Islam to justify its actions.

* * *

To what extent religion is involved when women are murdered in the name of honor varies greatly according to the legal and social environment in which they are committed.

In Turkey, officially a secular country, religion is less often mentioned as a reference in public life mainly because the state institutions, in particular the army which sees itself as the guardian of the Republic's secular principles, openly frown upon expressions of faith in any form. Until the Justice and Development party, which has a more devout following, came to power in 2002, civil servants were discouraged from praying publicly if they wanted to rise through the ranks of the administration and military officers who visited the mosque regularly could be dismissed for being "reactionaries" and for many decades.

Religion, pushed out of the way when Turkey's founder Atatürk abolished the Caliphate in 1924 and forced Muslim brotherhoods underground, slowly started to make its reappearance in public life in the 1950s. In 1996, Turkey acquired its first Islamist prime minister, Necmettin Erbakan, although the experiment was short lived: a year, later he was forced out in what was dubbed a "postmodern coup"—in contrast with three more traditional coups the army had staged in 1960, 1971 and 1980.

The Justice and Development party (AKP) was formed by former members of Erbakan's Welfare Party. Privately religious, they have been careful not to use religion in daily politics, but they are still viewed with great suspicion by Turkey's militant secularists and by feminists, who worry about creeping conservatism.

In such an environment, religion is rarely invoked directly when crimes are committed in the name of honor. More often, perpetrators justify their crimes with references to the *örf ve adet*—customs and traditions—of their community. Lenient court judgments suggest that their patriarchal prejudices are often shared by members of the judiciary, many of whom are staunchly secular.

Despite early reforms in the 30s that made women legally equal to men and gave them the right to vote and be elected, the pace of change slowed down in the following decades. In 2010, Turkey only ranked 126th out of 134 countries listed in the World Economic Forum's Gender Gap Index. In national politics, women occupied less than 9 percent of the seats in parliament and their representation in municipal and provincial councils amounted to less than 5 percent. Despite impressive achievements in some fields such as medicine, the law and academia, where women are found in large numbers, less than 20 percent of women are involved in paid work and therefore enjoy a degree of financial independence.

In recent years, efforts to improve the status of women in society have achieved some successes. The reforms of the penal and civil codes, for instance, were important milestones. The number of shelters for victims of violence also increased from four to over 40 within a few years. Changing the mentality in the society and in the justice system, however, may take long.

In 2006, the head of the Turkish language institute announced ambitious plans to erase several proverbs from Turkish dictionaries that showed women in a bad light.

Popular sayings that promote negative perceptions of women include "long hair, short on brains" or "a father who doesn't beat his daughter will beat his knees (in regret)."[11]

In the mid-80s, a judge in the northern city of Çorum had quoted a popular saying "Do not leave a woman's back wanting for beatings or a woman's belly wanting for babies" to justify denying divorce to an abused woman who was expecting her fourth child. The decision triggered widespread protests by women and marked the beginning of a nation-wide campaign against domestic violence and in favour of women's rights, which continues to this day.

The Turkish Directorate of Religious Affairs—which is akin to a Ministry of Religion, and employs the country's 60,000 imams—also launched another initiative, perhaps even more important than the linguistic purge, to review the Hadiths and filter out sayings attributed to Prophet Mohammed, but whose authenticity is in doubt, which are discriminatory to women.

Islamic Law or Sharia is largely based on the Hadiths, rather than on the Koran itself, and it is these edicts that most traditionalists rely on to denigrate women and justify their low position in society. Some prime examples include: " Women are imperfect in intellect and religion," "The best of women are those who are like sheep," "If a woman doesn't satisfy her husband's desires, she should choose herself a place in hell," "If a husband's body is covered with pus and his wife licks it clean, she still wouldn't have paid her dues," "Your prayer will be invalid if a donkey, black dog or a woman passes in front of you."[12]

Religious scholars, including female theologians like Hidayet Tuksal, who describes herself both as a conservative and as a feminist, have been poring over ancient texts to check their validity. "I can't imagine a prophet who bullies women. The hadith that portray him so should be abandoned," she said.[13]

This project was launched by Ali Bardakoğlu, who presided over the Directorate for Religious Affairs between 2003 and 2010 and was therefore Turkey's leading religious figure. "There are some traditions and customs ingrained in the culture that, with time, have acquired a religious tone," he told me when I met him in 2006.

Approaches that humiliate, belittle, oppress women and make them second-class citizens have become incorporated into religion over time, even though they are not linked to the Prophet's own statements. We want to remove the religious ground from these customs. This is a work we've started. We have to show that this thinking is wrong. With time, some "pollution" comes in and we have to clean up the religion and filter out the elements that have become contaminated. It's the same in all religions. The West too has been through such processes.

Since the Directorate dictates the text of the sermons delivered in the country's mosques, Ali Bardakoğlu's views carried a lot of weight. In recent years, tens of thousands of imams have, under his direction, preached against domestic violence, against honor killings and especially against linking honor to women's bodies. As Ali Bardakoğlu himself remarked, "women are the 'soft belly' in the Islamic world, and Turkey is no exception," before adding that in fact "it is also the case in the Christian world."

But changing the way people think, and the way they act, takes time, the theologian acknowledged. "Even when people realize that God doesn't approve of their actions, they explain that it is their traditions and customs. Religion alone cannot solve this problem. It has to go together with education, political participation and giving opportunities for people to develop themselves. Members of the media, bureaucrats and teachers all must play a role."

In Turkey, these forces have combined to increase awareness, but they have not yet succeeded in eradicating honor killings and other harmful practices that affect women's lives. For women's rights advocates and for women themselves, the struggle continues.

* * *

In Pakistan, the Hudood Ordinance, a set of laws allegedly based on Sharia introduced in 1979 by General Zia ul-Haq and frequently used against women, gave a religious stamp of approval to traditional practices. "Jinnah (Pakistan's founder) was a secular man and his sister Fatima was independent," Dr Jabbar Khattak, editor of the Sindhi daily *Awami Awaz*, told me during an interview in 2003. "But during Zia's period, social development stopped and fundamentalist elements came in. Now a religious misinterpretation is dominating our feudal society. Islam was polluted by tribal and feudal values, which have been wrongly labelled as Islamic."

The protections that the Koran offers to women falsely accused of adultery or improper behavior were not just removed in Pakistan, but they have been distorted and turned against them. The Koran requires four witnesses to prove adultery—a burden of proof that should be hard to meet—but Pakistan, under the Hudood ordinance, required on the contrary that a woman bring four male witnesses to back up claims of rape. If she failed to do so—and how likely is it that a woman will find four men willing to testify that she was indeed raped?—she could be accused of *zina* (adultery) and arrested, facing further abuse at the hands of police officers. Up to 80 percent of women detained in Pakistani jails were held on adultery charges, often a result of this twisted approach. Under Islamic rules, the alleged coconspirator should also be punished, if indeed adultery has taken place, but in Pakistan, women can apparently commit adultery on their own because men are not jailed for sexual misconduct in matching numbers. I am of course not advocating punishment for adulterers, be they male or female, but merely underlining the very selective and patriarchal interpretation of religious texts.

Riffat Hassan, a Pakistani Islamic scholar who teaches at the University of Louisville, Kentucky, has spent a lifetime studying the Koran and religion. In her view, the belief that men are superior to women stems from three assumptions common to Islam, Christianity and Judaism: God's primary creation was man and women, created from Adam's rib, are therefore secondary; Eve, a woman, committed the original sin which led to man's expulsion from the Garden of Eden; and finally woman was not only created from man, but also for man.[14]

"Very early in my study I realized that Islam, like the other major religions of the world (namely Judaism, Christianity, Hinduism and Buddhism) had developed a patriarchal culture in which its major sources, i.e. the Qur'an, the Sunnah, the Hadith literature and Fiqh, had been interpreted almost exclusively by men who had assigned to themselves the right to define the ontological, theological, sociological, and eschatological status of Muslim women," she wrote. "I spent the first decade of my research on Women in Islam reinterpreting the Qur'anic texts relating to women from a non-patriarchal perspective and came to the conclusion that the Qur'an does not discriminate against women in any way."

After the BBC documentary film "Murder in Purdah" outlining the practice of honor killings in Pakistan was shown on televisions worldwide, Riffat Hassan formed an association to fight the practice.

When I met her in the Pakistani city of Lahore in 2003, she acknowledged that Muslim countries, including Pakistan, were facing a major challenge. "The culture that has evolved in the past two or three decades is one that is more interested in punishing than reforming. There is a harshness to it. We have to transform this culture, and this transformation has to go through women."

In Pakistan, the way Islamic law and particularly the Hudood Ordinance has been used against women has often been debated. Attempts to introduce reforms were thwarted on many occasions, on the ground that Islamic law cannot be tampered with. As a theologian, Rifat Hassan believes Sharia is merely an umbrella concept, under which all Muslims live, that is often misunderstood and misused. "It was never intended to be used as a legal system," she wrote. "Of the four major sources of the Shariah—the Quran, hadith, ijma and ijtihad—three are human. Then how can we say that the Shariah is divine? It is not."[15]

In her views, legal distortions have to do with the patriarchal mentality, rather than with religion itself. "On empirical grounds, there is no question. These laws have been used against women," she said. "But discrimination did not start with the Hudood laws.

It started long before. Laws need to be addressed, but most important is the mentality. The Koran says you need four witnesses, Zia's
law says four male witnesses."

The mentality may not be religious in origin, but it often finds its
expression in religious sentiments. Human rights experts today are
divided on the role of religion in honor killings.

"Honor killings are sanctified by feudal precepts. This concept has
been given a veneer of belief in some cases, of caste in others such
as India where an affair between a lower caste man and upper caste
woman can lead to death," explained I.A. Rahman, the president of
the Human Rights Commission of Pakistan, when I met him in his
Lahore office in 2003. "Religion itself is not the cause. The political
system is going backward. The society is feudal, most lawmakers are
feudal lords and those who do not share their values are excluded."

While many of the conservative Pakistanis who uphold the notion
that honor is vested in women's behavior and who are prepared to kill
in its name generally consider themselves devout Muslims, they often
allow tribal traditions to trump religion if there is a clash of values.
"The unwritten code of Pashtunwali has certain standard values, with
minor variations between tribes. Even in urban areas, you cannot say
you don't believe in Pashtunwali," lawyer Afrasiyab Khattak, who lives
in Peshawar, the city closest to the Afghan border, explained to me. He
was familiar with Zia's harsh rule, having spent time in prison during
the General's tenure as Pakistan's ruler. Later Khattak had to leave his
country and he spent more than eight years in exile in neighboring
Afghanistan before returning in 1989 when Benazir Bhutto pardoned
political dissenters and allowed them to return from exile. "The honor
code clashes with family law. It even clashes with Islam. When tribal
rule clashes with Islam—for instance under tribal rule women get no
inheritance—tradition prevails. The mullahs accept it. If they see that
women can be victimized by Islam, they say Islam. If they can be
victimized by tradition, they say tradition."

In his city of Peshawar, within a stone's throw of the Afghan border,
the strict code of conduct that prevails is tough. Like in Afghanistan,
most women in the streets of the city wear the blue burqa that covers
them from head to toes, leaving only a meshed opening for them to
see where they are going. The "Talibanization" of Pakistani society,
which started with the influx of Afghan refugees during the Soviet
occupation of Afghanistan and gained new momentum after 9/11,
has given violence against women a new legitimacy. In February 2009,
after a protracted struggle with Pakistan Taliban in the Swat valley, the
government came to an agreement with the religious militants and

relinquished control over the region. In the months that followed, dozens of girls' schools were bombed and fewer parents were willing to risk their children's lives by sending them to be educated.

The new regional leaders immediately made their presence felt. The brutal flogging of a 17-year-old girl accused of adultery caused international uproar after it was captured on video and posted on the Internet.[16] An offensive by the Pakistani armed forces led to the Pakistani extremists' retreat, but their influence remains strong.

Religious leaders, all too often, remain silent when Islam is being co-opted and misused in defense of patriarchy. "Mullahs speak of general morality, rights for women, but where is the law? I can't think of a single instance of a mullah defending women who are killed," says Afrasiyab Khattak.

When in 2005 President Musharraf suggested amending the Hudood Laws to make rape a crime tried in civil courts, he faced strong opposition. As Maria Rashid, who ran the NGO Rozan in Islamabad, explained to me in 2003, "once you link something to Islam in Pakistan, it cannot be removed because it would be against religion. Religion is used to further the discrimination against women."

She explained the challenges rights activists face. Her organization had been running training programs for policemen and civil servants, to sensitize them to violence against women. "We were conducting a seminar with men on a Friday. At midday, they all went to the mosque for the Friday prayers. From our office, we could hear the imam's *khutba* (sermon). He was railing against women who don't cover themselves, saying they should be burned. If you look a woman in the eye, you'll go to hell, he said. Women are the source of all evil. His statements undid everything we had achieved in the morning session."

When the "Women's Protection Bill," designed to place rape in the context of the secular penal code rather than the Hudood Ordinance was submitted to the Pakistani parliament, the six Islamist parties gathered under the umbrella of the Muttahida Majlis-e-Amal (MMA) argued that the change would make Pakistan a "free sex zone." Despite their opposition, the legislation, which lifted the requirement to produce witnesses to the assault, was finally adopted in November 2008.[17] It was welcomed as a step in the right direction by women's rights activists but many expressed doubts about its successful implementation.

The radical and misogynistic interpretation of Islam that now has widespread currency in Pakistani has given a new religious legitimacy to ancient tribal practices like honor killings. "The underlying notion was that honor affected family respect and pride," explained Sohail Akbar Warraich, an activist with the Shirkat Gah association in Lahore. "What has emerged in recent years is a reference to religion."

In neighboring India, the caste system that continues to cause victims every year is also derived from Hinduism. Although officially banned, it continues to influence social behavior.

In February 2009, eight members of a poor Indian family were shot and beheaded in the northern state of Bihar, after their 21-year-old male relative eloped with the 18- year-old daughter of a wealthy family. "The girl's family invited the boy's family for a meeting on the pretext of settling the dispute (over the marriage) but they killed all eight and beheaded them," a police officer explained. Fifteen members of the teenage girl's clan were charged with murder after the bodies were found floating in the Ganges river.

Many honor killings that take place in Hindu or Sikh communities in India are motivated by such social transgressions. Women can marry above their station, but if men do, they can expect violent retribution. In Hindu, Sikh or Muslim India, as in Muslim and Christian countries, religion has often been invoked to justify blatant discrimination against women and horrendous forms of violence. The religion and the texts that inspire it may not be directly to blame, but they often inform a population's perception of what is right or wrong, and give harmful practices a cover of legitimacy and sanctity.

CHAPTER 13

HESHU

Many victims of crimes committed in the name of honor die anonymous or their death is only deemed worthy of a few lines on the back pages of a local newspaper. But in recent years, several cases have grabbed headlines around the world, largely because of the efforts of local activists seeking to raise awareness of these summary executions. From beyond the grave, the slain women have contributed to a crucial change in public perception.

Heshu Yones is one of these young women. A vivacious 16-year-old of Iraqi Kurdish descent raised in the United Kingdom, she was savagely stabbed by her father on October 12, 2002. Abdullah Yones, a Kurdish refugee who fled Saddam Hussein's Iraq at the time of the first Gulf War, found his daughter too "Western" and could not accept that she had a boyfriend. Many confrontations and frequent beatings had preceded the young girl's murder, as the gulf separating Heshu from her parents grew wider. Had Heshu or her friends dared to come forward, or signs of domestic tension and the young girl's inner turmoil been picked up by her school teachers, her death might have been averted. The danger signs were there all along.

Heshu's murder resulted in the first ever life sentence for an honor killing in Britain. It also triggered some critical soul-searching in the British police force. A special unit, led by Commander Andy Baker, was created to study crimes committed in the name of honor and develop adequate methods to protect girls at risk.

The Metropolitan Police estimates the number of honor killings in Britain to 12 a year. After Heshu's murder, over a 100 cases of murders that remained unsolved in the previous decade were reopened. The police force had worked with consultants of various backgrounds, who helped train officers to identify patterns of abuse that often lead to honor killings. They hoped that increased awareness of this specific form of violence against women might yield new clues.

The first inkling that something was wrong at 24 Charles Hocking House in the London suburb of Acton came when the police was informed that a man had fallen onto concrete from a sixth floor balcony. The officers who arrived at the scene found a man in serious condition, with broken legs, a broken pelvis and severe internal injuries. He was barely conscious but he told a police officer that he had "done a terrible thing," a confession later corroborated by the ambulance crew.

Using the keys they found in his pocket, the policemen entered the sixth floor duplex apartment. In the bathroom, they found Heshu lying in a pool of blood alongside the bathtub. She had been stabbed 17 times, with such rage that the knife had pierced right through her body. Her throat had also been slit. Heshu had obviously fought hard for her life, judging by the gashes the knife left on her arms when she lifted them to protect herself. The weapon found under her body—a standard Ikea kitchen knife—was twisted by the force of the blows and the tip had broken off. But the autopsy later concluded that none of the blows delivered by Abdullah Yones had been fatal and Heshu had probably taken 15 minutes to die as her blood slowly seeped out of her body.

For several weeks, Abdullah's life hung in the balance and it took several months until he was fit enough to be interrogated. "We put him under guard at the hospital, naively thinking that he might be in danger from the family," Detective Inspector Brent Hyatt, who had led the investigation into the murder, told me.

By the time I met him in London, shortly after the verdict of life imprisonment had been announced in the Yones's trial, Brent Hyatt and his colleagues had learned that a man who is head of a family is unlikely to be challenged by relatives if he decides to kill his daughter. But when Heshu's body was first found, the police knew little about the dynamics of these crimes. The investigation into the young girl's murder proved a sharp learning curve for the London Metropolitan police.

Previous cases had already lifted the veil on honor killings. Rukhsana Naz, for instance, was held by her mother and strangled by one brother, while another stood by, in 1998. Her body was later bundled into a sack. She had been forced to marry at the age of 16, but had refused to stay with her husband. She was seven months pregnant by her boyfriend at the time of her death.

But Heshu Yones's case marked a turning point not only because it triggered a review of investigation methods for this type of crime, but also because this time, the justice system made no allowance for Yones's cultural background and locked him up for life.

Throughout the investigation, Abdullah's wife, his eldest son, who was in his mid-20s, and the couple's 12-year-old son all denied the retired combatant was guilty of Heshu's murder. The teenager's mother, a teacher, claimed not to speak English and only communicated with police officers through an interpreter. "The translator once overheard her say 'she has disgraced us, it would have been better if we had killed her at birth,' " explained an Iraqi Kurdish women's rights activists who acted as a consultant to the Metropolitan police.

The family tried to paint a picture of harmonious home life sharply at odds with testimonies of people close to Heshu, who spoke of frequent physical abuse and arguments. The situation at home had in fact become so tense that Heshu had decided to run away. She had already written a goodbye note for her father, apologizing for being such a disappointment to him in a brief letter heavy with pain and sarcasm.

"Bye Dad, sorry I was so much trouble. Me and you will probably never understand each other, but I'm sorry I wasn't what you wanted, but there's some things you can't change." She also referred, with an attempt at black humor, to his brutality. "Hey, for an older man you have a good strong punch and kick. I hope you enjoyed testing your strength on me; it was fun being at the receiving end. Well done."

While Abdullah was recovering in hospital, his son visited him regularly in hospital. One day, he was overheard speaking to his father in urgent tones in Kurdish before switching to English.

The two men then summoned the duty officer and explained that Abdullah had been pushed off the balcony by four men from Al Qaeda, who had also killed Heshu because they believed her father worked for the intelligence service.

This version of events failed to convince the prosecution. Neighbors had seen Abdallah arriving at the flat, but his alleged assailants were never spotted. Heshu also had traces of her father's skin under her finger nails, proving that she had tried to fight him off.

Until a week before his trial began, Abdullah Yones persisted in denying all involvement in his daughter's murder. At the last minute, he changed his plea to guilty. "Heshu's mother visited our organization a few times. She tried to pass on the message that they had been the victims of a racist attack. Later they said Islamists were to blame, then the PKK (a Kurdish rebel organization from Turkey)," Nazand Begikhani told me.

The family tried to shield Abdullah from police questioning, alleging he was mentally unstable. Later they explored the possibility of using a defense of provocation to explain his sudden act of anger. In fact, there was plenty of evidence that Heshu's murder had been planned.

The girl's mother and her younger brother had gone off to visit friends and were conveniently away when the frenzied attack took place. Before his youngest son left the house with his mother, Abdullah made a point of telling him how much he loved Heshu. Police officers were convinced that the adult members of the family were aware that a murder would take place. Heshu was punished for having a boyfriend, but activists who attended Yones's trial said her elder brother often brought his girlfriend home and she was seen by her side during his father's trial: clearly the same standards did not apply to boys and girls in the Yones household.

Piecing together Heshu's life and understanding how she felt, torn between two cultures, was not easy but Heshu left some clues about her personality. Looking demure and childlike in her school photograph, she appears an attractive young woman in other pictures that show her made-up and looking more mature and sophisticated. Her prominent nose did not detract from the appeal of her laughing eyes and thick dark hair. Her friends described her as a bubbly and fun-loving teenager.

She also left pictorial evidence of the darker aspects of her domestic life. In the summer before he murdered his daughter, Abdullah Yones took his family to northern Iraq to visit relatives. He was hoping the trip would strengthen his children's bond with their Kurdish culture. During her stay in northern Iraq, Heshu used a camera to record a video diary. In the footage shown at a police conference in London, the teenager looked weary and older than her years, staring at the camera with heavy dark bags under her eyes. Clearly tense and unhappy, she expressed her longing for her friends back in England and spoke of the heavy pressure she was placed under by her relatives.

Yet Heshu was proud of her cultural roots and had joined a Kurdish folk dance group in London. Like many other young girls of migrant origin, she had one foot in each culture and wanted to enjoy them both.

Her father had hoped to find her a husband during the trip. Heshu, aware there was a risk that her parents might try to prevent her from returning to the United Kingdom, had taken the precaution to leave money with a friend in case she needed to escape. "The video shows her making self-deprecating remarks about the size of her nose. By our standards, she was a normal teenager, even a well-behaved one," said Dectective Inspector Hyatt. Heshu's friends testified that Abdullah Yones had pointed a gun to his daughter's head during the trip to Kurdistan. He would have killed her then had the girl's brother not intervened. Heshu's brother later denied the incident ever took place.

* * *

The judge in Abdullah Yones's case spoke of a "tragic story arising out of irreconcilable difference between traditional Kurdish values and the values of western society." Many Kurds beg to disagree. Although such crimes are still common in northern Iraq, the Patriotic Union of Kurdistan, of which Abdullah Yones was a member, had changed the law in the region of Kurdistan where it ruled and banned honor killings and women in Iraqi Kurdistan are actively fighting against entrenched patriarchy: they know that tradition alone is not a sufficient explanation for these murders. Traditions are not immutable: they are in constant evolution.

Ancient customs and traditional attitudes to women undoubtedly play an important part, but in many cases they have merged with modern factors. In migrant communities, social dislocation, unemployment and an inability to integrate in the host country often combine with a nostalgia for the homeland to create a powerful trigger.

"One cannot adopt a simplistic approach to honor crimes. Each case takes place in a very complex framework," activist Nazand Begikhani told me, deploring the fact that tragic cases were too often exploited by media organizations seeking sensational headlines. "The fact that Heshu's father had been a *peshmerga* (a Kurdish fighter) could have played a role, created a psychology of violence," she says. "He had also suffered chemical attacks." During his trial, 48-year-old Abdullah Yones was described as a "fish out of water" in Britain. Unable to work, he was depressed and unhappy while his children thrived in their new environment.

With migration to the West, the power dynamics within displaced families often undergo radical changes. In their home country, parents exercised strong control over their children and they enjoyed the respect of the community. When the migrants settle in a Western setting, the younger generation finds it easier to adapt. "The children are in constant touch with the host society," says Begikhani. "The parents are often isolated, jobless and do not speak the local language."

Parents then face the indignity of having to rely on their children to help them communicate or interact with the bureaucracy. Unable to blend into their new environment, members of the older generation turn inward and limit their social contacts to people from the home country, who suffer from the same sense of dislocation as they do. "Older people become stuck in a time warp," believes Begikhani. "There is also a disconnection with the reality of the country of origin, which continues to evolve."

This sense of helplessness and the feelings of inferiority can trigger violence. "People feel frustrated and they become defensive," says Sawsan Salim, a Kurdish member of the Independent Women Organisation, set up in 1993. "They then develop the belief that their own culture was better and their women cleaner and more honorable than British women."

Heshu's father Abdullah was generally considered a popular man by his party colleagues. Between 1980 and 1991, he fought for the Patriotic Union of Kurdistan (PUK), whose leader, Jalal Talabani, became president of Iraq, before being granted political asylum in Britain at the time of the Gulf War. He suffered sequels from a gas attack and was too ill to hold a job in London, but he remained an active member of the PUK, which has representation in Britain's capital.

Articles in the British press suggested Heshu's murder was motivated by the fact that she was a Muslim girl dating a Lebanese Christian. In fact, her boyfriend Nizam denied he was a Christian and Abdullah's friends say religion played no part in Heshu's murder. "Yones was a Marxist, not a religious fundamentalist," Sarko Mahmoud, deputy representative of the PUK in Britain at the time of trial, told me. "Most families in our community understand that they live in a different environment. But some still want their children to live like the old generation."

After Yones finally admitted having killed his daughter, he said he had been driven to murder by an anonymous letter he had received at work, denouncing Heshu as a "slut." But the letter, if it existed, was never found. At the PUK office, no one ever saw it. "He said the letter arrived on October 9," Mahmoud said. "I checked and found that he was the first to arrive at the office that day and he collected the mail. But we went out together that morning and I didn't notice anything unusual. He didn't seem preoccupied or upset. No one saw the letter."

Many in the Kurdish community were outraged by Heshu's murder, but others were ready to protect Abdullah Yones and cover up his
actions. The authorities decided against granting bail. "We had credible information that two people had come to the UK to help him
escape," explained Brent Hyatt.

In Britain, immigrant women have fought hard to make their voices
heard. Until not so long ago, when the authorities wanted to communicate with minority groups, they turned to community or religious
leaders, sometimes forgetting that women within the society might
have a different agenda.

Organizations like the Southall Black Sisters or the Kurdish Women
Action against Honor Killings (KWAKH), of which Nazand Begikhani
is a founding member, have done a great deal in Britain to expand the
cultural debate and highlight that strong differences of opinion exist
within communities and within cultures.

"Too often when culture is invoked, it is in favor of men," Rahila
Gupta of Southall Black Sisters explained to me. "Culture should not
be a mitigating factor for men, but it should help understand why
women feel they are the vehicle of honor and find it hard to leave
their family." Gupta believes the concept of *izzat* or honor is behind
most of the domestic violence committed by Asian immigrants.

The work of women's rights activists has already borne fruit.
Wives of asylum seekers and immigrants to the United Kingdom
often feared leaving an abusive husband, because their status was
tied to that of their husbands and they faced repatriation to their
home country in case of separation. After women's NGOs highlighted the injustice of forcing women to stay with violent partners
and campaigned for the authorities to change their policy, domestic
violence was recognized as a legitimate reason for separation and the
British government no longer deports wives who step out of abusive
relationships.

But domestic violence remains a thorny issue that is not always
addressed adequately in the society at large, let alone among immigrant communities. "What we would like ideally is for women to be
taken seriously when they complain, for the police to respond to actual
bodily harm and for pre-emptive action to be taken when needed,"
Rahila Gupta told me. "But there is a patriarchal approach to the
whole domestic violence issue. The best of them will give you tea
and sympathy or a cultural relativist argument: 'it would be wrong for
us to intervene.' "

*   *   *

Heshu Yones and Rukhsana Naz in Britain, Pela Atroshi and Fadime Şahindal in Sweden, Hatun Sürücü in Germany have all helped bring crimes committed in the name of honor to the attention of the European public and of law enforcement agencies. Honor killings are no longer an issue of developing countries: they also happen in the heart of the Western world. These young women's untimely deaths brought home the necessity to develop a better understanding of the social mechanisms that lead to these tragedies.

Each of these cases has highlighted a different aspect of the problem. Nineteen-year-old Pela Atroshi, for instance, was brought up in Sweden but she was lured back to Iraqi Kurdistan to be killed by her relatives in June 1999 because her strict parents had seen her talk with a Swedish boy.

For the Swedish police, this case presented a major challenge: the crime was committed in Iraq, but the perpetrators and the victim had Swedish passports. The grandfather, who is believed to have commandeered the murder and an uncle directly involved in the killing both lived in Australia. Pela's father Agid and his brother Rezkar received a one year suspended sentence in a court in Dohuk, in Iraqi Kurdistan. A medical report showed that Pela's hymen was broken and her killing was therefore deemed justified.

The testimony of Pela's sister Breen, who contacted the Swedish police from northern Iraq on the day of the murder, at great risk to herself, set the legal ball rolling and made the perpetrators' prosecution in Sweden possible. Breen and her mother had found Pela in an upstairs room after she was shot. The victim, still conscious, identified her uncle Rezkar Atroshi as her assailant. Pela, wounded, was brought downstairs by her female relatives, but her father and his brothers intervened and took them aside while Rezkar returned to finish the victim off with a bullet in the head.

Inspector Kickis Aahre Algamo traveled to the Turkish capital Ankara to pick up Breen, who had taken refuge at the Swedish embassy after Pela was shot. She was flown to Stockholm where she testified against her two uncles, who were picked up when they returned to Sweden in January 2000. Her father chose to stay in Iraq and was tried in absentia.

The main instigator of Pela's murder appears to have been her grandfather Abdulmajid Atroshi. A former Kurdish fighter, he resided in Australia but continued to rule over his extended family from a distance.

Pela, who had grown up in Sweden, had left home to escape the oppressive family atmosphere, which prevented her from living like a normal Western teenager. She eventually returned home and agreed to an arranged marriage in Iraqi Kurdistan because she missed her family too much.

But by then, her conservative grandfather had already traveled to Sweden and gathered the male members of the clan to rule over her fate. They decided that the young girl had to die. "When we counted all the ones involved in the planning, there were eleven," Inspector Algamo told a reporter from The Australian. "But some of them were Australian citizens and some of them Iraqi citizens—we could only prosecute three."[1]

The murder was planned to take place in Iraq, where laws were more lenient. Adbulmajid, the patriarch, announced he would stay in Sweden until Pela was dead. Although the Swedish police were in touch with the Australian authorities and Interpol became involved as well, the old man managed to evade capture.

It is not rare for honor killings to involve such a complex network of relations, which makes the work of law enforcement agencies particularly difficult when the suspects are refugees or migrants scattered across the globe under different jurisdictions, but still bound tightly by the ties of blood.

Fadime Şahindal was also a Kurd, but of Turkish origin, and she had been living under threat for several years by the time she was shot dead in Uppsala, Sweden by her father Rahmi Şahindal on January 21, 2002, while visiting her mother and her sisters.

Fadime, who was 26 at the time of her death, had lodged a police complaint against her brother and her father in 1998 after they attacked and threatened her. She had also testified about her experience in front of the Swedish parliament shortly before her death, urging Swedish lawmakers not to give in to cultural relativism and to provide better protection for young women of migrant origin. Because she had become a prominent spokeswoman for minority women's rights, her death shook Sweden to the core. Members of royal family and politicians attended her funeral, which took place in Stockholm cathedral.

Twenty-three-year-old Hatun Sürücü, brought up in Germany, may not have realized she was in danger. She had returned to Berlin after her marriage to a fellow Turk, arranged by her parents when she was 16, broke down. In Berlin, Hatun lived an independent life with her five-year-old son. She left her little boy tucked in bed on February 7, 2005, when a telephone call from a relative prompted her to leave her warm apartment in the early morning for a meeting at a bus stop: she clearly expected to be back within minutes.

Instead, she was found on the street shot to death. There were few credible leads in the investigation at first, but her three brothers aged 25, 24, and 18 were later arrested after the youngest bragged to his girlfriend[2] about the killing.

The trial, however, revealed how poorly equipped the German justice system was to deal with crimes of this kind, which involve not just a perpetrator but also coconspirators. Hatun Sürücü's youngest brother was sentenced to nine years and three months of imprisonment in 2006, but her two other siblings, Mutlu and Alpaslan Sürücü, were acquitted of conspiracy to murder for lack of evidence. The two men were later photographed, holding their fingers up in a victory sign and grinning after their acquittal, fuelling an already heated, and at time Islamophobic, debate in German society on migrant issues. In 2007, a German court ordered their retrial but the two brothers fled to Turkey.

Hatun Sürücü's family later launched a court procedure to gain custody of Hatun's son, causing further anger in Germany. Hatun's sister, Arzu, was the claimant but she failed to convince the courts who denied her request.

* * *

Cases of honor killings have also occurred in the United States, but until recently they were not flagged as deserving special recognition and were filed under the general label of domestic murders.

Public awareness that honor is sometimes used to justify the murder of family members greatly increased as a result of media interest in the killing of sisters Sarah Yaser Said and Amina Yaser Said, aged 17 and 18 respectively, in Lewisville, Texas in January 2008.

The two teenagers were apparently killed by their father, who disappeared after his daughters' murders. Their case could mark a turning point and encourage law enforcement officials to learn more about culture-specific forms of violence against women and review their investigation procedures, like their European colleagues have done in recent years.

In April 2002, a court in Brooklyn had convicted a 41-year-old Pakistani man from Britain, Manzoor Qadar, to life without parole for the 1996 killing of his niece's ex-husband, Shaukat Parvez.

Rubina Malik had married Parvez without the knowledge of her parents in 1994. When her father, a wealthy landowner, found out he forced her to marry a cousin. Rubina's new husband turned out to be sympathetic to her plight and fled with her to the United States, where Shaukat Parvez had already sought refuge.

They hoped that, far away from their relatives, they would be able to lead a normal life. Her influential father, incensed by the deception, was said to have offered a $60,000 bounty to have Shaukat, Rubina and her sympathetic cousin Khurram Khan killed. The killer only managed to carry out one of the murders. He was arrested in Britain and extradited to face trial.[3]

In February 2002, a computer expert and medical doctor from Columbus, Ohio, Nawaz Ahmed, was sentenced to death for killing his estranged wife, her father, her sister, and her two-year-old niece in 1999, a few days before a final divorce hearing.

His wife, Lubaina Bhatti, also a medical doctor, had put an end to their marriage, claiming that she had been physically and mentally abused. Her father, later joined by Lubaina's sister and niece from Canada, was staying with her to offer moral support and protection in the final days of the divorce.

They were found in the garage, their throat slit and bearing multiple stab wounds, after relatives alerted the police that repeated attempts to contact them by phone had failed. Ahmed was arrested the following day at JFK airport in New York, as he was preparing to board a flight to his native Pakistan.[4]

In April 2011, a court in Arizona sentenced an Iraqi immigrant, Hassan Almaleki, to 34 years of imprisonment for the murder of his 20-year-old daughter, Noor, whom he deemed "too Western." The mother of Noor's fiancé was also seriously injured when Almaleki deliberately ran over them with his Jeep. "The killing of one's own child is more than just a violation of the law," Maricopa County Attorney Bill Montgomery said in a press statement. "It is an offense against parenthood itself and the awesome responsibility parents have for nurturing and protecting their children."

The brutal beheading of Aasiya Hassan, 37, in Buffalo, New York, in 2009 illustrates how thin the boundary between domestic and honor-based violence can be, or rather how intertwined the two can become. Her Pakistan-born husband, Muzammil Hassan, aged 46, had been served divorce papers a week before he launched a frenzied assault on Aasiya, stabbing her more than 40 times before decapitating her. Ironically, Muzammil Hassan was the owner of Bridges TV, a television station he had launched to promote better intercultural understanding, and the attack took place as Aasiya stopped by to drop his laundry at the station.

While the horrific attack was taking place, the couple's four- and six-year-old children as well as Hassan's teenage son from a previous marriage, on their way to dinner with Aasiya, were waiting in the car parked outside the station.

During his trial, Muzammil Hassan alleged that his wife had been abusive, but he could provide no evidence of the violence he said he had suffered. Aasiya, on the other hand, had sought medical treatment on several occasions for injuries suffered during domestic arguments.[5] Muzammil's claims that he was the victim failed to convince the jurors who ruled against him. In March 2011, he was sentenced to 25 years to life for second degree murder.

One of the most horrific, and best documented, case of honor-based violence in the United States is the murder of 16-year-old Tina Isa, which took place in 1989. Tina's father was on an FBI surveillance list for suspected links to a Palestinian terrorist group. Microphones placed in the Isas house recorded the dialogue that took place when Zein Isa and his Brazilian-born wife, Maria, challenged his daughter as she came home one evening, but no agent was on hand to intervene and save the youngster. Against her traditional parents' wishes, Tina worked late nights at a fast food restaurant and went out with her boyfriend. An honor student, she played soccer—again, despite her father's objections—and felt perfectly at ease in St. Louis. The family had earlier lived on the West Bank, in Puerto Rico and in Brazil.

"You are a she-devil," Zein said. "And what about the boy who walked you home? He wants to sleep with you in bed, don't you have any shame? Don't you have any conscience? It's fornication."

What started as a fierce family argument quickly took a sinister turn when Zein announced that he would kill Tina.

"Listen, my dear daughter, do you know that this is the last day? Tonight you're going to die?" he asked.

Initially defiant and disbelieving, Tina soon realized her father meant it. She turned to her mother, begging her to intervene, but Maria remained impervious to her daughter's screams. Instead, she held her down why Zein stabbed Tina with a kitchen knife.

"Die! Die quickly! Die quickly!," Zein shouted as his daughter screamed. "Quiet, little one. Die, my daughter, die!" In court, he admitted he had placed his foot on his daughter's mouth to silence her.[6]

Jurors were shaken by the sounds of Tina's screams and her pleading with her parents in the seven-minute tape. The terms of endearment used by Zein as he savagely plunged a boning knife into his daughter's chest were particularly upsetting and out of place, uttered in such circumstances.

Killing someone you love is the ultimate contradiction, but as Canadian scholar Sharzad Mojab has pointed out, "honor killing is a tragedy in which fathers and brothers kill their most beloved, their daughters and sisters. Sometimes mothers and sisters participate in the crime or consent to it. Killing occurs in a family system where members are closely tied to each other in bonds of affection, compassion and love. Here, affection and brutality coexist in conflict and unity."[7] Zein eventually died of diabetes in prison in 1997, and his wife's sentence was commuted to life imprisonment.

* * *

Honor killings and other traditional forms of violence against women have fuelled a heated debated about multiculturalism and its impact on women's rights. Inevitably, racism has become involved and reports of crimes committed in the name of honor are frequently followed by calls for immigrants to be sent back "home," even if they have been living in the West for many years or were even born there. In Holland, for instance, a country that has seen its share of honor crimes, the assassination of controversial filmmaker Theo van Gogh in October 2004, after he produced a movie called "Submission," blaming Islam for women's abuse, caused strong anti-Muslim sentiments in this hitherto liberal country that had a negative impact on well-integrated migrants as well.

In a provocative essay entitled *Is Multiculturalism bad for women?*,[8] the late American political scientist Susan Moller Okin balanced minority rights against women's rights.

"In the case of a more patriarchal minority culture in a context of a less patriarchal majority culture, no argument can be made on the basis of self-respect or freedom that the female members of the culture have a clear interest in its preservation," she suggested. "Indeed, they *may* be much better off if the culture into which they were born were either to become extinct (so that its members would become integrated into the less sexist surrounding culture) or, preferably, be encouraged to alter itself so as to reinforce the equality of women—at least to the degree to which this value is upheld in the majority culture."

Her conclusion has been challenged by many of her peers. "Part of the reason many believe the cultures of the Third World or immigrant communities are so much more sexist than Western ones is that incidents of sexual violence in the West are frequently thought to reflect the behavior of a few deviants—rather than as part of our culture," wrote Leti Volpp, in a direct rebuttal of Okin's position. "In contrast, incidents of violence in the Third World or immigrant communities are thought to characterize the culture of entire nations."[9]

Another feminist author, Katha Pollitt, pointed out that majority cultures may be willing to accept accommodations because "gender and family are retrograde areas in most majority cultures too."

"How far would an Algerian immigrant get, I wonder, if he refused to pay the interest on his Visa bill on the grounds that Islam forbids interest on borrowed money?" she wrote.[10]

Not very far, one could argue. Yet culture is still routinely brought up in court as a mitigating factor to justify abuse of women in Western countries, although the efforts of women's rights activists are beginning to change perceptions.

Approaching violence against women from a racist perspective is both unhelpful and discriminatory. To blame "culture," often a euphemism for religion or Islam, is to ignore the wide varieties of views and lifestyles that coexist within any society. Politics, conflicts, wars, low levels of development combined with wide income discrepancies are all factors that contribute to a background of widespread gender inequality and discrimination against women.

Westerners are quick to focus on more "exotic" forms of violence such as honor killings and dowry deaths, but they do not always seen the more common forms of domestic violence or the growing number of rapes that take place in their own societies. While the institutional and social framework in Western countries undoubtedly offers women better protection with shelters where they can seek help, legal statistics show that abused or raped women still struggle to get heard. Even in the most liberal Western democracies, violence against women remains a social scourge that is far from being eradicated.

A British Home office report published in April 2005 showed that rapes marked a 27 percent increase in 2002 yet the proportion of rape allegations resulting in a conviction fell from 24 percent in 1985 to 5.6 percent in 2002. By 2008, conviction had barely reached 6.5 percent. Two women a week are killed in England and Wales by their partner or ex-partner. Data from other European Union countries is equally distressing. In the United States, 4 million women are believed to be abused by their partner every year, while 154 were killed in Texas alone in 2003.[11] Western societies too have their blind spots when it comes to the protection of women.

To blame an entire culture is to deny the struggle that women and men have been waging from within these different cultures to improve it. In all countries where honor-based violence is still common, many NGOs are actively fighting to increase awareness of violence against women and promote social change. In several countries, their efforts have already led to important legal changes.

Eastern women are often perceived in the West as submissive and accepting of their fate. This is a generalization that ignores the wide disparities that exist within societies. Some of the most charismatic and impressive female figures I have met in the course of my career as a journalist have been social activists fighting to close the gender gap and curb violence in Muslim countries.

In most of these countries, contrasting worlds coexist. Patriarchal values permeate the society but their impact on individuals is mitigated by many factors, including social status and income level. Families who kill their own are thankfully not the rule. In fact, the strong bond that links communities remains an attractive feature of traditional societies. Many of these characteristics have, to a large extent, been replaced in the West by an extreme individualism, which does not always promote happiness. The trend of consumerism and materialism is now sweeping through the world and transforming, for better or for worse, even the most isolated communities.

Activists campaigning for women's rights in Eastern nations do not necessarily embrace a Western lifestyle: they want rights, mobility, and protection from violence, but they do not want to sever community ties. They fight for rights principles to become incorporated within the existing culture. Those who have migrated to Western countries find a way of reconciling their double identities, holding on to the most positive aspects of their own culture and adding them to those of the host nation.

"Culture is not a homogenous, transhistorical, static entity. It is changing and changeable," Nazand Begikhani, who works in Paris and London, told me. "Not all Kurds condone honor killing and many of them condemn it. Those Westerners who prefer to see honor killing as a natural function of a barbaric alien culture and refuse to acknowledge the differences and dynamism within the minority communities share the same position as those Kurdish conservative forces who resist adaptation and internal change."[12]

CHAPTER 14

OLD TRADITIONS, MODERN CONTEXT

To what extent do ancient traditions really influence the behavior of men and women who today commit murder, allegedly to redeem their tarnished honor? The received wisdom was that honor killings were mainly taking place in remote corners of the world where local communities were stuck in a time warp. In reality, very few parts of the globe still fit this description today. Some rare rural outposts in developing countries may still be far removed from twenty-first century living, but few have been left untouched by aspects of modern life. Besides, as we have seen, honor killings also take place in modern cities of the West.

If people can adopt television, the internet, and other modern conveniences, is it reasonable to expect that the social structure that surrounds them has remain untouched and unchanged for millennia?

Turkish author Mehmet Faraç believed that modernization "increases the likelihood of honor killings" as the feudal and patriarchal system, challenged by a form of modernity that brings with it a quest for more individual rights, struggles to maintain the status quo.

Soap operas on television influence young girls, who start dreaming of a different life and become more assertive. "Such programs should not be broadcast when the society is not ready for them. Women here used to think that other women all over the world lived like them. They accepted their lot. But television shows young people holding hands, kissing," Faraç told me during a conversation in 2001.[1]

Limiting women's access to television broadcasts that show their peers making their own decisions is exactly what the patriarchal establishment would like to achieve. The solution lies not in keeping women locked up in their small world, oblivious to the freedoms that their sisters elsewhere enjoy. On the contrary, the obstacles and prejudices that hamper their empowerment need to be removed.

The contrast—but also the unlikely cooperation—between the old and the new were brought into sharp relief by the brutal murder of 17-year-old Du'a Khalil on April 7, 2007, in the town of Bashiqa, in the Nineveh province of Iraq. Her death demonstrated how selective patriarchy can be in its approach to contemporary life: it willingly embraces technological advances, while retaining archaic values when it comes to the family and the situation of women.

The young woman was one of the 70,000-strong followers of the Yazidi faith in Iraq, which combines a belief in reincarnation with elements of Islam, Christianity, and Judaism. She was accused of having an illicit relationship with a young man who was a Sunni Muslim.

As often happens in honor killings cases, the exact circumstances that led to her murder are shrouded in mist. Some reports suggested Du'a had converted to Islam to marry her Sunni boyfriend. The Yazidis tend to be strictly endogamous. Devout Sunnis, too, tend to marry their coreligionists. According to other claims, she had run away from home and was caught with her lover at a road block. Some rumors suggested that she had in fact merely been seen talking to a Sunni boy.

But most reports agree that Du'a knew she was under threat and had turned to the police, fearing for her safety. The local officers later released her into the custody of a Yazidi sheikh, a member of her extended family, after receiving assurances she would be safe. Did he betray her or, as some accounts suggested, did an angry mob forcibly enter his house to grab her?

While this point remains unclear, the brutal events that followed are well documented. Du'a was dragged out of the house and brutally stoned by a lynch mob of some 2,000 that included members of her own family. The frantic assault lasted half an hour.

Several participants in this arbitrary execution were equipped with state-of-the-art cell phones, which they used to record the atrocity in all its graphic detail. In a very modern twist on an old practice, the video and the photos were then circulated on the Internet for all to see. Viewers who could stomach the sickening scenes could hear Du'a's shouts for help as she fought for her life.

The video shows the young girl struggling to get up, her face bloodied, as she is repeatedly kicked and hit with concrete slabs. In the last frames, she is left prone on the ground having succumbed to the blows of her attackers. To underline their disrespect, her assailants lifted her skirt and pulled down her underpants.

Her body, said to have been buried with the remains of a dog to symbolize impurity, was later disinterred so that a pathology lab could conduct an autopsy and, in a final act of disrespect, determine whether she was a virgin at the time of her death. It turned out that she was, but the detail is hardly relevant to the barbaric assault.

Four men, including one of Du'a's cousins, were arrested for her murder. A couple of weeks later, Sunni militants said to be linked to Al Qaeda pulled 24 Yazidi men off a bus and massacred them in retaliation. Du'a's death was used as a pretext to fuel inter-factional fighting that had little to do with the wrongful accusations against her.

A year after her death, her father, Khalil Aswad, complained that none of the people responsible for his daughter's death had been charged. His family, on the other hand, was still ostracized by the tribe. "My daughter did nothing wrong," he said. "She fell in love with a Muslim and there is nothing wrong with that. I couldn't protect her because I got threats from my brother, the whole tribe. They insisted they were going to kill us all, not only Du'a, if she was not killed. She was mutilated, her body dumped like rubbish. "I want those who committed this act to be punished but so far they have not been, they are free. Honor killing is murder. This is a barbaric act."[2]

* * *

Honor is a value many people around the world remain attached to, but it is important not to see it as a sacred and untouchable notion that remains an intrinsic part of non-Western cultures and inevitably trumps common sense and family ties.

Sociologist Deniz Kandiyoti believes that the concept of tradition has to be treated with a degree of caution as, "what to Western eyes looks like tradition is in many instances the manifestation of new and more brutal forms of subjugation of the weak, made possible by a commodified criminal economy, total lack of security, and the erosion of bonds of trust and solidarity that were tested to the limit by war, social upheaval, and poverty."[3]

She made this assessment when commenting about the situation of women in Afghanistan, but her statements could apply to other parts of the world, including Iraq, Palestine, and Iraqi Kurdistan as well as Turkey's southeast, where conflict, displacement, and poverty have upset traditional structures and created new social tensions.

There is also plenty of evidence that motives more prosaic than the preservation of a family's reputation often lie behind the brutal suppression of women.

The need to control women's reproduction, particularly in rural communities, was always motivated in part by economic factors: ensuring they marry within the community prevented the division of assets. Until not so long ago, marriage among members of wealthy families or the aristocracy in Western cultures were often business deals as well. As Pakistani activist Rabia Ali from Pakistan wrote, "the connection between women, adultery, property and murder did not elude the Anglo-Saxons: English Common Law perceived women as chattel and, therefore, defined adultery as a crime against property. French Law, taking a more Gallic view, considered it an offence against honor."[4]

The commodification of women is certainly not a new phenomenon and the concept of honor has always been open to interpretation and gross abuse. "If someone commits a murder, he will then also kill a woman and say she was caught with the murder victim," Dr. Syeda Viqarun Nisa Hashmi, a lawyer who was at the time working on the National Commission on the Status of Women in Pakistan, told me in 2003. "He will be believed."

Old labels are now being applied to practices that owe little to tradition. Honor has been invoked to cover up greed, as the rise of consumerism has exacerbated the need for ready cash and led to new forms of exploitation.

In Pakistan, particularly in the province of Sindh, several of the people I interviewed in 2003 mentioned that greed had turned crimes allegedly committed in the name of honor into a new cottage industry. "It has become a complete business," Ali Qazi, a Sindhi media owner, told me.[5] "In ninety percent of the cases, it is about anything but honor."

To illustrate his point, he gave me some examples: "A man accuses his wife of committing adultery with a local businessman. The wife runs off to her parents for protection," he explained. "The *jirga* (feudal court) is called: the businessman is condemned to paying five lakhs rupees in compensation. Three months later, his wife returns and resumes marital life with her husband." In this particular case, the woman survives, members of the *jirga* get a commission, the husband is richer, and life goes on. But in other instances, the woman, just as innocent, is killed as part of the plot to claim financial compensation.

Feudal landowners often abuse their privileges. "If a woman is declared *kari*, she can go to the *serdar* (local landowner) and seek refuge. He can use her, then calls a *jirga*," Qazi told me. "If the woman is deemed *kari*, she is handed over to her relatives and killed. But even if she is innocent, she cannot return home. She will be auctioned off and handed over to the maximum bidder. Part of the money goes to the *haveli* (the landowner's estate) to recover his costs. The rest goes to her relatives."

Qazi saw this exploitation of traditional values as a transitory phase. "Before you can see change, you have to have a total collapse of values because something is evolving. It may take twenty or thirty years, but change will happen."

In the meantime, he acknowledged that the stigma of being accused of adultery never goes away, even if the woman is innocent. "Women in Sindh are treated as property," he said. "When there is a *faislo* (a *jirga* decision), compensation in money or other girls is usually awarded."

* * *

Mohammad*, who runs a grocery store in the bazaar of Larkana, in upper Sindh province, is familiar with these scams: his brother Amin became the target of false accusations and the entire family ended up paying a high price.

We sat at the back of his cramped store, surrounded by a great variety of wares piled up high on dusty shelves and on the ground. As flies buzzed around us, the grocer, who appeared in his early 30s, agreed to tell me his story, although he was clearly uncomfortable. "You have brought this lady to drag me in front of the court again," he joked with my translator, a local journalist. In this feudal part of Pakistan, few people dare challenge a *faislo*, or *jirga* verdict, and Mohammad was no exception.

For the grocer's family, the nightmare began shortly after the death of a young bride called Imrana*. Aged 14, originally from Sindh, she was killed by her husband in the neighboring province of Baluchistan on the morning after her wedding.

"Her husband cut off her nose and ears, and shot her with an AK-47 in front of the whole family. Her mother brought her body back" the grocer explained. The girl was declared *kari* but her alleged lover was not named at the time. "After two months, they blamed my younger brother and said he had been having an affair with her."

The girl, it appears, had grown up in the neighborhood where Mohammad's brother lived, but like most women in this traditional area, she lived in a segregated environment and Amin had never even met her. It was only several weeks after he killed his young bride that her husband "remembered" that she had confessed to an affair with the shopkeeper's brother during their wedding night.

A *jirga* was convened in Baluchistan—where *jirga* verdicts, I was told, apparently offer higher rewards—and the alleged lover was summoned in front of the tribal court to settle the matter. Amin never considered not turning up: his absence would have sealed his fate. Instead, he attended the feudal hearing where, his brother told me, he was threatened into accepting the judgment of the judges, who told him to keep silent. "They took 100,000 rupees (worth approx. 1,800 dollars in 2003) as a first installment, then another 100,000 a month later, then a third installment." For the grocer's family, the sums were considerable.

At the time, Mohammad was himself engaged and getting ready to get married. The money he had set aside for the occasion had to be used for the settlement and the ceremony was postponed. "Our family suffered mental, moral and financial difficulties," Mohammad told me. "But there is no way to challenge the system. If I rejected the private court's judgment publicly, a few armed men would come and kill me. The state would not protect me."

Mohammad did however make his feelings clear about the way the case had been handled in an interview he gave to a local Sindhi publication. Expressing his bitterness publicly turned out to be a mistake.

In an open warning to him, the accuser's family returned the money he had paid and raised the stakes. "We will fight, it will lead to war. You have defamed us," they said.

To prevent a blood feud from erupting between the two families and to save his young brother's life, Mohammad had to offer a groveling apology and he promised to keep silent about the matter. "Eventually they took the compensation money back, and I had to pay an extra 150,000 rupees (approx. 2,600 dollars)," he says with a dismissive gesture. In total, saving Amin's life had cost him 450,000 rupees (close to 8,000 dollars). The false accusation had affected their entire family, but the two brothers could now put the entire ordeal behind them and move on with their lives. Imrana, the forgotten victim, could not. She had long been dead and buried.

* * *

Since the weight of honor rests on women's shoulders, they are considered a vulnerable chink in a family's armor. Their body becomes a battleground, a site where social or political disputes are fought. The atmosphere of generalized violence that pervades in many conflict-ridden countries and the rising influence of a hard line interpretation of Islam have added to the discrimination and abuse women experience. They have also made it easier to blame all social ills on women and on immorality.

I met Shirin*, a school teacher, in the Sindhi town of Sukkur. She was introduced to me by one of her close relatives. Shirin shared a cramped apartment with her husband and their four children, where they received me with great warmth.

When asked to go out and buy a bottle of Coca-Cola for their foreign guest, their children's eyes lit up: the beverage was clearly a rare treat in this very modest household. Shirin and her husband Lateef* barely scraped together a living as primary school teachers: she earned 50 dollars a month while he was paid 90 dollars for a similar job.

They recounted their own brush with the "honor" culture. Eighteen months earlier, Shirin had been unjustly accused of adultery and been labeled a *kari*. Thankfully, her husband stood by her because he knew the allegations to be malevolent and false, but the scandal caused them both a lot of distress. Had it not been for her husband and her mother's steadfast support and their common determination to clear her name and resist community pressure, Shirin could have run into very serious trouble and possibly been killed.

The whole story began with a dispute that involved neither of the spouses. Lateef's brother, Jamal*, who lived in a house at the end of their street, had a running feud with one of his neighbors, a retired army officer who employed a manservant. Jamal was concerned that the officer's servant, who spent a lot of time standing idly in front of his employer's house, was staring at his female relatives when they walked past. For Jamal, it was a sign of disrespect to his family that a strange man, a servant at that, should ogle his female relatives. He therefore told his neighbor to keep his employee indoors. The request created tension between the two men, which erupted into a full-fledged feud.

"One evening during the winter, the officer visited Jamal and told him that a male stranger was staying at our house," Shirin explained. Her brother-in-law, appalled, turned up unannounced at their house where Lateef confirmed that he was indeed drinking tea with a colleague from school. Shirin was sitting in the next door room with the children and at no point had she been left alone with this close family friend. Nothing her brother-in-law could have considered improper had taken place.

For two weeks, Lateef's brother remained silent but the neighbor kept goading him about his relative's allegedly dubious reputation. Rumors about Shirin, though totally unfounded, continued to spread.

Eventually, Jamal could take it no longer. He confronted Lateef in the street. To his credit, Lateef staunchly defended his wife and tried to convince his angry brother than Shirin was innocent, but to no avail. Jamal demanded that the couple leave town immediately with their children, and he made his message clear by beating up his brother. With no savings and no other means of support than their poorly paid jobs, Lateef and Shirin were simply not in a position to comply with his order.

"I was crying all day long, I was very nervous and confused," recalled Shirin. "It was scary, it was constant harassment."

By incurring his neighbor's wrath, Jamal had unleashed the man's revenge on his entire family. In desperation, Shirin turned to her mother who, despite her lack of education, had a forceful and combative personality. The powerful matron enlisted support from other families living in the neighborhood and threatened to discredit the officer and his own family if they continued to persecute her daughter, who had done no wrong. Eventually, her intervention succeeded and the row abated.

Normal life resumed for Lateef and his family. Shirin, thankfully, did not suffer long-term consequences from this episode, but it left her feeling very vulnerable. "Honor is a weak point that everybody exploits," she told me. "The allegations were made to get back at Lateef's brother by humiliating him. As a result, I was mentally tortured. I suffered a lot over this."

∗   ∗   ∗

Tribal traditions may be objectionable, but they seem to have operated according to specific rules and conventions. Many of these guidelines have now been swept aside, perverted by a mixture of greed, opportunism as well as fundamentalist religious fervor. Killing, beating, raping or simply exploiting women is now easier than ever.

"In many landed families, girls are not married off, in order to avoid having to divide the property. They can be locked up in cellars, sent to a mental hospital, married to a close relative, which will cause no division of the land, or married to the Koran," Kamila Hyat, from the Human Rights Commission of Pakistan, told me in 2003.[6] "If a girl gets married anyway against the wishes of the family, they file a Hudood case. Then she gets arrested and has to prove she is legally married. But many don't even have marriage documents. According to the rules of Islam, if you have two witnesses, a marriage is valid. Then the case rests on the two witnesses, who can easily be bought."

In Sindh, several people I met mentioned local politicians and landed dignitaries who had married their sisters or daughters to the Koran. This practice, for which there appears to be no precedent in Islam, has conveniently developed among wealthy families. It seems to have no other function than to deny women a share of their inheritance. "Property of women married to the Koran remains under the legal control of their father or eldest brother, and such women are prohibited from contact with any male older than 14," explained a U.S. State Department Report on Pakistan.[7] "These women were expected to stay in the home and not maintain contact with anyone outside of their family."

This newly developed "tradition" ties in very neatly with the goal of cheating women out of their assets. It also shows that contrary to common perceptions, those who uphold harmful practices that condemn women to lives of misery are not always poor and uneducated. Customs and traditions are also skillfully exploited and manipulated by influential and wealthy people, some of whom benefited from a Western education. When the traditional division of gender roles allows them to exploit their female relatives, they do not hesitate to do so, invoking moral values and family reputation to ensure compliance.

* * *

In neighboring India, aside from honor killings that continue to claim the lives of hundreds of people every year, another "tradition" has been adapted to modern life with lethal consequences for women. In 2005, I was privileged to spend a few days with members of Vimochana, a women's rights organization based in the southern Indian city of Bangalore, the "capital" of the country's IT industry. There I met Madhu Bashan and her colleagues who for years have been working on documenting cases of women killed by their in-laws for failing to provide enough dowry, or pressured into committing suicide for the same reasons. The Vimochana women were an inspiring group, leading the fight against gender-based violence. Their passion and dedication confirmed to me, once more, that Westerners have nothing to teach to activists in developing countries.

At Victoria Hospital in Bangalore, three to four women are brought in every day to the Serious Burns unit. Most of the victims arrive at the hospital conscious and suffering excruciating pain, with burns so extensive that they eventually succumb to shock as their internal organs shut down. The few who survive are disfigured forever, and suffer an agonizingly long and painful recovery. India's national statistics reported 6,787 dowry-related incidents in India in 2005, an increase of 46 percent over the level ten years previously.[8] The British medical journal, *The Lancet,* had even more shocking figures, although not all the fire-related deaths it refers to were linked to dowry issues. "We estimated over 163 000 fire-related deaths in 2001 in India, which is about 2% of all deaths. This number was six times that reported by police. About 106 000 of these deaths occurred in women, mostly between 15 and 34 years of age. This age—sex pattern was consistent across multiple local studies, and the average ratio of fire-related deaths of young women to young men was 3:1."[9]

The tradition of providing dowry when a girl gets married used to be reserved to the upper echelons of society in the past, I was told in the state of Karnataka. Over the years, the practice spread and trickled down to the lower rungs of the society. Today, even the poorest bride is expected to bring substantial assets when she marries.

The rapid development of Western-style consumerism in India in recent years has only made the problem worse. Parents of well-educated young men submit long wish lists to families of potential brides. Washing machines, cars, motorcycles, computers are sought-after items.

And the gift-giving does not always stop after the wedding: new demands can be placed upon the bride's family at any point. If a young wife's parents are unable or unwilling to satisfy these requests, she can be beaten and harassed by greedy in-laws. The pressure can be such that young women choose to commit suicide, dousing themselves with kerosene. In many cases, in-laws or husbands are the ones who light the match when the wife's family fails to respond to this particularly egregious form of blackmail. Vimochana activists mentioned the case of one man who had gotten rid of three wives in quick succession in such a way without facing prosecution.

The police rarely bother to investigate such incidents thoroughly and too few cases result in a conviction. I spent an afternoon at Victoria Hospital talking to Satya, a staff member of Vimochana, whose job it was to convince the burn victims to testify and press charges against their husbands and in-laws. She spent her days in a small office, just off the burns ward, ready to intervene and comfort the injured women who were usually in critical condition when they arrived.

Passionate about her work, she managed to remain serene and optimistic despite the horrors she confronted on a daily basis. Yet she admitted her efforts rarely paid off. Most victims, raised to be dutiful wives, chose not to press charges against their husbands or other family members.

Modernity, far from eradicating the old dowry tradition, which had officially been outlawed with the Dowry Prohibition Act passed in 1961, has in fact strengthened it. "Marriage is now a commercial transaction. This came with the consumerism trend worldwide," Divya, an activist from Vimochana told me. "If the in-laws want a fridge, they send the daughter-in-law back home to get money from her parents. It is now a lifetime dowry."

The burden has become so heavy that many couples chose to abort female fetuses rather than face the financial cost of raising girls and getting them married. In the past two decades, India is thought to have "lost" 10 million unborn females despite a ban on selective abortion.[10]

The Indian authorities have banned doctors from disclosing the gender of an unborn child in an attempt to curb this practice, but enforcement has been extremely lax and most determined would-be parents can find a physician willing to take their money and reveal the sex of the fetus. Social activists told me of cases where microcredits, awarded to poor women to give them a chance to set up a small business and lift their household out of poverty, had been used to pay for an illegal scan and gender-selective abortion. Families too poor to determine the sex of their unborn baby through scientific means commit infanticide on their newborn daughters.

Discrimination against women used to start at birth. Modernity and tradition have joined forced to ensure that thanks to technology, it can now begin even earlier, when female fetuses are still in their mothers' wombs.

CHAPTER 15

SAMIA

The murder of Samia Sarwar Imran in Pakistan, on April 6, 1999, demonstrates that honor crimes do not only take place among the poor and the uneducated. At the time of the cold-blooded killing, the victim's father, Ghulam Sarwar Mohmand, was president of the Sarhad Chamber of commerce and industry in Peshawar. Her mother, a gynecologist, played an active role in the young woman's death.

Thanks to their influential position in society and to twisted legislation that allows charges to be dropped if relatives of the victims choose not to pursue the case, the victim's parents literally got away with murder. Members of Pakistan's parliament also showed their tacit approval of the crime when they rejected a bill condemning the event and pledging to get justice for the 28-year-old woman, who had two children.

Brought up in privileged circumstances in the city of Peshawar, Samia married the son of her mother's sister in 1989 at her parents' behest. The wedding was a grand affair with 1,000 guests, among them several ministers and a governor. The marriage itself, however, was less festive. Samia's cousin-cum-husband turned out to be a drug addict, prone to violence. After he pushed her down the stairs during her second pregnancy, the young woman, worn out by years of abuse, returned to her parents' home where she settled to bring up her two sons.

As long as their daughter was willing to preserve the status quo and remain officially married, her parents tolerated the separation. They supported her and her children financially, and allowed Samia to register at university to study law. But the young woman eventually met another man, Nadir Mirza, and fell in love. She wanted to marry him, but she knew that her parents were categorically opposed to her divorce. Besides, the man her heart was set on was not from her own Pathan ethnic group, which created an added obstacle.

In March 1999, while her parents were away performing their Muslim duty with a traditional pilgrimage to Mecca in Saudi Arabia, the young woman ran away to the city of Lahore. She sought refuge at Dastak, the first private shelter in Pakistan, set up in 1986 by lawyer Hina Jilani, who had also cofounded the country's first legal aid firm, AGHS, with her sister Asma Jahangir. The two lawyers are both internationally known as tenacious human rights advocates, relentless in their pursuit of justice. Hina Jilani agreed to help Samia obtain a divorce.

"Samia escaped from home while her parents were performing *haj*. Her uncle Yunus came here looking for her," Shahtaj Qazalbash, paralegal coordinator at AGHS, told me when I visited their offices in 2003. "We told him we were not going to keep her here by force. It was her decision to be here."

Yunus, Samia's uncle on her father's side, immediately informed the young woman's parents that their daughter had absconded. Her father, a prominent industrialist in the pharmaceutical sector, contacted an influential politician and asked him to intercede. He wanted a meeting with Samia and promised that she would be allowed to marry Nadir.

When contacted through the law firm, Samia, aware that she was in danger, refused at first to see her parents. She eventually relented and agreed to meet her mother, but only on condition that the meeting take place in her lawyer Hina Jilani's office. She saw her father as the main source of danger and felt she could trust her mother, who was going to bring some official papers needed for the divorce.

The murder was well planned. Mrs. Sarwar turned up at the busy AGHS law firm with her husband's brother Yunus in tow. He was asked to stay in the narrow hallway while Shahtaj Qazalbash showed Samia's mother into Ms. Jilani's office further down the corridor, where her daughter was already settled.

Claiming to need help because of a sprained ankle, Mrs. Sarwar insisted on bringing along a male attendant, who held her arm and supported her. Once inside the lawyer's office, the man greeted Samia: "Salam aleikum, Samia Bibi." But as the young woman got up to hug her mother, he pulled out a gun. The first bullet hit Samia near the eye. As she lay on the floor, bleeding heavily, he pulled the trigger a second time to make sure she would not survive. A stray bullet whistled past attorney Jilani's head, narrowly missing her.

Shahtaj Qazalbash emerged from her own office down the hall when she heard the gunshot and the commotion. "There was panic in our offices. Samia's mother was breathing hard," she said. In the corridor, Yunus, looking shaken, had pulled out his own weapon. He grabbed Shahtaj Qazalbash by the arm and forced her to come with them, to help secure their exit from the building. On the way out, there was a brief confrontation with a security guard, who ended up shooting Habibur Rahman, the hit man brought in by Mrs. Sarwar to kill her daughter.

Samia's mother, the victim's uncle Yunus, and the paralegal coordinator, now a hostage, climbed into a cramped rickshaw, the motorbike taxis ubiquitous in Pakistani cities. The open vehicle set off for Filetti's, a well-known historic hotel in the heart of Lahore. A remnant of the Raj era, it used to be a favorite haunt of Pakistan's founder, Jinnah. There they found Samia's father waiting for them in the hotel courtyard. "Yunus got off the rickshaw, put his arms up and waved. 'The job is done', he told Samia's father," Shahtaj explained. The paralegal was then released and sent back to her workplace in a taxi.

Later, as she sat down in the office with a glass of water, the full impact of the horrendous moments she had experienced hit her. "I could hardly drink, I was shaking so much," she said. "It was total betrayal on the part of the mother."

It is a measure of how skewed the judicial system has become in Pakistan that such a daring murder committed in front of several witnesses, including a lawyer who only just missed becoming the next victim, did not lead to a single conviction.

The Sarhad Chamber of Commerce issued a message of support for Samia's father, stating that honor killings were in line with religious and tribal traditions and demanding that Samia's two lawyers be arrested for "misleading women in Pakistan and contributing to the country's bad image abroad." In Peshawar, a demonstration was organised against "a dirty conspiracy against Islam, Pakistan, family life as we know it." Religious leaders even issued *fatwas* (religious edicts) against Hina Jilani and her sister Asma Jahangir.

Concerned that the shelter and their law firm could be attacked, the two lawyers filed a complaint against 16 people, including prominent businessmen from Peshawar, for issuing death threats but the authorities took no action.

Founding members of Pakistan's Human Rights Commission, the two lawyers had long been at the forefront of the struggle for democracy, human rights and women's rights. They were well known not just in Pakistan, but internationally. Ironically, at the time of Samia's murder, Hina Jilani's sister Asma Jahangir was UN Special Rapporteur on Extrajudicial Killings, Summary or Arbitrary Executions. She was due to fly to Geneva for a meeting at the time of Samia's murder, but heard about the shooting on her way to the airport and rushed back to the AGHS offices.

Samia's murder also triggered street protests against honor killings. A prominent member of Benazir Bhutto's Pakistan People's Party, Iqbal Haider, filed a draft resolution condemning such practices in the Senate, with the support of 19 senators.

But as the war of words in the senate grew more heated and scuffles erupted, the wording was amended and diluted four times. Support waned and the motion ended up not even being tabled, as the majority of the Upper House opposed it on the ground that "honor" matters should not even be discussed. "All the original supporters, except for three, had either backed down or were conveniently absent on the day," wrote columnist Ardashir Cowasjee in *Dawn* newspaper about the senate debacle.[1]

The threats did not stop Samia's courageous lawyers to pursue their fight for justice. They wanted the perpetrators of this horrendous crime to be punished. "We were not deterred, but the law stood against us," the bespectacled Hina Jilani told me in 2003, sitting in the very room where Samia had been gunned down four years earlier. "Since 1992, laws allow compromise. There is almost always one family member who kills, and one who forgives."

Indeed, despite overwhelming evidence, Samia's murderers got away. The hit man, Habibur Rahman, was dead. Samia's uncle Yunus was briefly indicted, "but the father and the mother forgave him, even before the case went to trial," explained Jilani. "The law allows murderers to get total impunity. The police bend to politically influential people. Even judges sometimes ask us why we bother."

*   *   *

Security measures were stepped up at the AGHS law firm after Samia Sarwar's murder. Security guards are now posted in front the building and a thick door prevents break-ins. But protecting potential victims is not easy. On the day I visited the firm, people were milling around the busy legal aid clinic. A queue of people, most of them women and men of limited means were waiting to get legal advice. For many plaintiffs, AGHS is the only hope of getting justice, but the lawyers often find their efforts frustrated by the strength of privilege and tradition, which carry more weight than the laws themselves.

Dastak, the shelter started by AGHS, is now run separately by a trust. Its location, in leafy suburb of Lahore, is not revealed for security reasons and members of staff are sworn to secrecy. "People are referred to us by police, judges or magistrates. If they have no reference, we have an initial interview to see if the girl needs legal aid, psychological support or medical examination. AGSH provides legal counselling and we also have a psychologist," Rubina, the shelter coordinator told me. On Fridays and Saturdays, residents who want to meet family members in the hope of achieving reconciliation are taken to AGHS office where the meetings are supervised.

In Rubina's office at AGHS, a mother was trying to convince her daughter to return home. She looked uncomfortable and spoke in a low voice but with an urgent tone, while her daughter listened attentively. The younger woman's body language made it clear that she was not convinced. She appeared on the defensive, and it looked unlikely that the two would come to an agreement.

Women who chose to leave their families often take an enormous risk and pay a heavy price for their bravery. No matter how bad the situation at home, a daughter or a wife is expected to accept her fate and follow the path traced by her male relatives.

Samia Sarwar is not the only Dastak resident who paid the ultimate price for her bid for freedom. When I visited the refuge, there were 35 women and 8 children sharing the crowded villa, designed to house between 25 and 30 women. The rooms were sparsely furnished and residents slept on bunk beds. The more educated among them organized classes to keep the children busy.

"Sometimes the women fight; sometimes they cry, but they also have fun," explained an attendant who had been working at the shelter for over a decade. "We provide newspapers, so educated women can read the news to those who are illiterate."

Their stay at Dastak is normally short. After three months, the rules dictate that they should have found a job and another place to stay, or reconciled with their families. The shelter helps them sort out their housing situation. Because it is still socially difficult for women to live on their own, residents sometimes team up to share lodgings. Dastak is a safe haven, where victims and potential victims of family violence can recover from their family traumas and start planning the rest of their lives. But the danger is never far off: Pakistani society is not kind to women who have challenged their relatives or live without the protection of a man, although many in the upper classes live a fairly free life.

"One girl was still staying at Dastak when she was killed at a bus stop, while out to look for a job. She wanted a divorce from her army officer husband and was killed by her brother," Shahtaj Qazalbash told me. "She was with another girl at the time, who returned to the shelter, upset and hysterical."

A thoughtful 19-year-old I met at Dastak, Lavina*, had moved into the shelter with her sister and their mother. Her father and her four older brothers were frequently abusive against the women of the house. After a few weeks at the refuge, she had found a job in a marketing firm that could help them all set up independent lives.

One day, she told me she had had a chance encounter with one of her brothers on the way back from her office. He set upon her, hitting her in the middle of the road, while trying to drag her away. There was a big scene and her *dupatta* (scarf) was torn.

"Whatever you have to do, do it here," she told her brother. "I am not coming with you." Fortunately, colleagues were by her side at the time, who insisted that she should contact ASGH to get legal representation. The public scuffle attracted the attention of police officers, who took the entire group to the police station. While her brother called other male relatives and telephoned an army friend, asking him to intervene and have his sister handed over to him, Lavina convinced the officers to protect her and contact Asma Jahangir. The lawyer arrived shortly after and a meeting was convened at the police station. The brother insisted that Lavina should marry the man her family had chosen for her, but she objected, pointing out that while she was educated, the potential husband was barely literate. Unusually, the police officers sided with her and defended her right to marry whomever she chose.

Shortly after the incident, a colleague proposed to her. She wanted to marry him, but he was a Christian and her brother had pledged to kill them both rather than allow them to be together. Life at the crowded shelter was not always easy, she said, but the world outside the gate was threatening. She felt safe behind the shelter's high walls, but she knew that her stay was coming to an end and she, her sister, and their mother would soon have to venture back into society, with all its inherent dangers.

CHAPTER 16

LEGAL MATTERS

Samia Sarwar's relatives in Pakistan benefited from the *Qisas* (retribution) and *Diyat* (compensation) ordinance promulgated in 1990 while Nawaz Sharif was Pakistan's prime minister.

This legislation allows victims or their relatives to retaliate and inflict equal punishment on the offenders. It also gives perpetrators a chance to come to an agreement with their victims or their heirs, and to pay compensation to avoid punishment. Homicides, in effect, have become private matters that can be settled out of court if the aggrieved relatives consent to it.

The *Qisas* and *Diyat* ordinance has proved particularly useful for perpetrators of honor-based killings, as the Sarwar case demonstrated: a family member can commit a murder and be swiftly pardoned by the victim's legal guardians who are complicit in the killing. The matter is usually settled before it even reaches court and life goes on, as if the victim had never existed.

The introduction of this law confirmed a trend of Islamification in the Pakistani legal system that had begun with Zia ul-Haq's Hudood ordinance in 1979. The veil of religion makes the *Qisas* and *Diyat* legislation, like the *Hudood* laws, extremely resistant to reform since religious conservatives view amendments as direct assaults on Allah's law.

Until Pakistan's parliament, after a fierce debate, narrowly voted in November 2006 to bring rape under the jurisdiction of the Pakistan Penal Code, declaring sexual assault a matter of secular rather than religious law, a woman who was raped and filed a complaint had to provide four male witnesses to back her claim. If she was unable to prove the assault, it was then assumed that intercourse had been consensual, and therefore, illicit. Any family or husband wishing to get rid of an unwanted wife or daughter can accuse her of *zina* (adultery) and have her imprisoned, where she would be unable to prove her innocence.

The new law addressing rape, known as the Women's Protection Bill, was adopted in spite of the strong opposition of conservative Muslims, who argued that the new legislation would promote loose morals. Human rights activists welcomed this development as a step in the right direction, but they expressed serious doubts as to its benefits in practice, particularly for women living in rural areas where male dominance and the feudal system are most deeply entrenched.

In Pakistan and in neighboring Afghanistan where the situation of women is dire, wives are also vulnerable to accusations of *zina* when their husband divorces them. A marriage can be dissolved unilaterally by a husband issuing the verbal statement—*talak*—three times: "I divorce you, I divorce you, I divorce you." In Pakistan, he is then legally required to file his decision with the authorities, but this step is often overlooked. If the woman later remarries, a vindictive ex-husband can easily find two witnesses to prove that she was still married to him at the time of her second union, and have her arrested for adultery.

Already discriminated against by the official legal system, women further suffer from the fact that Pakistani justice is so slow and ineffective that many people turn to tribal courts, which have been settling disputes for centuries on the basis of informal traditional codes. The judgments are often arbitrary, but they are swift and widely respected, particularly in the countryside where they have developed into a parallel justice system. In fact, few people dare challenge them.

A retired judge I met in rural Sindh in 2003, who did not want his name mentioned, acknowledged that the police force was often ineffectual and easily bought. The court system he had spent his entire career in, he stated with regret, was all but helpless.

We were sitting in the large and deserted garden of a kebab restaurant in Larkana on a hot August night. The sky was pitch black, lit only by a few stars. Despite the late hour, the heat remained stifling. The elderly judge was sitting ramrod straight, looking very dignified under his white hair. Thousands of mosquitoes whirled around the dim lantern that barely enabled us to identify the dishes that were brought to us. The food, whatever it was, tasted delicious.

The judge was a firm believer in the rule of law, but at the sunset of his career, he was also profoundly disillusioned. "The government has no interest in improving the system," he told me with a sigh. "Court cases take forever. Sometimes, advocates are using delaying tactics, particularly when we have to bring witnesses from remote areas. Eventually, the witnesses get tired of being summoned repeatedly and having to travel long distances, and they drop out."

No judiciary system can function without an effective police force. "What I have observed in my long career," he told me, "is that the courts are at the mercy of the police. Our police force is very corrupt. Officers receive very low salaries and they have to follow their superiors. In rural areas, they are under heavy pressure. There is unnecessary interference by local politicians and influential feudals. Without their consent, no police officer can be appointed. Honesty and merit don't count; the only criteria are the interests of the influentials."

The majority of the rural population in Sindh is extremely poor and often exploited by *zemindars* or landowners, who control most of the fertile land. The illiteracy rate hovers around 35 percent in the region, but it is much higher among women.

In the absence of a functioning justice system, other institutions fill the vacuum. "The community asserts its supremacy and autonomy over the state through other instances when it overrules the authority of the state itself," wrote Sindhi activist Nafisa Shah.[1]

Tribal courts are therefore doing brisk business in Upper Sindh and in other rural parts of Pakistan. Instead of chasing a case for years as it meanders through the official court system, a process both time consuming and costly, many plaintiffs prefer to rely on the local tribal leaders' brand of expedient justice, no matter how flawed.

When I met Aamir*, a local police chief, in his Sindhi headquarters, he was spending his last day at his desk: his attempts to enforce the law earnestly had ruffled a few feathers and powerful locals had arranged for him to be transferred to another city.[2] But, familiar with the inner workings of Sindhi bureaucracy and the pressures police officers are under, he did not seem overly bitter.

He admitted that a lack of cooperation from the community as a whole made police work difficult, particularly in honor-related crimes. A case is automatically opened when murder is committed, he explained, but this does not guarantee that the culprits will be punished. Without solid evidence or witnesses willing to testify, courts cannot sentence the perpetrators. "In simple murder cases, family members come as witnesses. They may not have been present at the scene of the crime, but they can lodge a complaint and bring two witnesses of their own. We then take their statements, even though we know they are false, according to the complainants' version," Aamir explained with matter-of-fact candor. "In cases of *karo kari*, however, witnesses are rarely available. Mothers and sisters will usually accept the crime and won't say anything."

While in tribal areas both man and woman are often killed, in Sindh, women alone were sacrificed to save a family's honor, on the flimsiest of suspicions, the police officer added.

He claimed that all murders were handled by official tribunals, but several lawyers I contacted denied this fact. The officer did however admit that the police routinely sent minor complaints to tribal courts. "For petty offences, we encourage people to go to private justice. After taking their matter to the *jirga*, they return and say 'we have settled the dispute.' They then change their statement and drop the case," he said. Although law enforcement officers may attempt to investigate honor-related crimes, most *kari karo* murders end up being compounded, meaning that the family of the victim(s) withdraws the charges and the case never reaches the court.

Human rights activists and lawyers, however, say *jirgas* do get involved in honor killings cases. "In the perpetuation of honor killing as custom and practice, the role of the local *waderos* or *sardars* (tribal chiefs or feudal lords, often both) cannot be underestimated ... Many of these gentlemen are well educated and well travelled; many sit in the country's parliament ... and serve in the government as ministers and advisers; they are all aware that the world beyond their fiefdoms has changed in the last hundred years. And they are not interested in changing the almost medieval world they themselves inhabit," wrote activist Rabia Ali of the Pakistani NGO Shirkat Gah. "It is the *sardars* who preside over tribal *jirgas* and secure an appropriate settlement between the two parties. The settlement, called a *faislo* in Sindh, is usually sought by the relatives of the man who has been declared a *karo*. The objective is to pre-empt revenge and therefore to appease the relatives of the *kari*."[3]

As several of my interlocutors in Pakistan pointed out, the parallel judicial system has also played a role in encouraging the development of a lucrative honor killing "industry."

Since killing a woman is often of no more consequence than swatting a fly, ruthless men can kill a female member of their family, sometimes an elderly woman, and then drag an unsuspecting, but usually prosperous male victim in front of a tribal court, alleging he had illicit relations with the deceased woman. The *jirga* members will order the male suspect to pay a hefty compensation to the victim's family to avoid being killed for his trespass, and will pocket a commission for their efforts.

Honor killings can cover a multitude of sins: if a man is killed in the course of a dispute totally unrelated to honor matters, the perpetrator can camouflage his crime by murdering a female relative. He can then announce that the two were caught together in flagrante delicto and that he acted to protect his reputation. While these scenarios may appear far fetched, such cases have in fact been reported.

I met Babu Sarfraz Jatoi in the summer of 2003 at his office next to the courthouse in Larkana. He was a practicing lawyer but, as a prominent member of a feudal family, he also sat on a *jirga* and dispensed informal justice one day a week. In fact, he appeared to favour this alternative system.

Clean shaven and wearing a carefully pressed shirt despite heat that glued our clothes to our bodies, Jatoi talked in a suave tone that belied the harshness of his comments. He gestured a lot and waved his hands, small and carefully manicured, to make his points.

He made a great display of hospitality, offering delicious chicken patties, fruit and chocolate cake to accompany the traditional milky tea that is commonly served in Pakistan. But his courteous behavior did not hide the underlying hostility. "Why are you interested in this region? There are honor killings in many other countries" he asked. "Seminars on honor killings are always being held in Sindh. Why always us? Such seminars promote womanizing. Illegal sex is very wrong!"

Honor killings, Jatoi explained, are "just a reaction": "someone sees their wife in a compromising position and they cannot control themselves. It's just like when people say something against religion. Then people will attack with any weapons at their disposal."

He defended tribal courts, claiming they could deliver just and fair verdicts much faster than official tribunals. "In *jirgas*, members are now shown postmortem reports," he said, thus confirming that the state outsources the judicial process to informal courts. "They also hear witnesses. If the witness is not believable, they dismiss him and bring another."

Women, however, cannot testify or give their version of any event, even if their own fate hangs in the balance. "Women do not appear before men. They are not educated to that extent," the Western-trained Jatoi explained patronizingly. "When people are not educated, their mind becomes the devil's mind. They become false witnesses."

In very rare circumstances, two members of a *jirga,* having obtained prior assent from the woman's male relatives, may go to a female witness' house to take her statement, but her testimony is unlikely to carry much weight against that of a man.

Since women have very limited access to a *jirga,* lodging a complaint in case of rape is particularly complicated. In order to have any hope of being believed when she reported a sexual assault— a slim hope that would be slim anyway—a woman or girl had to come forward before anyone had heard of the attack, the lawyer explained.

But a rape victim, who can only lodge her complaint through her male relatives—a husband, a father or a brother—is very unlikely to take the risk of drawing attention to her plight. She knows that they may "react," as Jatoi put it, and kill her for alleged adultery.

For female victims of rape, it is a lose-lose proposition: they risk being killed or locked up if they reveal they have been raped; but not speaking up is considered an admission of guilt, which exposes them to the same dangers. Going through official channels and filing a complaint at a police station is not much easier and often just as pointless. Poor, uneducated women in particular also face the risk of being abused at the police station. Their helplessness is exploited by all: young women from poor laborer families also suffer assaults from members of powerful landowning families, who know they can do so with total impunity.

Protecting the society's moral fabric, in appearance at least, was a priority goal in lawyer Jatoi's eyes and he viewed *jirgas* as serving a useful purpose. Illicit relations "have to be condemned," he thundered, launching into a long diatribe against immorality. "Womanizing is not allowed in our society, it is forbidden. Tell me what religion allows illegal sexual relations?"

The feudal attorney conceded that honor killings were often the result of forced marriage between partners who could not get along. "When there is no understanding between spouses, this leads to *karo kari.* The consent of the girl for the marriage is never required. This should be condemned. Sometimes a girl is a few days old when she is given in marriage."

He was also ready to admit that traditional concepts of honor were at times abused. "These sorts of things have occurred: when somebody needs money or they want to occupy land that belongs to another. Then they choose an old lady to kill and a young man. In this case, he has to pay *diyat* (compensation)."

But his statements and his general demeanor suggested that in his eyes, people wrongfully killed or whose lives were blighted by unproven allegations were mere collateral damage in a broader war against immorality.

* * *

The *jirga*-sanctioned gang rape of Mukhtar Mai from Meerwala is a particularly hideous case of traditional "justice" to have emerged from Pakistan. It is sadly not unique in its inhumanity. The bravery of the victim and the support she received from defenders of human rights are the main reasons why this story hit the international headlines in 2002.

The punishment meted out on Mukhtar Mai, who was 29 at the time, was meant to humiliate her family and punish it for an alleged honor violation committed by Mukhtar's 12-year-old brother, Shakoor, who had allegedly been seen with a female member of a richer clan. This is, at least, the version of events peddled by the perpetrators.

Several reports suggest that three men from the high caste Mastoi family had already punished Mukhtar's young brother, abducting him while he was asleep under a shaded tree outside their house in Meerwalla, southern Punjab and sodomizing him as punishment for allegedly having a relationship with their sister Salma.[4,5]

According to Mukhtar's court deposition, reported in Karachi-based *Dawn* newspaper, her family was told that Shakoor had been taken to the Mastois' house. They reported his kidnapping to police officers, who rescued the boy and took him to the police station, but they did not file a case against the kidnappers.

The powerful Mastois, not content with assaulting the teenage boy, called a *panchayat*—a tribal council of elders to discuss the alleged transgression. The boy's family was also represented and his relatives suggested that Shakoor could marry the Mastoi girl, if he had indeed tarnished her reputation. His sister Mukhtar could also be given in marriage to a member of the aggrieved Mastoi clan to soothe their anger.

But not all the Mastois agreed to a deal. Some wanted further retribution and demanded a "rape for a rape." They then announced that Shakoor's alleged crime would be forgiven if his sister Mukhtar came personally to apologize. A Baloch custom requires women to beg for forgiveness, thus symbolizing the helplessness of the family seeking the pardon.

Several of Mukhtar's male relatives, including her father and her uncle, accompanied her to the panchayat. But instead of accepting her apology, the council ruled that she should be raped. She was dragged to the house of one of her brother's kidnappers, and raped in turn by four men from the Mastoi family before being thrown out half naked and made to walk home in front of over 150 villagers.

Many women would have committed suicide after such an ordeal. A woman thus defiled is seen as damaged beyond redemption and she can even be killed by her family. But this combative lady chose instead to pursue her case in court, despite threats against her family issued by the Mastoi clan. She had already demonstrated her strength when she ended a three-year arranged marriage that went wrong at the age of 19.

Mukhtar's story was widely reported in the international press, but it was only one of 434 cases of gang-rape cases recorded by the Human Rights Commission of Pakistan in 2002. Media pressure ensured that Mukhtar's tormenters were brought to trial. The four men who raped her and two other members of the council that ordered her assault were sentenced to death while eight others were released.

The Pakistani authorities were not thrilled with the young woman's public stance, which they thought cast their country in a bad light. When she was invited to travel to the United States, she was initially denied a passport, until public pressure forced the government to issue the travel document. General Musharraf, who was at the time President of Pakistan, expressed his real feelings in a controversial *Washington Post* interview in 2005. "A lot of people say if you want to go abroad and get a visa for Canada or citizenship and be a millionaire, get yourself raped," he said. Although he later denied making these comments, they were confirmed when *The Washington Post* released a tape of the interview.

Despite his personal distaste for Mukhtar's battle for justice, President Pervez Musharraf eventually awarded the brave woman $8,300 in compensation, which she used to set up a school for girls and one for boys in her village, as well as 24-hour police protection.

Mukhtar believed knowledge would lead to social change and prevent other girls from meeting a fate like hers, and she has become one of the school's most enthusiastic students.

But if her case managed to put a dent in the patriarchal system, it was rapidly clear that the struggle was not over yet. On March 3, 2005, Appeals judges in Lahore decided to acquit the rapists because there was "insufficient evidence" to convict them. Their release reflected on how poorly justice is served in Pakistan. It also put Mukhtar and her family at great risk because the Mastois had vowed to kill her and her family. "There is a danger to my own life and also to my family," Mukhtar Mai told reporters in Islamabad after the men's conviction was overturned. "But I won't leave Pakistan or my village. I will continue my work in the schools."

The outcry that followed this decision led to a legal tussle. The Sharia (Islamic) court stepped in and suspended the acquittal, claiming the case fell under its jurisdiction and should have been tried under Islamic laws. To break the legal deadlock, the Supreme Court announced it would take over the case. Despite these cruel miscarriages of so-called justice committed by members of traditional courts, there is no sign that the government of Pakistan is seriously trying to curb their influence.

A high court in Sindh had declared *jirga* or *panchayat* illegal in 2004 and ordered the police to stop their gathering, but the order has been largely ignored. Tribunals of elders remain popular largely because the creaky Pakistani judiciary system is unable to cope with demand and deliver justice in an acceptable time frame.

On March 15, 2009 Mukhtar Mai married Nasir Abbas Gabol, one of the police constables who were brought to her village of Meerwala to protect her after her rape. She had resisted his advances for many months because Gabol was already married and she didn't want to be the cause of marital strife. But her suitor threatened to kill himself or to divorce his wife, Rukhsana, if the young activist did not accept his marriage proposal. His two sisters, who had married into Rukhsana's family as part of an exchange of brides, or *watta-satta,* begged Mukhtar to marry their brother.

If Gabol had indeed divorced his first wife, the marriages of his two sisters would have had to be dissolved as well. In the end, Mukhtar relented "on humanitarian grounds," she told the press, because she didn't want three families to be broken up on her account.[6] In April 21, 2011, the Supreme Court inflicted Mukhtar another blow when it acquitted 13 of the 14 accused in the case, only upholding the life sentence of one of the defendants, Abdul Khaliq.

*   *   *

There is a common misperception that countries where public support persists for killing in the name of honor are all ruled by Islamic law. This is not the case. While Pakistan has incorporated elements of Islamic law—distorted elements, many scholars would argue— into a legal system largely inherited from the British Raj, in many Mediterranean and Middle East countries, the legislation still bears the influence of French emperor Napoleon Bonaparte and the Penal Code he introduced in 1810, which also inspired the Ottoman Penal Code of 1858.

Legal provisions offering lenient sentences for honor killings are present in the legislation of several countries of the Middle East. They also existed in the laws of Spain, Portugal and Italy until not so long ago. In France, husbands who committed murder after catching their wives committing adultery in the marital bed legally benefited from mitigating circumstances until the 1970s, while adultery was considered a crime.[7] Adultery was seen as an insult to a man's honor in French law and judges were often willing to be understanding when a husband committed a crime of passion.

Italy had a similar approach: honor was an acceptable defence in court until 1981, and a man would get a reduced sentence of only three to seven years of imprisonment if he killed a wife, a sister or a daughter to uphold his family's reputation.

In Jordan, women's rights activists have been waging a long battle to have the Jordanian Penal Code amended. They focused in particular on Article 340 of the Code, which states that "he who discovers his wife or one of his female relatives committing adultery with another, and he kills, wounds or injures one or both of them, is exempt from any penalty." Another article also provides "a reduction of penalty" for a man who "discovers his wife, or one of his female ascendants or descendants or sisters with another in an unlawful bed, and he kills, wounds or injures one of them."

The public battle to change the law, headed by advocates of women rights such as journalist Rana Husseini and lawyer Asma Khader, who founded the organization Sister Is Global before joining the government and becoming a State Minister, contributed to raise awareness of honor killings in Jordan and around the world. They successfully alerted the international community to the fact that over 20 women a year are still killed every year in the name of honor in their tiny country, which only has a population of less than 6.5 million. While they successfully brought honor killings onto the political agenda, they have so far not succeeded in permanently changing the legal framework.

The Jordanian parliament rejected lifting Article 340 on several occasions. In December 2001, while parliament was suspended, the cabinet introduced a series of temporary bills including one imposing harsher penalties for perpetrators of honor crimes. Murderers were no longer exonerated in case of adultery, but they still benefited from mitigating circumstances. A new clause gave women the same right to hit if they caught their husband committing adultery, but this equal opportunity approach to murder did not satisfy women's rights activists.

"The amendment also gives women lenient sentences if they kill their husband for adultery, but this is not what we were seeking," Asma Khader told me in 2002. She acknowledged however that thanks to the campaign more women understood that defying patriarchal values did not always have to result in death. Public opposition to murders dictated by tradition also increased.

Limited though they were, these changes raised the hackles of conservative and religious politicians. Religion was invoked and religious groups railed that Jordan would sink into a cesspool of immorality if honor killings were condemned. The collapse of family values and the fight against immorality appear to be arguments used worldwide by conservatives when they seek to curb women's freedom.

In 2003, despite the fact that the Senate had upheld the changes introduced by the government, lawmakers of the lower house voted against the proposed reform and Article 340 reverted to its original form.

Queen Rania, King Abdullah's wife, has repeatedly urged parliament to curb honor killings, which she described in September 2003 as a "form of murder without trial, which is contrary to Islam." In that, she followed in the footsteps of her predecessor American-born Queen Noor, who had also been an outspoken opponent of traditional practices. Despite the Jordanian Royal Family's engagement, pushing through legal reforms has proved difficult.

Jordanian women's rights activists have admitted that Article 340 was perhaps the wrong target. Much more often invoked in Jordanian courts is Article 98, which focuses on the notion of provocation and states that "He who commits a crime in a fit of fury caused by an unrightful and dangerous act on the part of the victim benefits from a reduction of penalty."

A similar situation prevailed in Turkey until the country's old-fashioned Penal Code, introduced in 1926 and based on Italy's criminal laws, was thoroughly overhauled in 2005.

The Turkish Penal Code had also contained an article, 362, that specifically referred to honor crimes and offered lenient sentences. The legal provision shared similarities with Jordan's Article 340, even if it did not offer complete exoneration. Activists had already waged a fierce battle to have Article 362 repealed and its removal from the Penal Code had already been hailed as a major achievement in 2003.

But it turned out to be a Pyrrhic victory. As is the case in Jordan for Article 340, the offending clause was rarely used in court. Instead, Turkish defense lawyers usually relied on Article 51 which allowed sentences to be decreased by up to two-thirds in case of "severe provocation" to support their calls for leniency.

A coalition of women's organizations formed a platform to work on a thorough overhaul of Turkey's Penal Code. Rights activists lobbied lawmakers relentlessly and managed to have the article on provocation amended in the brand-new Penal Code that entered into force in 2005, making it harder for perpetrators of honor killings to evade justice or get off lightly.

Their coordinated efforts resulted in the comprehensive rewriting of 30 articles of the Penal Code that affect women. The amendments changed the entire legal perception of women: the distinction between girls and women—in effect between virgins and non-virgins—was removed, while sexual crimes, until then filed under "crimes against public morality" became "crimes against individuals." Marital rape, which had never been accepted as a crime in the past, also made its first appearance into the Turkish penal code as a result of this successful campaign for women's rights.

* * *

The importance of a sound legal framework to curb the practice of honor killings is obvious. But for harmful practices to be eradicated, general attitudes to women throughout society have to change.

No matter how tightly the legislation defines the crimes, judges still have to rule on the specifics of the acts of violence that are presented to them. Although legislations differ, entrenched misogyny is a common thread running through the judicial systems of most countries where honor killings are still practiced. It is not just embodied in the legislation itself but, more crucially, it persists in the mind of the magistrates and it is through the filter of their personal perceptions that the laws are interpreted.

This explains why verdicts handed down by courts for honor-motivated killings often remain soft on the perpetrators. "The interpretation of the judge is very important. He makes his own judgment with his mentality, his own prejudices," Judge Ali Güzel, former head of Bakirkoy Criminal Court in Istanbul, told me in December 2002.

Born in Gaziantep, close to the Syrian border, a region of Turkey where honor killings are still common, Ali Güzel was an enlightened magistrate who had spent his career fighting for the elimination of gender discrimination in the law. In 1990, he was among a group of judges who launched a petition and succeeded in having Article 438 of the Turkish Penal Code, which lowered the sentence for rape if the victim was a sex worker, lifted.

The retired judge and his wife were apparently thrilled to have a foreign guest when they received me in their apartment, in a housing estate near Istanbul's Ataturk airport. They plied me with delicious home-cooked food while answering my questions on the Turkish legal system's view of honor killings.

"Judges are educated and many of them have traveled abroad, but their thinking remains very conservative,"[8] Judge Güzel told me. To more open-minded members of the court like the judge, honor killings presented a serious challenge. "Sometimes we cannot even bring the case to court because we cannot find the culprits or a girl who was raped has been married off and the family tries to have the case closed," he told me. "There are many honor vigilantes in the community. The whole society works together to prepare the ground and cover up these murders."

Other judges opt for soft punishment because victims and perpetrators usually belong to the same family and they feel their relatives have "suffered enough already." "The killer is also a victim. We talk to them in prison, they're very sorry and yet they would do it again because of social pressure," Hakkar Karasu, who was president of the Criminal Court in the conservative Turkish city in Urfa, told me.[9] "When sentencing we have to take into account why they did it. We have to find the balance between being too hard and causing more hurt, and being too soft and encouraging the practice. You cannot change the *töre* (customs) with the laws. You have to educate people." These magistrates may mean well, but they unintentionally send the message that the judicial system condones their actions.

Prejudices against women, of course, are not limited to judges. In Turkey, as is the case in Jordan and elsewhere, potential victims who seek state protection are sometimes killed after the police or other representatives of the state hand them back to their families.

On July 1, 2004 a 26-year-old Jordanian woman, who had become pregnant out of wedlock a year earlier, was killed by her younger brother a day after she was released from protective custody and her family signed a document promising not to harm her.[10] She was one of 18 victims of honor killings committed, or at least documented that year, in Jordan.[11]

Protective custody is a euphemism used in Jordan to describe the practice of putting potential victims behind bars for their own safety. "Although they are referred to as 'administrative detainees', these young women under threat are kept in women's prisons or rehabilitation centers along with convicted criminals."

In its 2009 report, Amnesty International deplored the situation in Jordan where "tens of women were reportedly administratively detained without charge or trial. Some, including rape victims, women who had become pregnant outside marriage and women accused of extramarital sexual relations or of being prostitutes, were believed to be held to protect them from their family and community members."

Although a government-run shelter has been opened for victims of domestic violence, it housed few guests.[12] Instead of targeting the relatives who threaten them, the authorities find it more expedient to lock up the young women, who sometimes languish in jail for years. "Women stay in jail until a man the authorities trust comes to release them, but sometimes the men kill the woman as soon as she is out despite the fact that they have signed a paper promising to protect them," Asma Khader explained to me in 2002.[13]

In Pakistan, district judges can order women at risk to be transferred to state shelters known as Dar-ul Aman. Unlike in Jordan, these institutions are separate from the prison system, but they still operate very much like jails. Once admitted for their own protection, women have little or no freedom of movement.

Again, it is important to remember that such unfair treatment of women is not limited to the Muslim world. The Magdalene workhouses of Ireland, mentioned earlier in this book, functioned in much the same way until not so long ago. Young girls perceived to have strayed from the narrow path laid out for them by the Catholic society could be locked up and condemned to a life of drudgery until a compassionate relative eventually came to rescue them.

But walls are not always needed to create a prison. Millions of women around the world are still held firmly behind the bars of social norms and legal injustice, with no chance of an early release.

* * *

Occasionally, a verdict sets an example and proves that perpetrators of honor killings do not always get off lightly. In 2004, before the Turkish Penal Code was even amended, the Turkish press hailed the verdict given by Judge Orhan Akartuna in the traditional province of Urfa in a grievous case of honor killings. The open-minded judge handed down heavy sentences of 16 years and eight months to eight family members involved in plotting the 2002 murder of 14-year-old Emine Kızılkurt while the actual perpetrator, her cousin Mahmut, was imprisoned for life.

Emine was rumored to have been pregnant at the time of her death, the result of having been raped by a neighbor. Turkish documentary filmmaker Melek Ulagay investigated the circumstances of her death for her movie *Dialogues in the Dark*.

She found that Emine had in fact been killed for refusing to marry her paternal cousin Mahmut, who ended up murdering her. Searching through police files, the filmmaker found a moving letter Emine had written to the authorities. Born in the traditional village of Obali, near the Syrian border, the young girl knew she was at risk for rejecting her elders' choice of husband. After a malicious campaign was launched in her village to smear her, she wrote to the police, denouncing the slanderers:

> "My name is Emine Kızılkurt. If I die, my first enemy is Mustafa; my second enemy is Hilal; my third enemy is Isa; my fourth enemy is Ismail; my fifth enemy is Meryemel Ayşo. It is because of them that they find me guilty," the young girl wrote. "They say that I'm pregnant. But I'm not pregnant, nor did I have an abortion . . . I am too young to have had an abortion . . . I'm innocent, but they are Planning to kill me . . . They tell me that if I don't kill myself with electricity, poison or by hanging, they will shoot me."[14]

The teenager was brought to the city of Urfa for a pregnancy test. Three different doctors examined her to see if she was still a virgin. Violating their Hippocratic oath, which requires them to do no harm, they all told Emine's relatives that the young girl was "tainted."

Her parents did not want to kill her. They tried to save her by marrying her off to a distant relative, but the determination of their clan proved too strong. Emine's parents were overruled and the young girl was killed on June 12, 2002.

The judge recognized that many people had contributed to Emine's murder. The crime was the result of community pressure. It was a premeditated execution, and the person pulling the trigger was not the only culprit.

Another landmark judgment was served in the Başkale district of Van province, in eastern Turkey, in January 2009. Van province, which used to be populated mainly by Armenians before the massacres of 1915, is located at the eastern edge of Turkey, close to Iran.

The province is poor, but because of its proximity to the border, it is also a smuggler's paradise. Many illegal immigrants from Asia, as well as drugs on their way to Europe, transit through this area. Smuggling, however, is not an industry that spreads its wealth very broadly and the eastern provinces remain among the more deprived in Turkey. In these remote areas, tribal influences and a very traditional mentality remain quite strongly entrenched.

Naile Erdaş was killed in 2006, a day after she gave birth to a child conceived through rape. Until she delivered a healthy baby boy, the young girl had been able to conceal her pregnancy. She was brought to hospital by her relatives, allegedly suffering from a severe headache. When they realized she was pregnant and about to give birth, the doctors immediately notified the police and the prosecutor's office, aware that the young girl could be under threat from her own family.

But a week after she had given birth, Naile was sent home. Her father had pledged in front of a prosecutor to keep her safe, but shortly after she returned home, her brother killed her.

Naile was a victim of state negligence, but at least her killers did not go unpunished. On January 12, 2009, a judge sentenced the teenager's brother to life imprisonment for perpetrating aggravated murder in the name of tradition. The victim's father, who had made false promises, as well as her mother, her paternal and maternal uncles were found guilty of aggravated incitation to murder and jailed for life.

*   *   *

The concept of provocation, often raised in court in the context of honor killings, deserves closer examination. Provocation has proved just as contentious in Western democracies, where it can be a mitigating factor in domestic crimes.

The Pakistani lawyer who had argued Zahida Parveen' case in court and guided the mutilated woman through the long judicial process that led to her husband's conviction, complained about the way provocation was interpreted in her country's courts.

I met Nahida Mehboob Elahi, a fiery attorney with long dark hair who ran a private practice in Rawalpindi and also chaired the Women's Crisis Centre in Islamabad, at her law office late one evening in August 2003.

After a long day in court, Ms Mehboob Elahi received her clients at night in a small workplace overrun with files. Piled meters high, the documents created a maze in the antechamber where clients, clearly not drawn from the richest segments of the population, waited for their turn to consult the lawyer.

When she talked about her fight against gender discrimination in Pakistan, the lawyer's eyes burned with passion behind her glasses. She did her best to ensure that perpetrators of violent crimes against women were punished, but she admitted that the legal framework made her job very difficult.

"There is a cultural background to honor killings, and the Pakistani penal code, which is a legacy from the British, is not dealing properly with these cases," she explained. "In murder cases, most defendants argue either 'sudden and grave provocation' or 'self-defense', but people started misusing these concepts and courts accepted honor crimes as 'sudden and grave provocation'."

In a society as conservative as Pakistan's, mere suspicion that a woman has been unfaithful or has talked to a man who wasn't a relative is often considered sufficient to condemn her in the eyes of the community.

But even in the more progressive context of Western countries, the definition of provocation, used by many defendants tried for "crimes of passion," has also caused controversy. This is where the line that separates crimes committed in the name of honor and murders described in the West as "crimes of passion" becomes blurred.

Westerners may think of honor as an outdated notion far removed from our modern lives, but a close look at the motives behind so-called crimes of passion suggests that they are often not very far removed from the desire to possess and control that drives perpetrators of honor-based violence.

Australian law scholar Ian Leader-Elliott studied the legal history of provocation in Western courts and concluded that even in liberal democracies, the concept of "provocation" had a gender slant.

Provocation, he explained in an authoritative essay published in 1997, "offers men who kill from jealousy the possibility of a partial excuse for their crime." In eighteenth century British law, adultery was perceived as a wrong to property whereas the French system saw it as an insult to a man's honor.

In modern times, the concept of provocation in the legislation of many developed democratic nations has been extended "to ensure that women who kill violent partners avoid conviction for murder."[15] But, as Leader-Elliott underlined, there remains a fundamental difference between the male murderer who is "killing to possess the other"— the other being a wife or partner who was attempting to break up the relationship or was unfaithful—and "killing to preserve oneself," a scenario more common when women kill. Many female murderers are women who snapped after experiencing years of abuse.

Yet, the law, blind to such subtleties, makes no clear distinction between these different motives. "Modern courts are far more hospitable to pleas based on jealousy and possessiveness. Sexual provocation is a cultural defense which transcends religion or ethnic origin, and claims for itself a constituency almost exclusively masculine,"

Leader-Elliott claimed. "Given the disparity between the sexes in the matter of who kills whom, women may be far more likely than men to conclude that this particular claim to compassion is an anachronism."

In his conclusion, the Australian scholar wondered about the "unacceptable paradox that the progressive restriction of a husband's power to exert lawful control over his wife has been accompanied by a progressive enlargement of a partial excuse for killing her."

The bias against women is of course much stronger in countries where women's behavior is seen as affecting the reputation of their entourage as well as their own. Judges are too often ready to accept that a woman "severely provoked" her relatives simply by going out wearing a low-cut dress, by talking at length to a neighbor or even defying her parents' choice to marry a husband of her own choosing. The blame then shifts from the defendant to the victim, who is no longer able to defend her reputation and tell her own version of events in court.

Such unfair outcomes have also been recorded in South America. In August 1991, the State Court of Parana in Brazil acquitted Joao Lopes of the murder of his wife and her lover on the basis of a "legitimate defense of honor," although a Superior Court had earlier rejected this view. The defendant could hardly argue that he had acted in a fit of fury, because he had spent days tracking down the victims before killing them. Yet the magistrates were willing to accept that the double murder was justified by his need to defend his honor.

As recently as 2006, on the southern Italian island of Calabria, a member of a local mafia clan, Giovanni Morabito, aged 24, shot his 32-year-old sister, a law school graduate, who had given birth to a child conceived out of wedlock two weeks earlier. "It is a question of honor. I would have shot her in the back, but she turned round. I am not sorry. On the contrary, I am proud of what I did," he told the police. He was disappointed to hear that in spite of being hit by two bullets, the intended victim had actually survived.[16]

* * *

Westerners are quick to condemn entire cultures on the basis of discriminatory practices against women, but their sensitivity to brutality when it is committed against women in foreign countries has not always been accompanied by a similar awareness of the violence that goes on in their own societies nor by a show of strong legal support for immigrant victims at home.

The extensive investigations into the deaths of Heshu Yones in the United Kingdom and of Pela Atroshi in Sweden, and the strong verdicts that followed mark a new attitude toward honor killings in Western Europe.

Until the end of the twentieth century, Western judges were often willing to accept culture as an excuse for murder and violence. This attitude stemmed partly from political correctness and the desire not to offend immigrant communities, but also from a residual patriarchy which accepted, without questioning it, the influence of culture in family matters, forgetting that the victims were members of the very same cultures.

Women seeking shelter in developed Western democracies because they face death threats or a life of unrelenting abuse in their home country still face a major challenge. Gender-based persecution was not mentioned in the 1951 Convention on the Status of Refugees, but landmark court cases in several countries have sought to fill this gap.

In 2002, the Australian High Court overruled the immigration ministry in the case of a Pakistani national, a mother of three, who had fled constant abuse at the hands of her husband and in-laws four years earlier. Mrs. Khawar had been hospitalized on several occasions in her native country, but the authorities had paid no attention to her plight even after her husband and his brother doused her with petrol and threatened to light a match.

Although the Refugee Review Tribunal argued that the violence she suffered was directed at her personally and she was therefore not a member of a persecuted group, the High Court felt that the combination of violence perpetrated by non-state actors and the inaction of the authorities was enough to constitute persecution, as defined by the Convention on refugees.

A similar awakening had taken place in the United Kingdom a few years earlier when the House of Lords ruled in the case of Ms. Islam and Ms. Shah, two asylum seekers who had both been abused in the past and feared the consequences of false adultery allegations. The House of Lords held that given the lack of state protection, women in such circumstances may be considered "members of a particular social group" subject to protected status under the 1951 Convention Relating to the Status of Refugees.

This more liberal interpretation of asylum laws, which views entrenched violence against women and the threat of honor killing as a political issue, has only applied to a limited number of cases so far. In the United States, the Obama administration, shortly after its arrival in power, reversed the position adopted by courts under George

Bush, and cautiously opened the immigration door to victims of severe abuse, provided they meet stringent criteria and could prove that the authorities in their countries offer no protection.[17]

Courts in Western countries still often view honor killings and abuse of women from ethnic and religious minorities through the prism of cultural relativism. In March 2007, a female German judge refused to grant a speedy divorce to a German Muslim woman of Moroccan origin who had faced repeated domestic abuse. The judge, Christa Datz-Winter, argued that in Moroccan culture wife-beating was acceptable and, furthermore, that the Koran sanctioned physical punishment. The plaintiff should therefore have known what she was letting herself in for. "That's what the claimant had to reckon with when she married the defendant," the judge stated.[18] Her ruling caused strong reaction and the magistrate was given a leave of absence.

Greater awareness of violence against women in general, and crimes committed in the name of honor in particular, has gained ground in international institutions as well. In 1979, the Convention to Eliminate All Forms of Discrimination against Women was adopted (CEDAW), which requires states to work on modifying the social and cultural patterns of men and women in order to eliminate discrimination.

At the turn of the millennium, the United Nations General Assembly mentioned honor killings in the context of extrajudicial executions (Resolution 55/111, December 2000) and in Resolution 55/68 on the Elimination of All Forms of Violence, including Crimes against Women (December 2000).

In January 31, 2001, the United Nations General Assembly passed a resolution, entitled "Working Towards the Elimination of Crimes Against Women Committed in the Name of Honor," which focused exclusively on these crimes.[19]

Tabled by The Netherlands, the groundbreaking bill acknowledged "that crimes against women committed in the name of honor are a human rights issue and that States have an obligation to exercise due diligence to prevent, investigate and punish the perpetrators of such crimes and to provide protection to the victims, and that the failure to do so constitutes a human rights violation."

Several countries put up resistance, mainly because they felt that honor crimes were unfairly perceived to be linked to Islam. Twenty-six nations, including Pakistan, chose to abstain, but 146 countries voted in favour of the resolution. Jordan voted against, but later announced it had actually meant to back the resolution.

The UN General Assembly reaffirmed its commitment in December 2002 and again in December 2004 in a new resolution, which also stressed "the need to treat all forms of violence against women and girls, including crimes committed in the name of honor, as a criminal offence, punishable by law."[20] Eight Muslim countries, including Turkey, were among the cosponsors of this document.

The greatest challenge is still to find a way to transform these official pledges into a social reality. Reaching that goal involves a broad change of mentality, at the domestic as well as state level. Until then, many women will remain trapped in social perceptions that limit their freedom of choice and put them at risk of death and violence.

CHAPTER 17

GÜLDÜNYA

In Turkey, Güldünya Tören has posthumously become a powerful symbol of the fight against honor killings. Her name has been used in song lyrics, a street has been named after her, the Turkish chapter of Amnesty International held a "Letter to Güldünya" competition, and several Turkish pop stars teamed up to release an album of "Güldünya songs" to raise awareness of the silent war against women.

There are several reasons why Güldünya's murder on February 25, 2004, caught the public's attention. For a start, to borrow the title of novelist Gabriel Garcia Marquez's book, her murder can be described as a "chronicle of a death foretold."

The young woman knew that she was most likely to be killed. She had given birth to a baby son out of wedlock and knew that her family would never forgive her. She left behind photos of herself in the white wedding dress that she knew she would never wear in public, holding her baby son. Shortly after the photos were taken, she gave him up for adoption.

The photos show an attractive young woman, her face free of makeup, with dark hair tumbling down her back. But it is the intense way she stares straight at the camera, unsmiling and stern, that makes the images so haunting. She had no reason to smile: she knew herself to be under threat and securing her son's future meant letting him go. Despite her bleak prospects, she had not given up on life: her baby was named Umut, which means Hope.

Another striking aspect of Güldünya's case is that her death could have been prevented if the authorities had provided adequate protection. Her case is not the only example of bureaucratic shortcomings but the official neglect is particularly egregious in this instance, since Güldünya was attacked and shot not just once, but on two different occasions within a few hours, and no security measures were taken between the two attacks.

Güldünya's story began in Budaklı Köy, a small village of 60 households in Bitlis province, an underdeveloped region in southeast Turkey. She was one of 11 children. Her family was part of a large community, the Sşego tribe. Güldünya, who was 22 when she died, had developed a relationship with her cousin's husband, a 27-year-old named Servet Taşş.

When her parents learned that she was expecting a baby, her father, Serif Tören, asked Servet to take Güldünya as a *kuma* or second wife. The community would have accepted this marriage as legitimate in spite of the official ban on polygamy, but the young man objected and Güldünya did not want to be a mere concubine. Her lover left the village in a hurry, taking with him his wife and his two children, to avoid facing the wrath of her relatives.

When their face-saving plan proved unworkable, Güldünya's parents locked up their daughter in a room while they discussed what to do. They decided that sending her away was the best solution and Güldünya was dispatched to Istanbul, to stay with her uncle Mehmet Tören. Her relatives may have hoped the scandal would subside once the young woman and her swelling belly were no longer seen around the village.

Güldünya did not feel safe at her uncle's house—and her fears were justified. Her brother Irfan, aged 24, paid her a visit and tried to strangle her, but he did not have the nerve to go through with the murder. Instead, he gave his sister a rope and urged her to commit suicide. Güldünya wanted to live: she escaped through the window and sought protection at the police station.

Irfan and his uncle Mehmet Tören were summoned by police officers and they both pledged not to harm the young woman. Güldünya moved into the home of a retired imam, originally from her region, who sheltered her for the following months. She was still living with Alaatin Ceylan, his wife, and his six children, and she felt comfortable in their home in the Küçükçekmece district of Istanbul, when she gave birth to baby Umut on December 1, 2003.

But there was to be no happy ending to this story. Less than four months later, Irfan turned up at the Ceylans' house and announced that he wanted to take his sister to visit their aunt in the city of Bursa, three hours away from Istanbul.

When Alaatin Ceylan, the retired preacher, suggested that Güldünya should pack a few belongings for the journey, Irfan said that she would not need them. This made the imam suspicious of Irfan's motive and he offered to accompany Güldünya and her brother to the bus station. Once they reached the street, Irfan walked away, announcing that he was going to find a taxi.

As Irfan stepped aside, Güldünya spotted her 17-year-old brother, Ferit, who had been lurking in the street, waiting for them. She saw him approach, his hand in his pocket, and realized from his demeanor that he was about to pull out a gun. As she turned to run away, his shots hit her in the hip. Güldünya collapsed on the ground and her two brothers ran away.

Rushed to a local private clinic where doctors assessed her situation, the injured Güldünya was later transferred to the state hospital in the Bakırköy suburb of Istanbul, where she underwent an operation. As she lay recovering in her hospital bed, she was briefly interviewed by reporters and asked for police protection. "I know they won't want me to live. I'm scared," she told them.

When she testified to the police, she acknowledged that her brothers had shot her but she refused to press charges against them. Her siblings, however, were not as forgiving. Within hours of the first shooting, the two young men, who had hidden since their escape from the crime scene, made a second attempt on her life.

At 03:45 in the morning, Güldünya's youngest brother, Ferit, walked into the hospital where his sister had been left without protection. He pumped two bullets into her head before calmly walking out.

Güldünya did not die immediately, but was left brain dead. The last twist of irony was that it was left to her family to make the decision, two days later, to pull the plug on the machine that was keeping her body alive. *Sabah* newspaper reported that they refused to donate her organs for transplant, to ensure that "no trace would be left of her."

Güldünya's death, the result of official negligence, caused outrage in Turkey. A human rights lawyer and activist, Ergin Cinmen, filed a complaint against the police force for not protecting Güldünya.

Baby Umut, it transpired, had not been formally adopted. Güldünya had found a family to bring up her son, but she had kept their identity secret for fear that her family might try to harm the baby. Alaatin Ceylan's daughter, Keramet, who had become Güldünya's friend while she lived with their family, told reporters that the young mother had locked herself in her room after handing over her baby.

"She cried for two days and didn't eat," Keramet said. "But later her morale improved because she believed Umut would be safe. She even started looking for a job. But she missed her village and the tobacco fields."

The state minister in charge of social services at the time, Güldal Akşit, ordered the child taken into care but she said the couple Güldünya had chosen to bring up her child would still have a chance to bring him up once the vetting process and all adoption formalities had been completed.

Güldünya's relatives continued to deny that her death was the result of a group decision. Newspaper reports, unconfirmed, alleged that a meeting of tribe members had taken place in the village six weeks before the shootings. Some members wanted tradition to be upheld, but others had objected. Güldünya's father, Şerif Tören, had traveled to Istanbul, but his daughter refused to see him when he had shown up at Alaatin Ceylan's house. Only a few days later, his son Irfan retraced his footsteps and paid Güldünya a visit that would eventually prove fatal.

Victims of honor killings are rarely afforded a proper funeral in the presence of relatives. Güldünya's parents initially refused to claim her body, but the tide of public opinion had turned in Turkey and the case had generated widespread anger. After a few days, the family changed their mind, perhaps to lend their claims of innocence more credibility. Güldünya's remains were taken by ambulance to Bitlis province. Her body was given a police escort, which would have been more useful when she was still alive.

The vehicle was met by a large crowd of relatives, villagers, and officials at the province border, some 300 kilometers from the village. A convoy of 60 cars accompanied the young woman on her last journey. The funeral was attended by local dignitaries: the mayor of Bitlis was present and so was the *müfti* or district religious leader.

In total, more than 3,000 people turned up to bid Güldünya a last farewell. Many of those in attendance may well have been complicit in her death or have approved of it. In keeping with tradition, the women, including Güldünya's mother, watched from a distance and stayed away from the graveside.

For weeks after her death, a controversy raged on in Turkey and the victim's relatives faced a lot of media attention. Güldünya's father claimed that he had nothing to do with her death. "If my sons have killed my daughter, I disown them. There was no decision from the family council," he said. "As a father, would I tell my sons to go and kill their sister? Irfan and Ferit were not at the village. They were in Istanbul. I cannot understand why they would kill Güldünya, but maybe they were not the perpetrators. I do not believe my sons would kill my daughter."

Tören added that his family had struck a "peace deal" with the relatives of the man who had impregnated his daughter. "This young man wouldn't accept to marry my daughter," he explained. "But we tried to find a way to smooth the matter."

Umut's alleged biological father, who had fled the village, denied his relationship with Güldünya in a telephone interview with *Milliyet* newspaper. "I'm being libeled. I will lodge a complaint," he said. "I did not have a relationship with Güldünya. In order to put an end to the conflict, I paid 10 billion Turkish Lira (7,500 dollars) to the Tören family."[1]

The district official from Kaymakam of Guroymak district, Okan Leblebicier, confirmed that money had changed hands to keep the peace in the village. "When the relationship emerged—and I find the boy guilty—the tribe handled the issue and decided to seek peace."

Güldünya's two brothers were eventually arrested in April 2004, after two months on the run. The police found them in a small bed-sit that they had rented in Istanbul. Since the murder, they had stayed indoors most of the time, hoping to escape detection. During their trial, Ferit admitted that he had killed his sister. "I wanted to talk to my sister, but she said some harsh words," he explained. "I opened fire. In hospital, I shot her twice in the head. No one incited me to commit murder."

Their defense lawyers claimed that the defendants had acted under "severe provocation," triggering fresh outrage in Turkey. "Ferit acted because he faced the taunts of people who said 'your sister is dishonorable.' Güldünya's affair stained the family's pride; it devalued their honor. There are limits to sexuality. Ferit couldn't look people in the face, he acted under pressure," the lawyers said. "However you approach the matter of honor, in Turkey sexuality is not a minor matter; it can be a matter of divorce. One cannot say 'I'll have the sexual life I want.' It affects this family, and the society. The community punishes prostitution."

Although the defense argued that Irfan had not been present when the fatal shots were fired, the court sentenced him to life imprisonment for his role in the murder. His younger brother, the perpetrator, benefited from being under 18 and was sentenced to 11 years and eight months. But the Court of Appeal found the verdict too lenient and demanded a retrial.

In November 2007, the Fifth Criminal Court in the Bakırköy district of Istanbul sentenced Irfan to life imprisonment, twice, for "attempting to commit murder" and "premeditated murder." Because of his young age at the time of the crime, Ferit got reduced sentences totaling 23 years, including one year on an additional count of "illegal possession of a firearm."

The two young men will have plenty of time behind bars to reflect on their actions. Several years after her death, Güldünya continues to be a powerful symbol of the struggle to curb honor killings in Turkey.

CHAPTER 18

FATMA* AND FATIH*

Identifying who is responsible for a crime committed in the name of honor is rarely easy. All too often, the community as a whole is involved in the decision or goads the potential murderers until they see no way out and finally commit murder.

An Amnesty International report on honor killings in Pakistan pointed out that in some circumstances men "have virtually no other means of undoing a perceived infringement of 'honor' than to kill the women assumed to be guilty of it. Social pressures to eliminate the 'offending' woman are great and men who would rather ignore rumors of infringement of 'honor' are themselves considered dishonorable."[1]

Spilling blood is often the easiest way out of a scandal in communities where women are seen as carrying the burden of honor. But the decision to kill does not always make unanimity within the family group. Close relatives of a potential victim can oppose the decision to kill, but be overruled by more distant kin if they are in the majority.

The case of Fatma and Fatih suggests that, when proper support mechanisms are in place, families and potential murderers can find alternative solutions to their dilemma.

Nebahat Akkoç founded the Kamer Foundation in 1997 in Diyarbakir, the capital of Turkey's Kurdish region, to help abused women. The name Kamer is a contraction of the words *Kadın Merkezi,* which mean women's center.

Through her, I had heard about a young couple under threat.

Fatma was a young mother who had been unjustly accused of adultery. Her husband, Fatih, believed in her innocence, but both were under severe pressure from the village community. By the time Kamer called for a meeting of officials, academics, and nongovernmental institutions several months later, seeking their help to save the couple, tension had built to boiling point.

Fatma was only 12 when she married Fatih and the two had been together for 15 years when I met them in 2003. Aside from two boys aged 12 and eight, who were not present on the day of the gathering, the couple had a pretty, dark-eyed six-year-old daughter called Gül*, who had accompanied them. It was clear that they both doted on the little girl.

Their lives in the village had been fairly uneventful until Fatih's cousin Bülent* developed a crush on the beautiful Fatma. Over a two-year period, he harassed her through the telephone, making frequent nuisance calls. Fatma had mentioned the incidents to friends but, fearing her husband's reaction, she had not informed him.

At some point, Bülent's brothers started spreading the rumor that Fatma was having an affair with an unnamed soldier. Did they know at the time that their own brother, who was doing his military service, was infatuated with the young woman and was constantly calling her? Or were they trying to cover up his actions with counter-allegations? No one provided a rational explanation for the baseless gossip. It is also possible that Fatih, who worked as an electrician at the local gendarmerie station, was the real target of their wrath.

For 15 years, a violent conflict between separatist Kurdish guerrillas and government forces had torn Turkey's southeast. To fight the rebels, the government had set up a local Kurdish militia of "village guards" or *korucu,* despised as traitors by nationalist Kurds. By working for the *jandarma,* a paramilitary force attached to the Interior Ministry, even in a technical capacity, Hüseyin could have been perceived by some as a collaborator.

Fatma's harassment may have been politically motivated. Through her, the men who made accusations may have been trying to reach her husband. Fatih admitted that his cousins had recently put pressure on him to leave his job. "They threatened me. They said, 'you will leave the *karakol* (gendarmerie station); you won't work,' " he said. "If the problem is the fact that I'm a *korucu,* why did they wait ten years to say anything? I'm not harming anyone. I'm just an electrician."

Whatever the motive, it was increasingly clear that the malicious gossip was spreading rapidly. It soon threatened Fatma's life. The cousins, who were also the couple's neighbors, wanted the young woman punished for her alleged sins. One day, while her husband was away in Diyarbakir, some 20 kilometers away from the village, the cousins' wives warned Fatma that unless she left the village immediately, she would probably be dead within days.

* * *

When I met the youthful Fatma in the corridors of Kamer, I was at first surprised by her cheerfulness. I knew that she was living with a death sentence hanging over her head, yet she was chatting animatedly with the activists in the office and laughing, her daughter, Gül, by her side.

But when she started telling me her story, the mask fell and she revealed the enormous tension that had been welling inside her for months. Anguish was visible on her face as she spoke and she came close to tears several times during our conversation.

"I fled and went to my maternal aunt's house and stayed with her for five days. Then I moved to my paternal aunt and settled there," she explained. Fatma had run away in the middle of the night, in the dead of winter, with only the clothes she had on her back and flimsy slippers on her feet.

The young woman's sudden departure caused turmoil in the village and the elders gathered for a family council to decide her fate. When a woman leaves the family home, she is automatically assumed to be guilty. The elders ruled that Fatma would have to die.

The young woman would probably have been killed if one of the men sitting on the family council had not objected to the death sentence and discreetly contacted Nebahat Akkoç. She was well known and respected in the region, and he asked her to mediate to prevent an unnecessary death. Several weeks, and sometimes months, can go by between the decision to kill and the actual execution, leaving a window of opportunity to stage an intervention.

Nebahat and her colleagues took immediate action. On a cold winter's night, they traveled in the dark to a remote rural location where they met Fatma, who was sheltering with a relative.

"You should have seen this young woman. She was shaking with fear and didn't have any warm clothes on her back when I first met her," Nebahat had told me several months earlier, upset and clearly worried about Fatma's fate. "She doesn't weigh forty-five kilos, but dozens of big men gathered and decided to kill her."

After hearing the young woman's version of events, the activists got in touch with the family elders and eventually convinced the family that Fatma had done nothing to stain their honor. In fact, she was the victim of vindictive bullies. Their arguments were strong enough to convince the family elders that the young mother should be exonerated and allowed to return to her marital home.

Fatma's "acquittal" should have put an end to the incident, but Fatih's cousins continued their disinformation campaign. They went as far as alerting the local prosecutor that Fatma had run away with a soldier.

By the time I met Fatih, six months after the family council had officially reinstated his wife as a member of the extended clan, he was at the end of his tether: tongues were still wagging in the village and they could not be silenced. Constantly taunted in his community, he felt deeply ashamed, even though he knew, rationally, that neither he nor his wife had committed any social offence. He found himself unable to brush off the nasty rumors and ignore the people who were whispering behind his back. He could not sit in the village café holding his head high.

Fatih never doubted his wife's innocence, but he was becoming a danger to her, to their children, and even to himself. The aspersions against his honor were undermining his mental stability and he felt he could snap at any moment. Nebahat and her colleagues were particularly worried because the man whose name had been unjustly linked to Fatma's would soon be released from military service and return to the community.

"One of these days, this young guy will come back from the army and then we'll have trouble," Fatih told me, very agitated. "If he comes to my house or talks to my wife, I won't be able to contain myself." He then lapsed into a deep silence, looking at the floor, clearly wound up. There were tears of despair in his eyes.

"I am against the *töre* (customs) that comes from our ancestors. If a woman has committed an offence, the sentence is always death. But I'm against it. Even if they had found that Fatma was guilty, I still would have been against killing her. But if she had done something wrong, I might have divorced her," he said.

Fatih had firsthand experience of the impact that killing in the name of honor can have on a family. A few years earlier, his own brother had murdered his wife and an alleged lover in circumstances remarkably similar to the ones Fatih and Fatma were facing. Like Fatih, his brother had never taken the rumors of infidelity seriously. He even defended his wife in front of the family council and claimed her innocence, but he was overruled. The council had decided that the scandal was too damaging and the two people at the center of it needed to die to put an end to it. And although he did not believe that his wife was guilty, Fatih's brother was entrusted with the task of shooting her dead.

"It happened in 1995. Again the slander came from the same family. My brother believed it was slander, but he said 'I can't walk around the village, I can't hold my head high,' and he did it," Fatih explained, adding that his brother had used a rifle to commit the deed. "They had two daughters, who were little at the time. They're now 12 and eight. My mother and I look after them."

Fatih's brother only served 28 months in jail for the two homicides, but he was never able to forget his wife. "My brother is very sorry. How could he not feel sorry? But this is *namus* (honor)," Fatih told me. "Now his daughters won't come near him. They are angry with him. They say, 'you're not my father; I won't call you dad because you've killed my mother.' "

Fatma had also witnessed the terrible events: she knew how vulnerable women are to malicious talk. When she found herself the target of similar allegations, she knew the threat to her life was very real. "She was my maternal uncle's daughter and my sister-in-law. We were the same age," she told me. "I kept looking at our relatives afterward and thought: 'they have killed a woman.' I was very scared."

Fatma had never attended school and was illiterate but unlike most of the other women in the village, she didn't have to work in the fields because her husband received a government salary. Envy may have played a part in the campaign against her.

Fatih, under stress, was often short-tempered. Although he did not beat her, Fatma complained that his nerves were frayed and that he was often verbally abusive because he saw her as the source of his troubles. "It's very hard to be a woman. I can't tell you how much pain I've suffered," she said. "I wish he'd beat me rather than constantly reproaching me. I have children, where can I go? I have to think of them, especially my daughter who is still little. I'm sure his family is telling him to abandon me. They even paid my son to tell lies about me to my father. I don't trust anyone but Allah."

The activists at Kamer had kept in touch with the couple after Fatma returned to her village. They saw Fatih as a ticking time bomb. Increasingly depressed, he would not be able to contain himself if the man who had harassed his wife chose to return to the village. One of the couple's sons was also rumored to have been molested by his peers at school because of the cloud that hung over his family's reputation.

At this point, Nebahat Akkoç, who had launched a project aimed at preventing honor killings before they occur, decided that she needed to enlist the help of a broader group. A meeting was called to discuss concrete ways to help the couple. Her initiative paid off: Fatih, who was a public servant, was transferred to a new position in Diyarbakir.

This allowed him to relocate his wife and children to the city, away from nagging relatives and villagers. There was of course no guarantee that the couple would be able to leave the past behind them, but the move gave them a chance to make a fresh start.

A few months later, I asked my friends at Kamer how the two were doing. I was told all the family members had adapted well to their new circumstances and they were slowly overcoming the traumas of the past. The betrayal of their kin and the separation from their community would mark them forever, but at least they were given another chance. A potentially lethal situation had been defused and murder averted.

* * *

The intervention that saved Fatma and Fatih was part of an initiative launched by Kamer to demonstrate that potential honor killing victims could be saved.

When Nebhat Akkoç first founded the association, the Kurdish conflict was still raging and the region was tense. The early days proved difficult. Her initiative was opposed by everyone across the political spectrum: state institutions saw her as a Kurdish activist, not to be trusted. Kurdish militants felt her efforts were distracting attention from the "real" cause, that of Kurdish nationalism. For conservatives, and indeed for most men, she was an agitator trying to break up families.

Thankfully, she found that international donors were willing to support her efforts. Their confidence proved well placed. In 2003, the European edition of *Time* magazine named Nebahat Akkoç as a "Hero of our time." By then, she was attending international conferences on women's issues regularly and gaining recognition and influence within the borders of Turkey. The mistrust that many locals had displayed initially had been replaced by a grudging acceptance that she was doing necessary work. This evolution was largely the result of her tenacity and the efforts deployed by her inspiring team, many of them women who had experienced domestic violence themselves. Fatma and Fatih were rescued thanks to the useful contacts the Kamer foundation had established with local officials, convincing them that emergency measures needed to be developed to help women at risk.

Kamer is now a flourishing institution with branches in 23 provinces. Its activists promote female entrepreneurship and run restaurants and crèches. Local women are offered courses where they learn about their rights. Psychological counsel is also offered to victims of violence. Over the years, hundreds of women have called the Kamer hotline.

The Kamer project to prevent murders committed in the name of honor ran between 2003 and 2006. The organization had initiated this program in the belief that many families, wanting to avoid bloodshed, would welcome an alternative way to put an end to a socially sensitive situation. Its activists were aware that a window of opportunity usually opens between the moment when relatives sentence a woman to death and the actual homicide, as Fatma's case illustrated. In four years, Kamer proved that it was possible to intervene successfully. Altogether, its team handled 158 cases of women in imminent danger of being killed. Some of the women at risk contacted the organization through a hotline that had been set up. Others were referred by lawyers or police officers.

Disobedience was the "crime" most often cited as the motive for the death sentence: it was invoked in 23.4 percent of the cases handled by Kamer. Slander was the second most common threat, mentioned by 17.1 percent of applicants. Meeting or eloping with a lover accounted for 14.6 percent of the desperate pleas for help received at Kamer, while 12 percent of potential victims who contacted the activists stated that they faced execution following a rape.

In spite of the activists' efforts to save them, three of the 158 women who contacted Kamer for help were killed. In 34 instances, mediation allowed the families to reconcile and the potential victims to resume their normal life. Forty-two applicants, on the other hand, had to be removed from their environment for their own safety: they were sent to other parts of the country to start a new chapter with the help of social services.

*   *   *

The dedicated women of Kamer are only a few of the game changers I have met in the course of my research. Rana Husseini and Asma Khader in Jordan, Nadira Shahloub-Kevorkian and Aida Touma-Sliman in Palestine, and Asma Jahangir and Hina Jilani in Pakistan are other inspiring activists I have had the privilege to come across.

They have not only brought crimes committed in the name of honor to the attention of the international community, but, more importantly, they have also set the ball of change rolling in their own countries.

The Turkey-based organization Women for Women's Human Rights/New Ways formed a broad platform of women's rights organizations and successfully lobbied for sweeping changes in the Penal Code. They have also brought together civil society organizations from across the Muslim world to work on issues of sexuality, often considered taboo.

In Western countries, too, women from immigrant backgrounds successfully lobbied governments to ensure that voices other than those of male community leaders represent ethnic minorities. In Britain, for instance, Southall Black Sisters have been at the forefront of this campaign.

Far from being passive victims, women across the developing world are fighting back, planting the seeds of social transformation in their societies. They face an uphill battle. Poverty, feudal structures, inefficient justice systems, and autocratic leadership constitute formidable obstacles on the path to gender equality. Much work remains to be done to break the cycle of violence and dismantle the oppressive patriarchal system that continues to crush young women and turn men into killers.

Activists alone cannot change society. To achieve a mentality shift, governments must abide by their international commitments and play a leading role in the struggle against crimes committed in the name of honor and other traditional practices that threaten the lives of young women, and occasionally men, in their countries. No segment of the society can be left out of this fight. Religious leaders and conservative members of society, too, can help: change sometimes comes from unusual quarters.

In 2006, in the Turkish city of Diyarbakir, I met Sait Şanli, a balding butcher and community organizer who had acquired an unlikely reputation as a peacemaker and mediator. The soft-spoken Şanlı, who died in 2009, may never have heard of the Convention on the Elimination of All Forms of Discrimination Against Women (CEDAW) and he was certainly not an expert on human rights, but he had an innate sense of justice that earned him a reputation as a mediator in tribal disputes.

I have earlier mentioned the negative role played by some tribal courts in Pakistan. Şanli's role was not that of a judge and he was not a substitute for official justice. In fact, he insisted that if any incident referred to him involved bodily harm or homicide, he only accepted to get involved if the perpetrator surrendered to the police and faced the judicial system. But when a dispute erupted between two clans, or when a girl was kidnapped or chose to elope, his intervention allowed the matter to be resolved peacefully, without human loss.

Sait Şanlı, who sported a thick moustache, explained that he owed his vocation to an experience that marked him as a child. His extended family, which originated from another province of Turkey's southeast, Muş province, was forced into internal exile by an incident that caused long-term enmity between two clans and triggered a bitter conflict between them.

The event that triggered the dispute was so trivial that it is hard to imagine it could result in such tragedy, but perceived wrongs committed against women, land, or assets can have serious consequences in a feudal society.

In this case, the conflict began when a cow trespassed onto a field belonging to a neighbor. The irate landowner retaliated by cutting off the cow's tail. This "insult" could not be left without response and the matter escalated. One of Sait's uncles was killed in the fight with the rival family. Then the victim's clan turned to murder to avenge the collective honor.

Eventually, the only option to stop the deadly cycle of violence was to leave. Sait Şanlı's entire tribe—a total of 38 families—left their land to start a new life hundreds of miles away. The brutal uprooting Sait experienced as a child convinced him that dialogue rather than violence was the best way to resolve community disputes. "I suffered from this system, so I don't want other people to suffer as well," he explained.

Since 2000, Sait Şanlı proudly told me, he had successfully resolved 158 blood feuds and 88 cases of kidnapped girls, which could have led to honor killings. He also intervened in 57 cases of traffic accidents, which could have degenerated into lasting feuds as well as 144 cases of bodily injuries.

Şanli did not challenge the existing social order. He appealed to the elders' sense of fairness and sought to use dialogue to resolve tense situations involving women. When girls elope to marry the candidate of their choice, "I explain to the mothers that the girl loves the man," he explained, acknowledging that better access to education was slowly changing social attitudes. In one case, he managed to convince a father to lift his objection to his daughter's marriage by raising funds to help a potential groom deemed too poor furnish the marital home.

Sait Şanlı solved individual cases and did not attack the roots of the problem. But thanks to his commitment to fairness and his innate compassion, he had an impact on the lives of dozens of people. The French news agency *Agence France Press* nominated Şanlı for the Nobel Peace Prize, saluting his efforts to shift deeply entrenched social attitudes from within the traditional structure. He could only be a part of the solution, but in the fight against honor-based violence, every contribution counts.

CONCLUSION

Is it important, or even useful, to identify honor killings as a separate form of violence against women? After all, as the tragic and outrageous cases described in this book show, honor killings are homicides, and honor-based violence is often an extreme form of domestic abuse. Yet there is little doubt that some of these murders share common patterns and that some families act in the mistaken belief that killing will restore their reputation, deemed to have been damaged by one of their members.

Honor killings can only be averted, or adequately punished when they have taken place, if the social triggers that cause them and the environment in which they occur are well understood. As I have tried to explain in the preceding chapters, many different factors usually combine to cause a tragedy.

The stories of young women killed in the prime of life in the name of outdated patriarchal norms make painful reading. But there are hopeful signs to suggest that change is on its way. Awareness of honor-based crimes has risen in recent years throughout the world. More women have access to a support infrastructure when they feel under threat and perpetrators no longer systematically get away with murder.

But much more still needs to be done. Throughout Europe, and more recently in North America, honor killings have been singled out as an issue that needs to be addressed urgently. Unfortunately, this particular form of violence has at times become caught in the crossfire of the debate on immigration and the challenge of integrating immigrants from non-Western cultures, in particular Muslims. As xenophobia rears its ugly head, honor killings are cited as proof of the unredeemable barbarity of "other" cultures and used as ammunition against multiculturalism.

Honor killings are murders, and they have to be punished as such. Singling out crimes committed in the name of honor is only useful for the purpose of developing strategies to combat them. Using them to tar entire cultures with the brush of condemnation is counterproductive.

For a start, honor crimes no longer enjoy the widespread social acceptance they once commanded in traditional or tribal communities, and a growing number of people within the communities in which they occur are engaged in the fight to eradicate them. Furthermore, when an entire social group is targeted and stigmatized, defensiveness sets in, making the task of local activists who are fighting to effect change from within even harder.

To approach violations of women's rights from a racist perspective also ignores the fact that even in the most liberal Western democracies, violence against women remains a major social scourge and women continue to be victims of homicides committed by those close to them.

Whatever form of violence is being targeted, the right approach needs to be developed to ensure that perpetrators are caught and punished.

Homicide detectives throughout the world look for a motive and seek clues at the murder scene when they are investigating a crime. Spouses and partners are usually prime suspects who have to be eliminated from inquiries before the investigation explores other avenues.

Investigators need to be aware that aside from greed, jealousy, and other common motives for murder, families may also kill in the belief that slaughtering one of their own involved in a social scandal will restore their reputation in the eyes of the community.

It is also crucial that law enforcement agencies, schools, and social services understand that honor is often perceived to rest in a women's body and what constitutes a violation of social mores is often interpreted very broadly by conservatives.

When a teenager turns up at a police station claiming that her parents are going to kill her, she may not be using the hyperbolic language common to adolescents who fear being grounded for violating their curfew. She may be speaking literally and harbor legitimate fears that need to be taken seriously. Law enforcement officials have to tread carefully and not send young women home without seeking community advice and ensuring that the family environment is safe.

They must, however, be careful not to fall into the trap of racial profiling. The majority of Eastern migrants in Western countries have found a happy medium between their cultural roots and the social mores of the host culture. The tragedies that still occur highlight the challenges of integration and the need for further action, but they should not be used to fuel racist reflexes that will only ostracize entire ethnic groups and further their sense of alienation.

In developing countries where killing in the name of honor is an old practice that has survived and even taken modern forms, law enforcement officials and magistrates often share the prejudices of the community. Legislators have the responsibility to provide a more women-friendly legal framework, in line with their country's international commitments, particularly with the Convention on the Elimination of All Forms of Discrimination Against Women (CEDAW). But governments also have the responsibility to ensure that the laws are properly implemented. To succeed, they need to provide adequate training to law enforcement personnel and members of the judiciary. Impunity and lenient sentences create a climate of tolerance that allows harmful practices to thrive.

Pressure from activists has already led to the introduction of legal amendments and policies to offer better protection to women in several countries. These developments suggest that popular pressure is having an impact on politicians, who can no longer afford to ignore violence against women, even if they personally don't see the issue as a priority. But the gap remains wide between enacting a law and ensuring that it is strictly applied.

Almost everywhere, the tide has begun to turn but the battle has yet to be won. Many women fighting to free themselves from the shackles of patriarchal values face a backlash. Terrorist attacks, conflicts, and increased tension between the East and the West have strengthened the position of religious and nationalist hard-liners. Rapid social change brought on by globalization and economic turmoil is at times fuelling violence: conservative men invoke honor when they hit out against women who have become more assertive and no longer accept abuse and total obedience as an inescapable fate.

Honor-based violence clearly amounts to a violation of the victim's most basic human rights, but at the grassroots level, the rights discourse may not always be the most effective tool to promote change.

There are pros and cons to approaching crimes committed in the name of honor from a human rights perspective. While this approach may mobilize a sense of shame, expose endemic violations of women's basic rights, and emphasize state responsibility in combating these crimes, invoking human rights, still perceived by many in the developing world as a concept imposed by the West, can also trigger resistance.

Local activists are best placed to lead the battle and determine what methods are most likely to yield the best results. Often, it is not about focusing on a single policy, but rather adopting a multipronged approach. Some victims of gender-based violence have themselves become powerful agents of change, and use their own experience to contribute to the struggle.

No single model offers a ready-made solution. Most civil society associations based in the developing world understand that the solution lies in action at different levels. Women at the grassroots level need to learn about their rights, but empowering them and giving them the means to protect and support themselves is only a first step. Dialogue has to be established with all segments of society, including religious leaders and tribal chiefs, who still wield a lot of influence. Brandishing a copy of CEDAW or the Universal Declaration of Human Rights may be less effective at community level than appealing to the leaders' sense of justice and fairness in the first instance, even if in the long run the aim is to ensure that the group understands and adopts the principles enshrined in these documents.

States must be encouraged to face up to their international obligations, and allocate enough resources to train law enforcement agencies to become more sensitive to gender issues, and ensure that judges rule according to the spirit of legal amendments that seek to improve the situation of women.

Above all, I believe it is crucial to recruit men in the fight against honor-based crimes. At conferences on violence against women, usually attended by an overwhelmingly female audience, I have witnessed men attempt to make a contribution or to ask questions. Instead of being encouraged for showing an interest in a social problem that many men still regard as a "women's issue" and therefore not worthy of interest, some of them were rebuffed by radical feminists, who had already concluded that men were the enemy. Segregation is not the solution to gender-based violence. Instead, the solution rests on fine-tuning social balances to ensure a more peaceful coexistence.

Hot-blooded young males may still want to prove their virility by killing for honor, but many in the younger generation, particularly those who have had more exposure to the outside world, want change and are ready to challenge social norms. While patriarchy undoubtedly favors men, this rigid system also demands that they conform to strict social rules. Few men question the roles that have been assigned to them. Most of them accept them as normal, unaware that gender roles, and masculinity, are largely social constructs.

Judging from my conversations with young men in the course of my research, and the stories of many others who, in recent years, have resisted the call to kill, I believe that the younger generation provides a fertile ground for change. Rather than just blaming men, it would be more useful to help young people understand the constraints that the patriarchal system places on members of both genders through educational programs that promote better practices.

I do not believe that young boys anywhere in the world grow up with the ambition of killing their sisters or their wives. For every murder, there are dozens of cases that have taken a different course because individuals, men and women, who were determined to avoid a lethal outcome, sought and found help along the way.

Many of the female activists I have encountered have also made it clear that while they claim the right to make their own choices and to live in an environment free of violence, their vision of an ideal society may not exactly mirror that of Western feminism.

The relentless individualism that characterizes most Western societies is seen by many in the East as lacking in warmth and communal solidarity. Women in the developing world want to be respected as individuals, they defend their rights, but they want to achieve these goals without sacrificing the community or the extended family. Achieving the right balance requires delicate social fine-tuning. For these women, as for their counterparts in the West, gender equality is still very much a work in progress. Constant vigilance is also required to consolidate the gains achieved.

Women's rights defenders around the world are working tirelessly to put an end to honor killings and the underlying discriminatory practices. Their efforts have already borne fruit, but they cannot win the battle alone.

Opposition to honor-based violence is on the rise, but the protests have not yet coalesced into a single voice. To eradicate honor killings and other discriminatory gender practices, a consistent message must be heard from all segments of society. Nongovernmental associations, government institutions, the judicial system, law enforcement agencies, and above all, politicians must express publicly and repeatedly that killing is never an acceptable or an "honorable" solution.

NOTES

CHAPTER 1

1. Education Reform Initiative, *Education Monitoring Report 2008,* Sabanci University, Istanbul, June 2009.

CHAPTER 2

1. Leila Ahmed, *Women and Gender in Islam: Historical Roots of a Modern Debate,* New Haven: Yale University Press, 1992.
2. Rabia Ali, "The Dark Side of 'Honor': Women Victims in Pakistan," *Women Living under Muslim Laws,* Special Bulletin 2001, http://www.shirkatgah.org/violence-against-women.html.
3. Eliza Grisworld, "Faith of Her Fathers," *The New Republic,* February 26, 2001.
4. European Stability Initiative, Sex *and Power in Turkey,* June 2007.
5. Nafisa Shah, "Role of the Community in Honor Killings in Sindh," in *Engendering the Nation-State, Vol. 1,* N. Hussain, S. Mumtaz and R. Saigol (eds), Simorgh Women's Resource and Publication Centre, Lahore, 1997.
6. Human Rights Watch, Oral Intervention at the 57th Session of the UN Commission on Human Rights, April 5, 2001.
7. Lama Abu-Odeh, "Crimes of Honor and the Construction of Gender in Arab Societies," in Mai Yamani (ed.), *Feminism and Islam: Legal and Literary Perspectives,* Ithaca Press, Berkshire, 1996.
8. Sahrzad Mojab and Nahla Abdo, Introduction to *Violence in the Name of Honor, Theoretical and Political Challenges,* Bilgi University Press, Istanbul, 2004.
9. Emniyet genel Müdürlüğü Asayiş Dairesi Başkanlığı Töre ve Namus Cinayetleri Raporu (Police General Directorate report on Honor and Customary Killings), 2008.
10. CEDAW, Combined initial, second and third periodic reports of States parties, Pakistan, August 3, 2005.
11. Frontline Magazine, Volume 24—Issue 04, Feb. 24-Mar. 09, 2007.
12. Clare Murphy, "Jordan's Dilemma over Honor Killings," *BBC News Website,* September 10, 2003, retrieved on July 30, 2009.
13. N.V. Baker, P.R. Gregware & M.A. Cassidy, "Family Killing Fields," *Violence against Women,* Vol. 5: 164–184, 1999.

14. Aysan Sev'er & Gökçeçiçek Yurdakul, "Culture of Honor, Culture of Change," *Violence against Women*, Vol. 7, No. 9: 964–999, 2001.
15. United Nations Commission on Human Rights, Report of the Special Rapporteur on violence against women, its causes and consequences, Ms. Radhika Coomaraswamy, E/CN.4/1997/47, February 12, 1997.
16. Mehmet Faraç, *Töre kıskancında kadın*, Istanbul: Günizi Yayıncılık, 2002.
17. Sev'er Aysan and Yurdakul Gökçeçiçek, see note 14.
18. Lila Abu-Lughod, *Veiled Sentiments—Honor and Poetry in a Bedouin Society*, University of California Press, 1988.
19. Nafisa Shah, "A Story in Black: Karo Kari Killings in Upper Sindh," *Reuters Foundation Paper 100*, Green College, Oxford 1998.
20. Asma Khader, interview with the author, February 2002.
21. Nafisa Shah, "Honor Killings: Code of Dishonor," *Dawn* daily, *Karachi*, November 19–25, 1998.

CHAPTER 4

1. Riffat Hassan, Interview, Lahore, August 16, 2003.
2. Douglas Jehl, "Arab Honor's Price," *The New York Times*, June 20, 1999.
3. Fatma Uma, Interview with the author, May 8, 2002.
4. "Koca dayağı haklı olabilir mi?" *Milliyet newspaper*, November 28, 2004.
5. Yeşim Arat and Ayşegül Altınay, "Türkiye'de Kadina Yönelik Şiddet," *TUBITAK*, November 2007.
6. Ibid.
7. Rabia Ali, "The Dark Side of 'Honor': Women Victims in Pakistan," *Women Living under Muslim Laws*, 2001.
8. Fatima Mernissi, "Virginity and Patriarchy," in *Women and Sexuality in Muslim Societies*, ed. Pinar Ilkkaracan, WWHR/New Ways, 2000.
9. Serpil Karacan, "Turkey's Test of Blood Slammed as Violence against Women," *IPPF*, January 2001.
10. Timur Soykan and Demet Bilge, "Bir resmi bile yoktu," *Radikal newspaper*, March 6, 2001.
11. Carol Delaney, *The Seed and the Soil: Gender and Cosmology in Turkish Village Society*, University of California Press, 1991.
12. Germaine Tillion, *Le harem et les cousins*, Editions du Seuil, 1966.
13. Ibid.
14. Ayesha M. Imam, "The Muslim Religious Right ('Fundamentalists') and Sexuality," in *Women and Sexuality in Muslim Societies*, ed. Pinar Ilkkaracan, WWHR/New Ways, Istanbul, 2000.
15. Ibid.

16. Fatima Mernissi, *Beyond the Veil: Male-Female Dynamics in Modern Muslim Society, Revised Edition,* Indiana University Press, 1987.
17. Karen Armstrong, "Eve of Destruction," *The Guardian,* January 24, 2004.
18. Laila Ahmed, , *Women and Gender in Islam: Historical Roots of a Modern Debate,* Yale University Press, 1992.
19. Germaine Tillion, see note 12.
20. Pascale Harter, "Divorce Divides Morocco and W Sahara," *BBC News website,* August 4, 2004.
21. UN Commission for Human Rights, Report of Ms Radhika Coomaraswamy, UN Special Rapporteur on violence against women.
22. Nafisa Shah, "A Story in Black—Karo Kari killings in Upper Sindh," *Reuters Foundation Paper 100,* Green College Oxford.
23. Deniz Kandiyoti, "Identity and Its Discontents: Women and the Nation," in *Colonial Discourse and Post Colonial Theory,* ed. Patrick Williams and Laura Chrisman. New York, 1994.

CHAPTER 6

1. "Ceza mı ödül mü," *Hürriyet newspaper,* March 26, 2003.
2. Mehmet Yildirim, interview with the author, Urfa, May 2002.
3. "Töre vahşetinde mucize," *Hürriyet,* February 14, 1998.
4. BBC Radio Five Live broadcast, January 16, 2005.
5. Tom Rawstorne, "Across the cultural divide," *The Daily Mail,* September 2, 2009.
6. "Father rejects child bride criticism," *BBC News website,* September 30, 2003.
7. "Meclis erken evliliklere el atti," *Taraf newspaper,* June 15, 2009.
8. "Sırtında bebeğiyle kendini astı," *Nethaber.com,* December 1, 2006.
9. UN Population Fund, *Virtual Slavery: The Practice of Compensation Marriages Fund,* retrieved on October 16, 2010.
10. Ibid.
11. Kutcha Chohan, "Court awards hand of girl aged two to 40 year-old," *The Guardian,* April 20, 2004.
12. Amnesty International, *Afghanistan: Women Still under Attack—A Systematic Failure to Protect, http://www.amnesty.org/en/library/info/ASA11/007/2005,*accessed on October 25, 2007.
13. *The Guardian,* see note 12.
14. Declan Walsh, "15 child brides used to settle Pakistan feud," *The Guardian,* June 5, 2008.
15. "Victims of 'honor killings' recall horror," *The Hindu,* January 13, 2004.
16. Monobina Gupta, "Veil ripped off honor killings," *The Telegraph,* January 13, 2004.

CHAPTER 8

1. Fadia Faqir, "Intrafamily femicide in defence of honor: The case of Jordan," *Third World Quarterly*, Vol. 22, No. 1, 65–82, 2001.
2. Rabia Ali, "The Dark Side of 'Honor'," *Women Living under Muslim Laws*, 2001.
3. Nafisa Shah, "Karo Kari: Ritual killings in the name of honor," *Newsline*, January 1993.
4. "Pakistan: Insufficient protection for women," *Amnesty International*, 2002.
5. "Supreme Court orders re-arrest of Imam, 20-year jail sentence," *Dawn newspaper*, February 1, 2002.
6. *Dawn newspaper*, February 9, 13 and March 12, 2004.
7. *The Nation*, "Killings in the name of honor," August 5, 2001.
8. Rabia Ali, see note 2.
9. "Gözlerimi bağla abi," *Sabah newspaper*, June 9, 2000.
10. "Tecavüze uğrayan kadın affeldilmiyor," *Sabah newspaper*, May 4, 2004.
11. "Pantolon giydi, öldü," *Milliyet newspaper*, January 10, 2005.
12. "Pidenin içine fare zehiri katti," *Radikal newspaper*, November 6, 2003.
13. Nadera Shalhoub-Kevorkian, "Femicide and the Palestinian Criminal Justice System: Seeds of Change in the Context of State Building?," *Law and Society Review*, January 1, 2002.
14. Germaine Tillion, *Le harem et les cousins*, Editions du Seuil, 1966.
15. NTVMSNBC website, November 3, 2003.
16. "Töre vahşeti ne zaman bitecek!," *Radikal newspaper*, January 8, 2003.
17. Batman intiharları çoğunun cinayet olabilir!," *Milliyet newspaper*, October 17, 2003.
18. Progressive Women's Association website, www.pwaisbd.org, retrieved on July 25, 2009.
19. "Why are Kurdish women dying of burns?," *Newsweek*, September 18, 2007.

CHAPTER 10

1. Amir Hossein Kordvani, "Hegemonic Masculinity, Domination, and Violence Against Women," paper presented at conference on *Understanding the Complexities of Violence against Women*, Sydney, February 18–22, 2002.
2. "'Afet beni anne' diyerek öldürdü," *Milliyet newspaper*, May 18, 2001.
3. "Aile 'namusu' ona ihale edildi," *Hürriyet newspaper*, May 16, 2001.
4. Amnesty International, *Pakistan: Insufficient Protection of Women*, April 2002.

5. Alam Fareena, "Take the Honour out of the Killing," *The Guardian*, July 6, 2004.
6. "Kızını ölmesi gerektiğine inandırmış," *Taraf newspaper*, February 5, 2009.
7. Nadera Shalhoub-Kevorkian, "Femicide and the Palestinian Criminal Justice System: Seeds of Change in the Context of State Building?, *Law and Society Review*, January 1, 2002.
8. "Korkunç görumceler," *Hürriyet newspaper*, March 8, 2000.
9. "Anne de kendine astı," *Hürriyet newspaper*, March 3, 2003.
10. "Tetikçinin isyanı," *Hürriyet newspaper*, March 31, 2004.
11. "Katil olmamak için kaçiyorum," *Milliyet newspaper*, January 10, 2005.
12. "Karımı öldürmem," *Sabah newspaper*, November 11, 2005.
13. "Genç, töre baskısını mahkemeye götürdü," *Nethaber.com*, March 4, 2009.
14. "Kardeşini öldürten ağabeyden töreye lanet: Bize yazıklar olsun," *Radika newspaper*, November 16, 2009.
15. "Sevdiler diye yaşatmadılar," *Hürriyet newspaper*, March 13, 2005.

Chapter 12

1. Rafif Sida Sidawi, Interview with the author, January 2002.
2. Susan E. Pritchett Post, *Women in modern Albania*, McFarland 1998.
3. Eleanor Beardsly, "Despite progress in the republic's fledgling democracy, women still have an uphill struggle for equal treatment," *The Boston Globe*, December 9, 2001.
4. Riffat Hassan, "Islam and Human Rights in Pakistan: A Critical Analysis of the positions of three contemporary women," *Media Monitors Network*, August 23, 2002.
5. "Hitmen charge $ 100 a victim as Basra honour killings rise," *The Guardian*, November 30, 2008.
6. "If a woman runs around and if a man runs around with her, both of them are killed," www.MSNBC.com, February 28, 2009.
7. "Gallup Coexist Index 2009: A Global Study of Interfaith Relations," www.abudhabigallupcenter.com, accessed on August 22, 2011.
8. *The Guardian*, January 15, 2004, "The Eve of Destruction," Karen Armstrong.
9. The Bible, Deuteronomy 22:13–21.
10. Karen Armstrong, "The Eve of Destruction," *The Guardian*, January 15, 2004.
11. "Eksik etek çıkmasın, Şener," *Radikal newspaper*, July 13, 2006.
12. Mustafa Akyol, "Sexism deleted in Turkey," *The Washington Post*, July 16, 2006.
13. Ibid.
14. Riffat Hassan, see note 4.

15. Riffat Hassan interview, *The Herald*, May 2001.
16. Jane Perlez, "Pakistan's Chief Justice Assails Attorney General Over Taliban Flogging," *The New York Times*, April 6, 2009.
17. "Pakistan votes to amend *rape* laws," BBC news website, November 15, 2006.

CHAPTER 13

1. Sian Power, "Australian links in honor killing of Pela Atroshi," *The Australian*, April 26, 2008, retrieved on news.com.au on Aug. 8, 2009.
2. "The whore lived like a German," *Der Spiegel online*, March 2, 2005.
3. "Love triangle hitman gets life," www.thisislancashire.co.uk, April 18, 2002, accessed August 22, 2011.
4. State v. Ahmed, case no. 2001–0871, *Supreme Court of Ohio*, Belmont County.
5. "US TV Executive convicted of beheading wife," *The Guardian*, February 8, 2011.
6. "Terror and Death at Home Are Caught in F.B.I. Tape," *The New York Times*, October 28, 1991.
7. Shahrzad Mojab, " 'Honor killings': Culture, Politics and Theory," *Middle East Women's Studies Review*, Spring/Summer 17 (1&2): 1–7, 2002.
8. Susan Moller Okin, "Is Multiculturalism Bad for Women?" in *Is Multiculturalism Bad for Women?* ed. Joshua Cohen, Matthew Howard, and Martha C. Nussbaum, Princeton University Press, 1999.
9. Leti Volpp, "Feminism versus Multiculturalism," *Columbia Law Review* Vol. 101, No. 5, 1181–1218, June 2001.
10. Katha Pollitt, "Whose Culture?" in *Is Multiculturalism Bad for Women?* ed. Joshua Cohen, Matthew Howard, and Martha C. Nussbaum, Princeton University Press, 1999.
11. Texas Council on Family violence, www.tcfv.org/pdf/womenkilled/2003.pdf, accessed August 21, 2011.
12. Nazand Begikhani interview, www.KurdishMedia.com, March 2002.

CHAPTER 14

1. Mehmet Faraç, interview with the author, November 2001.
2. Terry Judd, "Barbaric 'honor killings' become the weapon to subjugate women in Iraq," *The Independent*, April 28, 2008.
3. Deniz Kandiyoti, "Old Dilemmas or New Challenges? The Politics of Gender and Reconstruction in Afghanistan," *Development and Change*, Vol. 38, no. 2, 2007, 169–199.
4. Rabia Ali, "The Dark Side of 'Honor," *Women Living under Muslim Laws*, 2001.

5. Ali Qazi, interview with the author, August 2003, Larkana.
6. Kamila Hayat and I.A. Rehman, interview with the author, Lahore, August 2003.
7. Human Rights Report Pakistan, *U.S. Department of State*, 2008.
8. "Domestic violence against women in India," presentation by Dr. S. Varalakshmi, at the conference of the *International Association for Feminist Economics*, Boston, June 26–28, 2009.
9. Claudia Garcia-Moreno, "Gender inequality and fire-related deaths in India," *The Lancet*, Vol. 373, no. 9671, April 11, 2009, 1282–1288.
10. Raekha Prasad and Randeep Ramesh, "India's missing girls," *The Guardian*, February 28, 2007.

CHAPTER 15

1. Ardeshir Cowasjee, "Are we inhuman?," *Dawn newspaper*, February 23, 2003.

CHAPTER 16

1. Nafisa Shah, "Role of the Community in Honor Killings in Sindh," in *Engendering the Nation-State, Vol. 1*, Simorgh Women's Resource and Publication Centre, Lahore, 1997.
2. Interview with senior police officer, August 2003.
3. Rabia Ali, "The Dark Side of 'Honor," *Women Living under Muslim Laws*, 2001.
4. Nicholas Kristof, "Sentenced to be raped," *The New York Times*, September 29, 2004.
5. Nadeem Saeed, "Chief juror also guilty, says gang-rape victim," *Dawn newspaper*, August 3, 2002.
6. "Pakistan rape victim gets married," BBC news website, March 17, 2009.
7. Nadera Shalhoub-Kevorkian, "Femicide and the Palestinian Criminal Justice System: Seeds of Change in the Context of State Building?," *Law & Society Review*, No 3/577, 2002.
8. Judge Ali Güzel, interview with the author, December 2003.
9. Hakkar Karasu, interview with the author, May 2002.
10. Jordan Human Rights Report 2004.
11. Ibid.
12. Amnesty International Report 2009—Jordan, *Amnesty International*, May 28, 2009.
13. Asma Khader, interview with the author, Amman, February 2002.
14. *Dialogues in the Dark*, produced by Melek Ulagay and Ulla Lemberg, 2006.
15. Ian Leader-Eliott, "Passion and Insurrection in the Law of Sexual Provocation," in Ngaire Naffine and Rosemary J. Owen (eds.): *Sexing the Subject of Law*, Sydney, Sweet and Maxwell, 1997.

16. "Mafioso shoots sister over 'dishonor,' " *The London Times* online, March 27, 2006.
17. Julia Preston, "New Policy Permits Asylum for Battered Women," *The New York Times,* July 16, 2009.
18. Kate Connolly, "German judge invokes Qur'an to deny abused wife a divorce," *The Guardian,* March 23, 2007.
19. UN Resolution, Working towards the elimination of crimes against women committed in the name of honor (A/RES/55/66, of December 2000).
20. UN Resolution, Working towards the elimination of crimes against women and girls committed in the name of honor (A/RES/59/165, of December 2004).

CHAPTER 17

1. "Vurmadan önce de boğmayı denemişler," *Milliyet,* February 28, 2004.

CHAPTER 18

1. "Pakistan: insufficient protection of women," *Amnesty International,* April 2002.

BIBLIOGRAPHY

Abu-Odeh, Lama. "Crimes of Honour and the Construction of Gender in Arab Societies," in *Feminism and Islam: Legal and Literary Perspectives,* ed. May Yamani, Reading: Ithaca Press, 1996.

Abu-Lughod, Lila. *Veiled Sentiments—Honor and Poetry in a Bedouin Society,* Berkeley: University of California Press, 1988.

Ahmed, Leila. *Women and Gender in Islam: Historical Roots of a Modern Debate,* New Haven: Yale University Press, 1992.

Ali, Rabia. *"The Dark Side of 'Honor': Women Victims in Pakistan."* Women Living Under Muslim Laws, Special Bulletin, 2001.

Amnesty International. *Afghanistan: Women Still Under Attack—A Systemic Failure to Protect,* 2007.

Amnesty International. *Amnesty International Jordan Report,* 2009.

Baker, N., Gregware, M. and Cassidy, M. "Family Killing Fields," *Violence Against Women,* Vol. 5 No. 2, 164–184, 1999.

Committee on the Elimination of Discrimination against Women (CEDAW). "Combined Initial, Second and Third Periodic Reports of State Parties," *Pakistan,* August 3, 2005.

Education Reform Initiative, *Education Monitoring Report 2008,* Istanbul: Sabanci University, June 2009.

Emniyet Genel Müdürlüğü Asayış Dairesi Başkanlığı. *Töre ve Namus Cinayetleri Raporu (Report on honour and customary killings),* Ankara, 2008.

European Stability Initiative. *Sex and Power in Turkey,* June 2007.

Faqir, Fadia. "Intrafamily Femicide in Defence of Honor: The Case of Jordan," *Third World Quarterly,* Vol. 22, No. 1, 65–82, 2001.

Faraç, Mehmet. *Töre kıskacında kadın,* Istanbul: Günizi Yayıncılık, 2002.

Garcia-Moreno, Claudia. "Gender Inequality and Fire-related Deaths in India," *The Lancet,* Vol. 373, No. 9671, 1282–1288, April 2009.

Human Rights Watch. Oral intervention at the 57th Session of the UN Commission on Human Rights, April 5, 2001.

Kandiyoti, Deniz. "Old Dilemmas or New Challenges? The Politics of Gender and Reconstruction in Afghanistan," *Development and Change,* Vol. 38, No. 2, 169–199, 2007.

Kordvani, Amir Hossein, "Hegemonic Masculinity, Domination, and Violence against Women." Paper presented at a conference on Understanding the Complexities of Violence Against Women, Sydney, February 18–22, 2002.

Leader-Elliot, Ian. "Passion and Insurrection in the Law of Sexual Provocation," in *Sexing the Subject of Law,* ed. Ngaire Naffine and Rosemary
J. Owen, Sydney: Sweet and Maxwell, 1997.

Mernissi, Fatima. *Women and Gender in Islam,* New Haven: Yale University
Press, 1992.

Mojab, Shahrzad. " 'Honor Killing': Culture, Politics and Theory." *Middle East Women's Studies Review,* Spring/Summer, Vol. 17, No. 1&2, 1–7,
2002.

Okin, Susan Moller. "Is Multiculturalism Bad for Women?", in
Is Multiculturalism Bad for Women? ed. Joshua Cohen, Matthew Howard,
and Martha C. Nussbaum, Princeton: Princeton University Press, 1999.

Post Pritchett, Susan E. *Women in Modern Albania,* Jefferson NC: McFarland,
1998.

Mojab, Shahrzad and Abdo, Nahla. Introduction to *Violence in the Name
of Honour, Theoretical and Political Challenges,* Istanbul: Bilgi University
Press, 2004.

Sev'er, Aysan and Yurdakul, Gökçicek. "Culture of Honor, Culture of
Change," *Violence Against Women,* Vol. 7, No. 9, 964–999, September
2001.

Shah, Nafisa. "A Story in Black: Karo Kari Killings in Upper Sindh." *Reuters
Foundation Paper 100,* Green College Oxford, 1998.

Shah, Nafisa. "Role of the Community in Honour Killings in Sindh," in
Engendering the Nation-State, Vol. 1. ed. Neelam Hussain,Samiya Mumtaz
and Rubina Saigol, Lahore: Simorgh Women's Resource and Publication
Centre, 1997.

Shalhoub-Kervorkian, Nadera. "Femicide and the Palestinian Criminal Justice
System: Seeds of Change in the Context of State Building?" *Law and Society
Review,* Vol. 36, No. 3, 577–606, 2002.

United Nations Commission on Human Rights, *Report of the Special
Rapporteur on Violence Against Women, Its Causes and Consequences
Ms. Radhika Coomaraswamy,* February 1997.

United Nations Population Fund, *Virtual Slavery: The Practice of Compensation Marriage.* www.unfpa.org/gender/docs/fact_sheets/marriage.doc,
accessed August 20, 2011. US Department of State, *Human Rights Report
Pakistan,* 2008.

Volpp, Leti, "Feminism versus Multiculturalism," *Columbia Law Review,*
Vol. 101, No. 5, 1181–1218, June 2001.

INDEX

CPSIA information can be obtained at www.ICGtesting.com
Printed in the USA
LVOW10s1440100114

368788LV00011B/210/P

9 781137 371430